THEORY AND INTERPRETATION OF NARRATIVE
James Phelan, Peter J. Rabinowitz, and Robyn Warhol, Series Editors

A Poetics of Unnatural Narrative

EDITED BY
JAN ALBER
HENRIK SKOV NIELSEN
BRIAN RICHARDSON

THE OHIO STATE UNIVERSITY PRESS
COLUMBUS

Copyright © 2013 by The Ohio State University.
All rights reserved.

Library of Congress Cataloging-in-Publication Data

A poetics of unnatural narrative / edited by Jan Alber, Henrik Skov Nielsen, and Brian Richardson.
p. cm. — (Theory and interpretation of narrative)
ISBN 978-0-8142-1228-8 (cloth : alk. paper) — ISBN 978-0-8142-9330-0 (cd)
1. Narration (Rhetoric) 2. Poetics. I. Alber, Jan, 1973– II. Skov Nielsen, Henrik. III. Richardson, Brian, 1953– IV. Series: Theory and interpretation of narrative series.
PN212.P644 2013
808'.036—dc23
2013005782

Cover design by Greg Betza and Despina Georgiadis
Text design by Juliet Williams
Type set in Adobe Minion Pro

∞ The paper used in this publication meets the minimum requirements of the American National Standard for Information Sciences—Permanence of Paper for Printed Library Materials. ANSI Z39.48–1992.

9 8 7 6 5 4 3 2 1

Contents

Acknowledgments vii

Introduction
JAN ALBER, STEFAN IVERSEN, HENRIK SKOV NIELSEN, and
BRIAN RICHARDSON 1

1. Unnatural Stories and Sequences
   BRIAN RICHARDSON 16

2. The Whirligig of Time: Toward a Poetics of Unnatural Temporality
   RÜDIGER HEINZE 31

3. Unnatural Spaces and Narrative Worlds
   JAN ALBER 45

4. Naturalizing and Unnaturalizing Reading Strategies:
   Focalization Revisited
   HENRIK SKOV NIELSEN 67

5. Unnatural Minds
   STEFAN IVERSEN 94

6. 'Unnatural' Metalepsis and Immersion: Necessarily Incompatible?
   WERNER WOLF 113

7. Realism and the Unnatural
   MARIA MÄKELÄ 142

8. Implausibilities, Crossovers, and Impossibilities: A Rhetorical Approach to Breaks in the Code of Mimetic Character Narration
   JAMES PHELAN   167

9. Unnatural Narrative in Hypertext Fiction
   ALICE BELL   185

10. The Unnaturalness of Narrative Poetry
    BRIAN McHALE   199

Contributors   223

Index   227

Acknowledgments

THE EDITORS would like to thank Peter Rabinowitz, Robyn Warhol, and the anonymous reader for their extensive and perceptive comments on the manuscript. We thank James Phelan for additional judicious help along the way. Our gratitude also extends to Sandy Crooms, Maggie Diehl, Malcolm Litchfield, and Kathy Edwards for expertly guiding this collection to the finish line. Finally, we would like to thank Nancy Stewart for editorial assistance and help with the proofreading.

Introduction

JAN ALBER
STEFAN IVERSEN
HENRIK SKOV NIELSEN
AND BRIAN RICHARDSON

IN RECENT YEARS, unnatural narratology has developed into the most exciting new paradigm in narrative theory and the most important new approach since the advent of cognitive narratology. A wide range of scholars have become increasingly interested in the analysis of unnatural texts, that is, texts that feature strikingly impossible or antimimetic elements.[1] Such works have been consistently neglected or marginalized in existing narratological frameworks.

Generally speaking, unnatural narrative theorists oppose what one might call "mimetic reductionism," that is, the claim that the basic aspects of narrative can be explained primarily or exclusively by models based on realist parameters. This has been the default position for most narrative theory since Aristotle and has recently been given new prominence by many cognitive-

---

1. See the publications by the following authors: Alber; Heinze; Iversen; Mäkelä; Nielsen; Richardson; Tammi. See also the joint essay by Alber, Iversen, Nielsen, and Richardson as well as the debates with Monika Fludernik and Tobias Klauk/Tilmann Köppe in *Narrative* and *Storyworlds*; the joint essay by Alber/Bell; the entry to the *Routledge Companion to Experimental Literature* by Alber, Nielsen, and Richardson; and the collections edited by Alber/Heinze and Hansen/Iversen/Nielsen/Reitan. In November 2008, Jan Alber and Rüdiger Heinze organized a conference called "Unnatural Narrative" at the Freiburg Institute for Advanced Study (FRIAS) in Germany, and unnatural narratology also features regularly at the Narrative conference which is organized by the International Society for the Study of Narrative.

oriented theorists.[2] Scholars working within the tradition of unnatural narrative argue instead that narratives are particularly compelling when they depict situations and events that move beyond, extend, challenge, or defy our knowledge of the world. According to Jan Alber, narratives "do not only mimetically reproduce the world as we know it. Many narratives confront us with bizarre storyworlds which are governed by principles that have very little to do with the real world around us" ("Impossible" 79).

Many innovative practices and projected storyworlds differ radically from those of the actual world. The narrator may be an animal, a mythical entity, an inanimate object, a machine, a corpse, a sperm, an omniscient first-person narrator, or a collection of disparate voices that refuse to coalesce into a single narrating presence. A fictional narrative may have the structure, purpose, and development of a traditional realist narrative, or it may resist or refuse many of these features of tellability, and seem instead (from a conventional or "natural" perspective) relatively plotless, pointless, arbitrary, unconnected, or contradictory.

Similarly, fictional characters often resemble human beings, but we should never lose sight of the fact that they are not people but verbal constructs acting in a fictional world. A character (such as Cora in Clarence Major's *Reflex and Bone Structure*) can die several times; a human dies only once. One character may merge into another, or may try to escape from the author that created him. Also, fictional storyworlds are often fundamentally different from the world we inhabit. Many invented domains differ radically from actual places, as is evident by merely glimpsing into the worlds of Aristophanes, Jonathan Swift, E. T. A. Hoffmann, Jorge Luis Borges, Vladimir Nabokov, Samuel Beckett, Italo Calvino, Angela Carter, Mark Z. Danielewski, and the more anomalous spaces in Shakespeare's plays. Fictional narratives can easily and radically deconstruct our real-world notions of time and space.[3] As Lubomír Doležel affirms, fictional entities "are ontologically different from actual persons, events, places. . . . It is quite evident that fictional persons cannot meet, interact, or communicate with real people" (*Heterocosmica* 16; see also Richardson "Nabokov's Experiments").

Unnatural narratology seeks to challenge general conceptions of narrative by accentuating two points: (1) the ways in which innovative and impossible narratives challenge mimetic understandings of narrative, and (2) the consequences that the existence of such narratives may have for the general

---

2. One important work that does include several antimimetic examples is Herman and Vervaeck's *Handbook of Narrative Analysis*.

3. See Richardson "Beyond Story and Discourse," as well as the essays by Rüdiger Heinze and Jan Alber in this volume.

conception of what a narrative is and what it can do. Unnatural narrative theory regularly analyzes and theorizes the aspects of fictional narratives that transcend the boundaries of conventional realism. Unnatural narrative practices may be flagrant and widespread, as in much postmodern fiction, or the practices may be more restrained, intermittent, or submerged, as when, at the beginning of the otherwise mimetic *Adventures of Huckleberry Finn,* the fictional character Huck complains about the verisimilitude of his representation in Mark Twain's earlier novel, *Tom Sawyer.*

Many theorists of the unnatural are particularly interested in texts that present extremely implausible, impossible, or logically contradictory scenarios or events. Unnatural narratologists affirm the distinctive nature of fiction, gravitate toward unusual and experimental works, and seek to comprehend theoretically the strategies of narrative construction that are unique to fiction. But even though many theorists are particularly interested in non- and antimimetic kinds of narrative such as postmodern texts, they also draw attention to the many unnatural and unrealistic features that can be found in literary realism.[4] These include paralepsis, or a character narrator's knowledge of events he or she cannot have learned, and what James Phelan refers to as "redundant telling," that is, a narrator's apparently unmotivated report of information to a narratee that the narratee already possesses. They are also interested in probing conventional strategies of realistic narratives that nevertheless are impossible or wildly unlikely in everyday experience: phenomena such as omniscience, a streamlined plot, and literary dialogue. Furthermore—as has been claimed by Stefan Iversen in the context of Holocaust narratives ("'In Flaming Flames'")—unnatural and impossible elements may also occasionally be found in nonfictional narrative. In short, unnatural narrative analysis seeks to draw attention both to the unnatural in defiantly antimimetic texts as well as to the largely invisible unnatural elements cached within ostensibly mimetic works.

The term "unnatural" was originally derived from its antithesis to what William Labov called conversational natural narratives. Brian Richardson used it in the title of his book *Unnatural Voices: Extreme Narration in Modern and Contemporary Fiction* as an allusion to Monika Fludernik's *Towards a "Natural" Narratology.* By doing so he indicated that his work was intended to both complement and move beyond the framework that Fludernik had developed and applied. Unnatural narrative theorists like the looseness of the term as well since it provides a kind of umbrella word that all can comfortably utilize, even as each individual occupies a slightly different space and offers adjacent yet overlapping definitions (see, for example, Alber, "Impossible" 80).

4. See, for example, the essays by Maria Mäkelä and James Phelan in this collection.

Unfortunately, the word "unnatural" carries a large amount of cultural baggage that has nothing to do with these narratological investigations, which are "unnatural" only in the socio-linguistic sense just indicated. Unnatural narratology has no position on the nature/culture debate and does not designate any social practices or behavior as natural or unnatural. This term will inevitably cause a certain amount of confusion among the uninformed, but since the name is now fairly well established all are prepared to live with its natural (and unnatural) consequences.

Narrative theory has always had a pronounced mimetic bias. Fictional works are largely treated as if they were primarily lifelike reproductions of human beings and human actions and could be analyzed according to real-world notions of consistency, probability, individual and group psychology, and correspondence with accepted beliefs about the world. This kind of analysis is for the most part perfectly appropriate for substantially mimetic genres such as Menandrine comedy and parts of the realist tradition in the novel, as well as mimetic aspects of works such as Homeric epics, Euripidean drama, and Shakespeare's more realistic plays. An insistently mimetic narrative theory, however, is largely useless when faced with the rich tradition of works by non- or antimimetic authors that stretch from Aristophanes and Apuleius through Rabelais and Shakespeare to the innovative fiction of romanticism, late modernism, and postmodernism.

The unnatural approach is usually an inductive one—beginning with the full range of the literature that exists and then going on to construct theories around it. This is different from approaches such as structuralism that start with a linguistic or rhetorical model and then proceed deductively, often ignoring the many innovative texts that elude the model. We, however, take seriously unusual and experimental texts. Many unnatural works are designed to flout realist models and conventions; they cannot by definition be circumscribed by theories that limit themselves to the forms they are designed to transgress. We feel that a theory of narrative that cannot do justice to non- and antimimetic practices is as impoverished as a theory of art that cannot account for nonrepresentational painting.

In the twentieth century, the tradition of antimimetic narrative theory begins with the insights of the Russian formalists and their analyses of anti-realist texts and techniques (see Shklovsky, for instance). Mikhail Bakhtin ("Forms") is another important theoretician, especially in his work on Rabelais and nonrealist chronotopes of the novel. Theorists and practitioners of experimental French fiction between 1950 and 1980 are also very instructive: these include Nathalie Sarraute, Alain Robbe-Grillet, and Jean Ricardou. We would also like to mention the important work of Brian McHale and Werner

Wolf, who both deal with the specific techniques that are used in postmodern and anti-illusionist narrative texts, as anticipations of unnatural narratology.[5] Since 2000 there has been an explosion of new work in the field by a large number of scholars, many of them represented in this volume, who are keen to theorize the unnatural and who are skeptical about unified theories and universal narratological categories that try to comprehend all narratives whether fictional or nonfictional, written or performed, literary or nonliterary.

The distinctiveness of unnatural narratology, then, is in the object, aims, and approach rather than any specific theoretical framework. Indeed, there is no inherent reason why rhetorical or cognitive theorists could not extend their work to include the rhetoric or cognitive function of non- and antimimetic narrative. In fact, the essays by James Phelan and Jan Alber in this volume show how this fusion might be achieved. At the same time, sustained analyses of antimimetic texts often reveal the limitations of existing narratological accounts: to comprehend the kinds of texts discussed by Heinze and Richardson, for example, one needs to modify and extend existing conceptions of the *fabula*.

This brings us to an outline of some of the most important points of disagreement within the field. These differences concern (a) the definition of the term "unnatural," (b) the choice of methodology and tools, and (c) the question of interpretation. In other words, the differences within unnatural narratology concern the questions of *what* and *how*: what is an unnatural narrative, and how can we approach and/or make sense of it? These divergences affect which texts get included as unnatural, how they are conceptualized, and how their reception is understood.

For Brian Richardson the fundamental criterion of unnatural narratives is their violation of the mimetic conventions that govern conversational natural narratives, nonfictional texts, and realistic works that attempt to mimic the conventions of nonfictional narratives. Robert Coover's "The Babysitter" is an entirely unnatural text as a result of its depictions of contradictory events. The temporality of Shakespeare's *A Midsummer Night's Dream* is unnatural since it has a dual chronology: four days pass for those in Athens while, at the same time, two days pass in the enchanted forest (see Richardson "Time"). Samuel Beckett's *The Unnamable* is a narrative that travesties "the mimesis of actual speech situations" (*Unnatural* 5): the narrator of this novel is a semihuman figure who keeps merging with the contradictory narrative he is telling. Richardson goes on to argue that "if a narrative is, as commonly averred, someone relating a set of events to someone else, then this entire way of looking at nar-

---

5. See also the studies by Heise, Orr, Sherzer, and Traill.

rative has to be reconsidered in the light of the numerous ways innovative authors problematize each term of his formula, especially the first one" (5).

Jan Alber, on the other hand, restricts the use of the term "unnatural" to physically, logically, or humanly impossible scenarios and events. That is to say, the represented scenarios or events have to be impossible by the known laws governing the physical world; accepted principles of logic (such as the principle of noncontradiction); or standard human limitations of knowledge and ability (see also Alber, "Impossible" 80).[6] The speaking breast in Philip Roth's *The Breast,* for instance, is physically impossible because in the real world, breasts do not speak, that is, produce lexemes. Meanwhile, the coexistence of mutually exclusive storylines, as in Robert Coover's short story "The Babysitter," is logically impossible: in the projected storyworld, the contradictory sentences "Mr. Tucker went home to have sex with the babysitter" and "Mr. Tucker did not go home to have sex with the babysitter" are true at the same time, and this feature of the text violates the principle of noncontradiction. Finally, Saleem Sinai, the telepathic first-person narrator in Salman Rushdie's novel *Midnight's Children,* transcends standard human limitations of knowledge and ability because he functions like a radio receiver and can literally hear the thoughts of other characters, which is also impossible in the real world. Moreover, Alber discriminates between unnatural elements that have already been conventionalized, that is, turned into cognitive frames, during the course of literary history (such as the speaking animal in beast fables, the talking objects in eighteenth-century circulation novels, the omniscient narrator in much realist fiction, and time travel in science fiction) and unnatural segments that have not yet been conventionalized and still strike us as being odd, strange, or defamiliarizing (Alber "Diachronic").[7]

For Henrik Skov Nielsen, unnaturalness can appear on the representational level as well as on the level of the act of narration. For him, unnatural narratives are a subset of fictional narratives that may have temporalities, storyworlds, mind representations, or acts of narration that would have to be construed as physically, logically, mnemonically, or psychologically impossible or implausible in real-world storytelling situations.

In his essay in this volume, Stefan Iversen ties the notion of the unnatural to narratives that present the reader with clashes between the rules governing the storyworld in the narrative and events producing or taking place inside

---

6. The unnatural in Alber's sense may concern the level of the story but also discrepancies between the level of the story and the level of the narrative discourse. An example of the latter would be the child narrator in John Hawkes's *Virginie: Her Two Lives* who speaks like an unusually eloquent adult.

7. In most cases, Richardson would refer to these two types as, respectively, nonmimetic and antimimetic.

this storyworld, in other words, clashes that defy naturalization. While many of these events become conventionalized over time, some remain resistant to familiarization, such as the unnatural transformation in Franz Kafka's "The Metamorphosis," which confronts the reader with an unresolvable fusion of a bug and a human mind, situated in an otherwise conventionally realist storyworld. Iversen's model allows for explaining the fact that some narratives change status along the natural–unnatural axis over time as new methods of conventionalization are developed and become widespread.

A fifth definition sees any kind of fictional and/or artificial representation of human life as unnatural in the capacity of its character as a representation that is tied to one or more specific types of media. In Maria Mäkelä's terms, "we don't have to resort to avant-garde literature to notice that the unnaturalness—or the peculiarly *literary* type of cognitive challenge—is always already there in textual representations of consciousness" ("Cycles" 133). To Mäkelä, the unnatural does not only emerge from broken conventions or impossible scenarios; it must also be recognized as a fundamental feature of *any* fictional representation of human life. A very broad notion of the unnatural results from this approach, in that in effect any type of art is, as Mäkelä puts it, always already not natural, in the sense of being artificial.

The question of methodology (b) and the process of interpretation (c), then, concern the question of how to make sense of unnatural narratives. Richardson has argued in favor of the development of concepts and models that are sensitive to the fluidity and dichotomy-resistant nature of unnatural narratives. Thus, the simple opposition between story and discourse is often dismantled or problematized by experimental works, as the essays by Brian Richardson and Rüdiger Heinze here make clear. According to Richardson, "we will be most effective as narrative theorists if we reject models that, based on categories derived from linguistics or natural narrative, insist on firm distinctions, binary oppositions, fixed hierarchies, or impermeable categories" (*Unnatural* 139).

Jan Alber instead argues that "ideas from cognitive narratology help illuminate the considerable, sometimes unsettling interpretive difficulties posed by unnatural elements" and advocates using "cognitive-narratological work to clarify how some literary texts not only rely on but also aggressively challenge the mind's fundamental sense-making capabilities" ("Impossible" 80). Alber argues that since we are always bound by our cognitive architecture, unnatural narratives can only be approached on the basis of cognitive frames and scripts.[8] He therefore proposes a number of reading strategies designed

8. Frames are static, while scripts are dynamic cognitive parameters: "frames basically deal with situations such as seeing a room or making a promise while scripts cover standard

to help readers explain or make sense of the unnatural.⁹ According to his approach, the reader's job is to demonstrate how the unnatural urges us to create new cognitive frames that transcend our real-world knowledge (such as the unborn narrator, the speaking corpse, the reversed causality, or the shapeshifting room), and, in a second step, to address the question of what the unnatural says about us and our being in the world. Alber's second step closely correlates with what Stein Haugom Olsen calls the "'human interest' question" (67), that is, the argument that fiction focuses on "mortal life: how to understand it and how to live it" (Nagel ix).

By contrast, what one might call unnaturalizing readings leave open the possibility that unnatural narratives contain or produce effects and emotions that are not easily (if at all) explainable or resolvable with reference to everyday phenomena or with reference to the rules of the presented storyworld.¹⁰ In his contribution to this volume, Stefan Iversen elaborates on ideas presented by H. Porter Abbott, who—when discussing what he calls "unreadable minds"—claims that they "work best when we allow ourselves to rest in that peculiar combination of anxiety and wonder that is aroused when an unreadable mind is accepted as unreadable. In this regard, my stance is at odds with efforts to make sense of the unreadable, as, for example, Jan Alber's effort" ("Unreadable" 448).¹¹

Similarly, Henrik Skov Nielsen argues that when readers face unnatural narratives, they have two options: they can either try to naturalize or they can apply unnaturalizing reading strategies. Unnaturalizing reading strategies, for him, resist the application of real-world limitations to all narratives and refrain from limiting interpretations to what is possible in literal communicative acts and representational models. Accordingly, for Nielsen, unnatural narratology investigates the interpretational consequences of the employment of unnatural techniques, scenarios, and strategies insofar as they are *different* from the interpretation of natural narratives. For example, he argues that readers will be led astray if they judge first-person narration unreliable only on the basis that information is revealed that the protagonist could not realis-

---

action sequences such as playing a game of football, going to a birthday party, or eating in a restaurant" (Jahn, "Cognitive" 69).

9. See also the essays by Jan Alber and Werner Wolf in this collection.

10. This point is also made by Henrik Skov Nielsen and Maria Mäkelä in this volume.

11. Abbott is here rephrasing what the Romantic poet John Keats calls "*Negative Capability*": the state of remaining in "uncertainties, mysteries, doubts without any irritable reaching after fact or reason" (Forman, *Letters* 72). Along the same lines, Jan Alber proposes "the Zen way of reading," which might be adopted by an attentive reader who repudiates cognitive-rational explanations, and simultaneously accepts the strangeness of unnatural scenarios and the feelings of discomfort, fear, or worry that they evoke in her or him ("Impossible" 83).

tically possess. Likewise, he argues, if we begin to ask in second-person narratives who is telling this story to the "you" that seems completely unaffected by and even ignorant of the uttered words, we will miss the point of most literary second-person narratives that explore the possibility of designating while not addressing a specific person through the "you"—a possibility that is different from oral, natural storytelling situations in which the "you" simply refers to the audience being addressed (or is used in the sense of "one").

Even though their individual formulations and specific interests may vary, it should be underscored that these approaches within the new paradigm of unnatural narratology are all drawn to the same basic features and qualities of narrative fiction: the impossible, the unreal, the preternatural, the outrageous, the extreme, the parodic, and the insistently fictional.

Let us turn to the individual contributions. Brian Richardson's essay examines the nature and narrative status of a number of unnatural stories and progressions. He begins with texts that test the very concept of narrative: extreme works by Beckett and Robbe-Grillet that play with or aspire to the status of a minimal narrative and David Shields's unusual collection of actual bumper stickers that he has assembled into a text called "Life Story." Richardson goes on to explore unnatural narratives' innovative practices and challenges to traditional conceptions of story (*fabula*) and text (*syuzhet*), investigating works that refuse to provide fixed or retrievable stories, a stable presentation of the text, or both. His analysis of Ana Castillo's *The Mixquiahuala Letters* discloses the way readers are invited to construct three different possible stories by using any of three different reading sequences. He goes on to discuss works that refuse to offer fixed beginnings or single endings. Richardson then discusses challenges to the identity of a single narrative in the case of texts that produce variant sequences and multiple plot trajectories (*Lola rennt*). In the course of this investigation, he argues for the extension and reformulation of conventional narratological concepts, calls for the inclusion of the important analytical category of multilinearity, and makes the case for still other essential analytical tools for postmodern narrative progressions.

Moving along a parallel path, Rüdiger Heinze discusses the many paradoxes of unnatural temporality in fictional narratives. After a compelling discussion of time as understood by physicists and time as constructed by novelists, he identifies two major types of unnatural temporality: one located in the story, the other in the work's discourse. The former can be found in H. G. Wells's *The Time Machine*, which depicts an unnatural temporal scenario at the story level that is quite unobtrusive at the level of discourse. In the latter camp, he points to antichronological and fragmentary texts that present perfectly realist events in an unnatural manner. And there are also texts that do both. He explains how readers come to naturalize and narrativize these unusual texts, and goes on to discuss works that cannot be broken down into the fabula/syuzhet model, something that can be done with every natural narrative. Heinze discusses the role of medium and genre in the construction and perception of unnatural temporalities, and points out some surprising paradoxes that ensue from these modes.

In his contribution, Jan Alber seeks to further our understanding of narrative spaces by determining the potential functions of representations of physically or logically impossible space. In a first step, he shows that narratives may denaturalize our real-world knowledge of spatial organization in a wide variety of different ways. For instance, narrative texts may present us with shapeshifting locations; burning lakes; insubstantial castles; impossible planets; visions of the infinite universe; unnatural geographies; two-, one-, and nondimensional worlds; literal manifestations of internal processes; houses that are bigger on the inside than they are on the outside; and so forth. In a second step, he addresses the potential purpose or point of these simulations of impossible space. For Alber, unnatural spaces fulfill determinable functions and exist for particular reasons. He thus proposes seven reading strategies that concern the cognitive reconstruction of spatial impossibilities on the one hand, and their subsequent interpretation on the other. Furthermore, his navigational tools constitute options to help readers cope with the unnatural in general and impossible spaces in particular.

Henrik Skov Nielsen argues that it is sometimes necessary, often profitable, and nearly always possible to apply unnaturalizing reading strategies when faced with unnatural narratives. He contends that Genette's separation of voice and mood (who speaks? vs. who perceives?) and Genette's understanding of focalization as a restriction of access to point of view are more radical proposals than previous narratologists have recognized—and that they are in line with unnatural narratology insofar as they allow for the development of unnaturalizing reading strategies. Furthermore, Nielsen argues that Genette's separation of mood and voice and the possible combinations that follow from it are connected to the no-narrator thesis. These combinations of narration and focalization are attributable not to a fact-reporting narrator but rather to a world-creating author. The consequences of this assumption are tested in a range of examples, and, finally, he offers a simple rhetorical model in which the real author (rather than the narrator) is the main agent of the telling.

Stefan Iversen takes unnatural minds as his topic, and examines the nature of subversive, impossible, and metamorphosed minds in narrative fiction. He provides a definition of unnatural minds and goes on to evaluate approaches to theories of mind that have recently been set forth in cognitive studies and philosophy, showing the inherent limitations of most of these accounts when confronting antimimetic narratives. To demonstrate his argument, he applies it to Marie Darrieussecq's *Pig Tales,* the story of a woman who is miraculously transformed into a pig.

Werner Wolf addresses the important question of whether metalepsis, an inherently unnatural phenomenon, and aesthetic illusionism are necessarily incompatible. He shows that there are indeed cases in which the unnaturalness of metalepsis appears to be compatible with immersion and aesthetic illusion, and hence there is not a *necessary* incompatibility in all cases. On the other hand, it is worth noting that metalepsis generally has a strong antiillusionist effect as a common function. However, Wolf shows that this is a generalization which must be relativized—at least with regard to the cases he discusses in his essay.

Maria Mäkelä's essay attempts to recover the unnatural essence of the conventional in narrative fiction. She argues that classical realist novels are often far from being natural. Focusing in turn on the topics of perception, psychological verisimilitude, anti-immersion, and discursive agency, she shows how the works of classical realists such as Flaubert, Tolstoy, and Dickens are permeated by dislocated or unnatural perceptions, conflicted or arbitrary motivation, and the frequent impossibility to derive cognitive agency from novelistic representation. In the end, this essay calls for nothing less than a reevaluation of the project of realism.

Meanwhile James Phelan studies character narrators in mimetic fiction but zeroes in on some salient violations of mimetic conventions. His essay provides a rhetorical account of these unnatural acts of narration, focusing on "implausibly knowledgeable" narration in *Huckleberry Finn* and *The Great Gatsby,* and on the "impossible" phenomenon of simultaneous first-person present-tense narration. Phelan also introduces an unnatural narrative technique that has hitherto gone unnoticed and coins it "crossover narration." In "crossover narration," an author transfers the effects arising from the narration of one set of events to the narration of a second independent set of events. Phelan proposes some rules of thumb about the reading of mimetic character narration that explain why most readers do not notice these violations of the mimetic code and why they are so rhetorically effective.

Alice Bell's analysis may be placed at the intersection of unnatural and transmedial narratology. More specifically, Bell analyzes two examples of unnatural narrative in Stuart Moulthrop's 1991 hypertext fiction *Victory Garden.* Her first analysis shows how the multilinear structure of a hypertext creates contradictions in the narrative. In her second analysis, Bell demonstrates that the fragmented structure of the text allows the unnatural status of a scene to change depending on the reading route through which it is accessed. She ends her discussion by arguing that any narratological analysis must be alert to the media-specific features present within these unique texts.

The protagonist of Borges's story "The Secret Miracle" chooses to write his drama in verse because, as he puts it, verse "does not allow the spectators to forget unreality, which is the condition of art" (159). In the same spirit, Brian McHale investigates the unnaturalness or artificiality of narrative poetry. More specifically, he analyses William Shakespeare's *Venus and Adonis* as well as Les Murray's *Fredy Neptune* to show that artificial segmentation functionalizes and semanticizes nonsemantic patterns, such as rhyme, that are irrelevant and even inaudible in unsegmented prose. Furthermore, artificial segmentation occasionally coincides with narrative segmentation, enhancing and amplifying it. Sometimes, instead, it cuts across segmentation, setting up counter-rhythms, syncopating and counterpointing narrative shifts. In any case, by introducing a series of minuscule gaps and interruptions, artificial segmentation jars us out of our automatic (or "natural") attitude toward such a narrative. For McHale, artificial segmentation counters the template of natural narrative with a competing unnatural one.

It will be readily apparent that the essays in this volume are not simply dutiful reapplications of the same general formula. Instead, the contributors develop the poetics even as they are expounding it. The editors are interested in assembling a dialogue of overlapping perspectives and watching them enrich, modify, and extend each other's insights. We are happy to leave the differences in a productive tension, a normal enough situation at the birth of a new theoretical approach. Furthermore, we feel that diversity has proven productive for the field of narrative theory as a whole, and it would be surprising if this were not also the case with regard to the thriving subdiscipline of unnatural narratology.

In addition, we hope this volume will achieve several other goals. We believe it will help us refigure literary history by connecting postmodern experiments with earlier unnatural work in Aristophanes, epics, romances, Rabelais, German romanticism, Gothic fiction, metadrama, science fiction, theater of the absurd, *écriture féminine,* and many avant-garde experiments. We expect these essays to help provide a rethinking of literary realism, and to suggest important new perspectives on narrative poetry, nonfictional narratives, and hyperfiction.[12] Above all, we hope to fill an important gap in exist-

---

12. See, for example, the essays by Brian McHale and Alice Bell.

ing narrative theory by including the wide range of texts it has historically ignored, and by producing expanded theoretical models that are able to incorporate these recalcitrant texts. Furthermore, we wish to identify, comprehend, and theorize the numerous unnatural elements within seemingly realistic or largely mimetic works and thereby provide a more comprehensive account of narrative fiction in general.

Works Cited

Abbott, H. Porter. "Immersions in the Cognitive Sublime: The Textual Experience of the Extratextual Unknown in García Márquez and Beckett." *Narrative* 17.2 (2009): 131–41.
———. "Unreadable Minds and the Captive Reader." *Style* 42.4 (2008): 448–70.
Alber, Jan. "The Diachronic Development of Unnaturalness: A New View on Genre." In Alber and Heinze, *Unnatural Narratives, Unnatural Narratology*, 41–67.
———. "The Ethical Implications of Unnatural Scenarios." In *Why Study Literature?* ed. Jan Alber, Stefan Iversen, Louise Brix Jacobsen, Rikke Andersen Kraglund, Henrik Skov Nielsen, and Camilla Møhring Reestorff. Aarhus: Aarhus University Press, 2011. 211–33.
———. "Impossible Storyworlds—And What to Do with Them." *Storyworlds* 1 (2009): 79–96.
———. "The 'Moreness' or 'Lessness' of 'Natural' Narratology: Samuel Beckett's 'Lessness' Reconsidered." *Style* 36.1 (2002): 54–75. Reprinted in *Short Story Criticism* 74 (2004): 113–24.
———. "Pre-Postmodernist Manifestations of the Unnatural: Instances of Expanded Consciousness in Omniscient Narration and Reflector-Mode Narratives." *Zeitschrift für Anglistik und Amerikanistik*, forthcoming 2013.
———. "Unnatural Narrative: Impossible Worlds in Fiction and Drama." Habilitation, University of Freiburg, Germany, 2012.
———. "Unnatural Narratives." *The Literary Encyclopedia.* www.litencyc.com, 2009.
———. "Unnatural Narratology: Developments and Perspectives." *Germanisch-Romanische Monatsschrift*, forthcoming 2013.
———. "Unnatural Temporalities: Interfaces between Postmodernism, Science Fiction, and the Fantastic." In *Narrative Interrupted: The Plotless, the Disturbing and the Trivial in Literature*, ed. Markku Lehtimäki, Laura Kartunen, and Maria Mäkelä. New York et al.: de Gruyter, 2012. 174–91.
Alber, Jan, and Alice Bell. "Ontological Metalepsis and Unnatural Narratology." *Journal of Narrative Theory* 42.2 (2012): 166–92.
Alber, Jan, and Rüdiger Heinze, eds. *Unnatural Narratives, Unnatural Narratology.* Berlin and New York: de Gruyter, 2011.
Alber, Jan, Stefan Iversen, Henrik Skov Nielsen, and Brian Richardson. "Unnatural Narratives, Unnatural Narratology: Beyond Mimetic Models." *Narrative* 18.2 (2010): 113–36.
———. "What is Unnatural about Unnatural Narratology? A Response to Monika Fludernik." *Narrative* 20.3 (2012): 371–82.
———. "What Really Is Unnatural Narratology?" *Storyworlds* 4, forthcoming 2013.
Alber, Jan, Henrik Skov Nielsen, and Brian Richardson. "Unnatural Voices, Minds, and Narration." In *The Routledge Companion to Experimental Literature*, ed. Joe Bray, Alison Gibbons, and Brian McHale. London: Routledge, 2012. 351–67.

Bakhtin, Mikhail. "Forms of Time and the Chronotope in the Novel [1938–73]." In *The Dialogic Imagination: Four Essays*, ed. Michael Holquist. Austin: University of Texas Press, 1981. 84–258.
Borges, Jorge Luis. *Collected Fictions.* Trans. Andrew Hurley. New York: Penguin, 1998.
Doležel, Lubomír. *Heterocosmica: Fiction and Possible Worlds.* Baltimore and London: Johns Hopkins University Press, 1998.
Fludernik, Monika. *Towards a "Natural" Narratology.* London and New York: Routledge, 1996.
———. "How Natural is "Unnatural Narratology"; or, What Is Unnatural about Unnatural Narratology?" *Narrative* 20.3 (2012): 357–70.
Forman, Maurice Buxton, ed. *The Letters of John Keats.* London: Oxford University Press, 1935.
Hansen, Per Krogh, Stefan Iversen, Henrik Skov Nielsen, and Rolf Reitan, eds. *Strange Voices in Narrative Fiction.* Berlin and New York: de Gruyter, 2011.
Heinze, Rüdiger. "Violations of Mimetic Epistemology in First-Person Narrative Fiction." *Narrative* 16.3 (2008): 279–97.
Heise, Ursula K. *Chronoschisms: Time, Narrative, and Postmodernism.* Cambridge: Cambridge University Press, 1997.
Herman, Luc, and Bart Vervaeck. *Handbook of Narrative Analysis.* Lincoln: University of Nebraska Press, 2005.
Iversen, Stefan. "'In Flaming Flames': Crises of Experientiality in Non-Fictional Narratives." In Alber and Heinze, *Unnatural Narratives, Unnatural Narratology,* 89–103.
———. "States of Exception: Decoupling, Metarepresentation, and Strange Voices in Narrative Fiction." In Hansen, Iversen, Nielsen, and Reitan, *Strange Voices in Narrative Fiction,* 127–46.
Jahn, Manfred. "Cognitive Narratology." In *Routledge Encyclopedia of Narrative Theory,* ed. David Herman, Manfred Jahn, and Marie-Laure Ryan. London: Routledge, 2005. 67–71.
Klauk, Tobias, and Tilmann Köppe. "Reassessing Unnatural Narratology: Problems and Prospects." *Storyworlds* 4, forthcoming 2013.
Labov, William. *Language in the Inner City: Studies in the Black English Vernacular.* Philadelphia: University of Pennsylvania Press, 1972.
Mäkelä, Maria. "Cycles of Narrative Necessity: Suspect Tellers and the Textuality of Fictional Minds." In *Stories and Minds,* ed. Lars Bernaerts, Dirk de Geest, Luc Herman, and Bart Vervaeck. Lincoln: University of Nebraska Press, 2013. 129–51.
———. "Possible Minds: Constructing—and Reading—Another Consciousness as Fiction." In *FREE Language INDIRECT Translation DISCOURSE Narratology: Linguistic, Translatological, and Literary-Theoretical Encounters,* ed. Pekka Tammi and Hannu Tommola. Tampere: Tampere University Press, 2006. 231–60.
———. "Who Wants to Know Emma Bovary? How to Read an Adulterous Mind through Fractures of FID." In *Linguistic and Literary Aspects of Free Indirect Discourse from a Typological Perspective,* ed. Pekka Tammi and Hannu Tommola. Tampere: University of Tampere Press, 2003. 55–72.
McHale, Brian. *Postmodernist Fiction.* New York and London: Methuen, 1987.
———. *Constructing Postmodernism.* London and New York: Routledge, 1992.
Nagel, Thomas. *Moral Questions.* Cambridge: Cambridge University Press, 1979.
Nielsen, Henrik Skov. "The Impersonal Voice in First-Person Narrative Fiction." *Narrative* 12.2 (2004): 133–50.

———. "Natural Authors, Unnatural Narratives." In *Postclassical Narratology: Approaches and Analyses*, ed. Jan Alber and Monika Fludernik. Columbus: The Ohio State University Press, 2010. 275–301.

———. "Unnatural Narratology, Impersonal Voices, Real Authors, and Non-Communicative Narration." In Alber and Heinze, *Unnatural Narratives, Unnatural Narratology*, 71–88.

———. "Fictional Voices? Strange Voices? Unnatural Voices?" In Hansen, Iversen, Nielsen, and Reitan, *Strange Voices in Narrative Fiction*, 55–82.

Olsen, Stein Haugom. *The End of Literary Theory*. Cambridge: Cambridge University Press, 1987.

Orr, Leonard. *Problems and Poetics of the Nonaristotelian Novel*. Lewisburg, PA: Bucknell University Press, 1991.

Richardson, Brian. "Beyond Poststructuralism: Theory of Character, the Personae of Modern Drama, and the Antinomies of Critical Theory." *Modern Drama* 40 (1997): 86–99.

———. "Beyond Story and Discourse: Narrative Time in Postmodern and Nonmimetic Fiction." In *Narrative Dynamics: Essays on Time, Plot, Closure, and Frames*, ed. Brian Richardson. Columbus: The Ohio State University Press, 2002. 47–63.

———. "Beyond the Poetics of Plot: Alternative Forms of Narrative Progression and the Multiple Trajectories of *Ulysses*." In *A Companion to Narrative Theory*, ed. James Phelan and Peter Rabinowitz. Malden, MA: Blackwell, 2005. 167–80.

———. "Denarration in Fiction: Erasing the Story in Beckett and Others." *Narrative* 9.2 (2001): 168–75.

———. "Nabokov's Experiments and the Nature of Fictionality." *Storyworlds* 3 (2011): 73–92.

———. "Narrative Poetics and Postmodern Transgression: Theorizing the Collapse of Time, Voice, and Frame." *Narrative* 8.1 (2000): 23–42.

———. "Plot after Postmodernism." In *Drama and/after Postmodernism*, ed. Christoph Henke and Martin Middeke. Trier: WVT, 2007. 55–67.

———. "'Time Is Out of Joint': Narrative Models and the Temporality of the Drama." *Poetics Today* 8.2 (1987): 299–310.

———. *Unnatural Voices: Extreme Narration in Modern and Contemporary Fiction*. Columbus: The Ohio State University Press, 2006.

———. "Voice and Narration in Postmodern Drama." *New Literary History* 32 (2001): 681–94.

Richardson, Brian, David Herman, James Phelan, Peter Rabinowitz, and Robyn Warhol. *Narrative Theory: Core Concepts and Critical Debates*. Columbus: The Ohio State University Press, 2012.

Sherzer, Dina. *Representation in Contemporary French Fiction*. Lincoln and London: University of Nebraska Press, 1987.

Shklovsky, Victor. "Art as Technique." In *Russian Formalist Criticism*, ed. Lee T. Lemon and Marion J. Reis. Lincoln: University of Nebraska Press, 1965. 3–24.

Tammi, Pekka. "Against 'Against' Narrative (On Nabokov's 'Recruiting')." In *Narrativity, Fictionality, and Literariness: The Narrative Turn and the Study of Literary Fiction*, ed. Lars-Åke Skalin. Örebro: Örebro University Press, 2008. 37–55.

———. "Against Narrative ('A Boring Story')." *Partial Answers* 4.2 (2006): 19–40.

Traill, Nancy H. *Possible Worlds of the Fantastic: The Rise of the Paranormal in Literature*. Toronto: University of Toronto Press, 1996.

Wolf, Werner. *Ästhetische Illusion und Illusionsdurchbrechung in der Erzählkunst. Theorie und Geschichte mit Schwerpunkt auf englischem illusionsstörenden Erzählen*. Tübingen: Niemeyer, 1993.

Unnatural Stories and Sequences

1

BRIAN RICHARDSON

A CONVENTIONAL, realistic, or conversational natural narrative typically has a fairly straightforward story of a certain magnitude that follows an easily recognizable trajectory. Unnatural narratives challenge, transgress, or reject many or all of these basic conventions; the more radical the rejection, the more unnatural the resulting story is. For me, the fundamental criterion of the unnatural is its violation of the mimetic conventions that govern conversational natural narratives, nonfictional texts, and realistic works that attempt to mimic the conventions of nonfictional narratives. In what follows, I will focus on works that are decidedly antimimetic, but I will also look at some other extremely unusual sequences whose startling unconventionality situates them at the edge of the unnatural. Thus, the most striking aspect of Nabokov's *Pale Fire* is not the invention of the fictitious country of Zembla but the narrative that emerges from the unlikely source of a poem and the mad commentary it inspires. These examinations will in turn allow me to explore the larger implications of such texts, examining how they test or defy the concept of narrative itself, of a single self-consistent story, of a fixed presentation (*syuzhet*) of the story (*fabula*), of beginnings and endings, and of the idea of a single story.

1. Narrativity

The most fundamental interrogation of traditional story is that of narrative itself: does a given assemblage of words constitute a narrative, does it constitute a different kind of text, or does it hover somewhere at the very border of narrativity? A number of recent works navigate just this boundary. Rick Moody's story "Primary Sources" consists solely of an alphabetical list of titles in the narrator's library and a series of thirty footnotes that comment on each book. This sketchy and selective bibliography is really an autobiography, the narrator avers; as we read more and more of the footnotes, we get more information about the narrator's life. Thus, the annotation to the first book, William Parker Abbé's *A Diary of Sketches*, begins: "Art instructor at St. Paul's School when I was there ('75–'79)" (231). The narrative bits accumulate to the point where we can indeed place a number of episodes into a causally related temporal sequence and thereby construct a partial, fragmentary, episodic narrative. Other texts similarly challenge narrative practices and limits. J. G. Ballard's "The Index" is merely an index to a fictional biography that nevertheless divulges the entire, unbelievable life history of a certain Henry Rhodes Hamilton (sample entry: "Churchill, Winston, conversations with HRH, 221; at Chequers with HRH, 235; spinal tap performed by HRH, 247; at Yalta with HRH, 298; 'iron curtain' speech, Fulton Missouri, suggested by HRH, 312; attacks HRH in Commons debate, 367"). Ballard has also written another story that is composed solely of a single sentence, each word of which is annotated ("Notes Towards a Mental Breakdown"). And there are even more extreme examples of such experiments, such as the set of annotations to a text that has been erased in Jenny Boully's "The Body" (2003). As its second footnote states, "It is not the story I know or the story that you tell me that matters; it is what I already know, what I don't want to hear you say. Let it exist this way, concealed" (437).

Other writers play with but may not quite attain narrative status; that is, the assemblages fail to cohere into an identifiable story. This is arguably the case in David Shields's unusual piece "Life Story," a collection of actual American bumper stickers arranged in thematic clusters along a vaguely temporal trajectory. It begins:

> First things first.
> You're only young once, but you can be immature forever. I may grow old,
>   but I'll never grow up. Too fast to live, too young to die. Life's a beach.
> Not all men are fools; some are single. 100% Single. I'm not playing hard to
>   get; I am hard to get. I love being exactly who I am.

> Heaven doesn't want me and Hell's afraid I'll take over. I'm the person your mother warned you about. Ex-girlfriend in trunk. Don't laugh; your girlfriend might be in here.

The text goes on to assemble a number of other clusters concerning activities, personal predilections, and sexual identifiers. The latter include a number of insistently erotic ones: "Girls wanted, all positions, will train. Playgirl on board. Party girl on board. Sexy blonde on board. Not all dumbs are blonde." More philosophical statements about the nature of human existence appear later in the text: "Love sucks and then you die. Gravity's a lie; life sucks. Life's a bitch; you marry one, then you die. Life's a bitch and so am I. Beyond bitch." Culturally coded female voices emerge with greater frequency, some crass, others cynical: "So many men, so little time. Expensive but worth it. If you're rich, I'm single. Richer is better. Shopaholic on board. Born to shop. I'd rather be shopping at Nordstrom. Born to be pampered. A woman's place is the mall. When the going gets tough, the tough go shopping. Consume and die. He who dies with the most toys wins. She who dies with the most jewels wins. Die, yuppie scum." The entire cycle of family life is represented, from "Baby on board" to "My kid beat up your honor student" to references to grandchildren. Bumper stickers involving aging are collected later in the text: "I may be growing old, but I refuse to grow up. Get even: live long enough to become a problem to your kids. We're out spending our children's inheritance." The text ends with references to dementia and death: "Of all the things I've lost, I miss my mind the most. I brake for unicorns. Choose death."

If a narrative is a representation of a causally connected series of events of some magnitude, then it is not clear that this collection qualifies as a narrative. The subject seems too scattered, too contradictory; the narrative too unconnected, often because it is too specific in identifying antithetical predilections and its incompatible target audiences. I see this rather as a pseudonarrative, a collection that mimics but does not comprise a genuine narrative, however minimal.

Samuel Beckett challenges the boundaries of narrative in a different manner. His story "Ping" presents a series of descriptions that are repeated and slightly varied throughout the text. Other oddities of this piece are the absence of any active verbs and the irregular interjection of the syllable "ping." The reader is challenged by a number of interpretative questions, a central one being whether the text is a narrative or not; that is, does it simply display a group of descriptions, or do those images constitute a narrative; that is, can one derive a fabula from these images? The space is a confined, white enclosure: "White walls one yard by two white ceiling one square yard never seen"

(*Prose* 193). The central figure is human or humanoid: "bare white body fixed one yard legs joined like sewn" (193). The body is immobile in a semigeometrical position: "hands hanging palms front white feet heels together right angle" (193). The only nonwhite entity seems to be the figure's eyes: "Only the eyes only just light blue almost white" (193).

James Knowlson and John Pilling even aver that "it is impossible to read *Ping* in the consecutive manner in which we read a narrative that is ongoing in its syntax (say, *Ulysses*). It resembles rather a piece of sculpture that we contemplate from outside, attuning ourselves to the shape and texture of the materials" (169). Nevertheless, as these descriptions recur, the reader, like the narratologist, looks for signs of life and movement: if there is no change, there can be no narrative. Beckett teasingly offers a few scraps of possible, if minimal, transformation. The light is sometimes described as "light grey almost white" (193); this could mean that the light source changes or merely that the original depiction is being slightly modified. There seems to be a sound: "Murmur only just almost never one second perhaps not alone" (193). This is our first indication of any passage of time; the murmur would presumably be coming from the supine figure. Then there is the irregularly occurring word "Ping," which may be a repeated mechanical sound in the storyworld or simply an aspect of the work's strange discourse. The blue eyes seem to turn black and a possible fleeting memory may appear as the ping syllable recurs with greater frequency: "Ping perhaps not alone one second with image same time a little less dim eye black and white half closed long lashes imploring that much memory almost never" (195). It is not immediately clear what the phrase (if it is a single phrase) "imploring that much memory" means (the figure has enough memory to enable him to implore?); the two terms "imploring" and "memory" do suggest a temporal passage, if only a brief, painful one. This reading seems confirmed by the text's last sentence: "Head haught eyes white fixed front old ping last murmur one second perhaps not alone eye unlustrous black and white half closed long lashes imploring ping silence ping over" (196). This text plays at the edges of narrative, suggesting the most minimal possible narrative of an immobile figure in pain, with memories, imploring; however, we are never able to say definitively that it does in fact cross over the boundary into narrative.

Robbe-Grillet challenges narrativity from the opposite end of the spectrum. If Beckett's text has too few events, Robbe-Grillet's has far too many contradictory ones. His story "The Secret Room" presents several depictions of what superficially appears to be the same scene at different times. Sometimes they appear to be a series of actions, scrambled in time; at others, the text seems to depict several visual images, presumably paintings, which either can form a narrative or else are merely variations on a theme. Both interpretations are right and wrong: characters are described as moving, which indicates the presence of a narrative, though other images are depicted as painted. The reader is challenged to actively assemble from the pieces of the text a narrative of a gothic murder and the escape of the killer. However, because of contradictions in the descriptions of the setting, it remains a quasi-story; the fabula will not stay fixed, it does not endure as a representation of a single set of events. In other words, the only way a narrative can emerge is if a reader disregards the contradictions, takes up the events and, forcibly adding the narrativity, turns them into a story. The governing (or generating) figure is the spiral, which is manifested in numerous spatial patterns as well as in the work's temporality. It becomes clear that the text is not a realistic representation of a series of events that could occur in the world, but rather a uniquely fictional creation that can only exist as literature.

2. Fabula

One of the most foundational concepts in narrative theory is the dyad of fabula and syuzhet, or the distinction between the story that we infer from a text and presentation of that text itself. This distinction, established by the Russian formalists, has been around for nearly a century and is referred to in a variety of ways, including the French structuralist terms *histoire* and *récit*, and story and text. (In this essay, I will retain the Russian formalist terms for analytical precision.) Meir Sternberg has indicated the importance of this distinction for narrative theory, asserting that "actional discourse, whether literary or historical or cinematic, presupposes temporal extension [which] provides a natural principle of coherence, one that enables the narrator to construct his presentational sequence, [. . .] according to the logic of progression inherent in the line or chain of events themselves; from earlier to later and from cause to effect" (60–61).

As his metaphors of line and chain indicate, Sternberg here reveals himself to be trapped by mimetic presuppositions. As Monika Fludernik has pointed out, "the story vs discourse opposition seems to repose on a realist understanding of narrative" (334). A noncontradictory fabula can indeed be derived from every correctly formed nonfictional or conversational natural narrative, as well as the mimetic or realist works of fiction that strive to resemble these discourse types.[1] There remain, however, a number of varieties of unnatural

---

1. It may be objected that an unreliable narrator of a realist novel or an incompetent or

fabulas that elude the mimetic model which narrative theory needs to account for. A narrative can circle back on itself, as the last sentence becomes the first sentence, and thus continues for eternity (Joyce's *Finnegans Wake*, 1939; Nabokov's "The Circle," 1936); such a fabula is infinite. In other works, time passes at different speeds for different groups of people. Thus, in Shakespeare's *A Midsummer Night's Dream*, four days pass for the nobles in the orderly city while—at the same time—two days pass in the enchanted forest (see Richardson "Time"). In Virginia Woolf's *Orlando* (1928), twenty years pass for the protagonist while three and a half centuries pass for those around him (her); similarly, in Caryl Churchill's play *Cloud Nine* (1979), twenty-five years pass for the characters while a full century passes for the rest of the world. These cases result in dual or multiple fabulas.

Other texts have several contradictory sequences of events (Robbe-Grillet's *La Jalousie*, 1957; Robert Coover's "The Babysitter," 1969). Some of the different, incompatible endings all present in Coover's text include the following: the babysitter accidentally drowns the baby, the husband who hired her comes back early to have sex with her, the babysitter is raped and murdered by neighborhood boys, the family returns to find all is well, and the mother learns from the television that the children are murdered, her husband is gone, there is a corpse in the bathtub, and her house is destroyed. Ursula Heise has observed that such novels "project into the narrative present and past an experience of time which normally is only available for the future: time dividing and subdividing, bifurcating and branching off continuously into multiple possibilities and alternatives" (55). Instead of one event precluding several other possible options, all possibilities can be seen to have been actualized. In none of the examples noted in this section can one easily extract a single, consistent story from a fixed syuzhet the way one might in any natural or realistic narrative.[2] Alain Robbe-Grillet, referring to the contradictory fabula in *Jealousy*, stated: "It was absurd to propose that in the novel . . . there existed a clear and unambiguous order of events, one which was not that of the sentences of the book, as if I had diverted myself by mixing up a pre-established calendar the way one shuffles a deck of cards" (*New* 154) and went on to state that for him there existed no possible order outside of that found within the pages themselves. This text does not mimic realistic narratives whose syuzhets

---

deceptive conversational narrator can have inconsistencies in their stories; this fact does not invalidate the larger principle I am developing. In such cases, the inconsistencies are epistemological, based on faulty narration of a fixed set of events, not ontological, denoting incompatible realities.

2. For additional discussions of many of these forms, see my essay "Beyond Story and Discourse" and Rüdiger Heinze's essay in this volume.

will divulge a single fabula; here one has only an indeterminate, contradictory fabula.

Still other kinds of unnatural fabula also exist. Some of Lorrie Moore's stories mimic the form of the self-help manual and provide hypothetical sequences of possible events: "Begin by meeting him in a class, a bar, at a rummage sale. Maybe he teaches sixth grade. Manages a hardware store. Foreman at a carton factory. He will be a good dancer . . . A week, a month, a year. Feel discovered, comforted, needed, loved, and start sometimes, somehow, to feel bored" (55). Matt DelConte has suggested that texts like this "do not have a story in the traditional sense: the entire action consists of discourse because the prescribed events are hypothetical/conditional; nothing has actually happened" (214). For him, there is no actual fabula. Nevertheless, I argue that there are finite though variable indications of how much time elapses: "a week, a month, a year," is not the same as "after ten seconds" or "after twenty years"; radically different temporal parameters would produce a very different narrative. It is also the case that the story proceeds as if the originally hypothetical events had in fact taken place, as possible future events become transformed into an incontrovertible past.

Two other experimental techniques employ features of the discourse to create or destroy the fabula. These two are textual generators and denarration (see Richardson, "Beyond the Poetics of Plot," and *Unnatural* [87–94]). Both appear prominently at the beginning of Robbe-Grillet's *In the Labyrinth*: first we learn that "outside it is raining [. . .] the wind blows between the bare black branches" (141); in the next sentence this setting is denarrated as we are informed instead that "outside the sun is shining: there is no tree, no bush to cast a shadow" (141). Inside the room there is fine dust that coats every surface; this dust in turn generates what will become the definitive weather beyond the walls of the house: "Outside it is snowing" (142). Similarly, other surface images on the inside generate objects in the storyworld: the impression of a letter opener becomes a soldier's bayonet; a rectangular impression produces the mysterious box that the soldier carries; a desk lamp gives rise to a street lamp outside in the snow, which in turn yields up a soldier leaning against it, clutching a box; and a realistic painting, "The Defeat at Reichenfels," literally brings to life the military events it depicts. The descriptions here bring into being the events they suggest, as the discourse creates the story; in the case of denarration, by contrast, the discourse abolishes both the setting and the fabula.

In other works both the fabula and the syuzhet are variable. In "choose-your-own-story" texts such as Raymond Queneau's 1961 "A Story as You Like It," the reader is offered a series of options to choose from; both fabula and syuzhet are multilinear and variable, though once a particular event is selected, it becomes fixed; this is the principle around which many hyperfictions are constructed. Ana Castillo's *The Mixquiahuala Letters* (1986) operates along similar principles. The book consists of a series of letters sent by one of the characters, but not all are intended to be apprehended by the reader. Instead, the author offers three different reading sequences depending on the reader's sensibility. Thus, the conformist is told to begin with letters 2 and 3 and then to go to number 6, while the cynic is to start with letters 3 and 4 before going on to number 6. The quixotic reader is offered yet another different sequence: 2, 3, 4, 5, 6. It is important to note that each sequence produces a different story. Thus, we have a partially variable syuzhet that, once selected, produces different fabulas.

3. Syuzhet

In the last section I examined antimimetic elements of a narrative's fabula; in this section we will discuss some mimetic stories the telling of which defies natural and realist conventions. In virtually every natural, realistic, or mimetic narrative, the syuzhet of a work is always linear. In the words of Shlomith Rimmon-Kenan, "the disposition of elements in the text . . . is bound to be one-directional and irreversible, because language prescribes a linear figuration of signs and hence a linear presentation of information about things. We read letter after letter, word after word, sentence after sentence, chapter after chapter, and so on" (45). For the most part, she is correct: the syuzhet of a text is simply the sequence of pages you hold in your hand or the events you experience in performance. But this statement does not apply to all experimental and unnatural stories, whose reception is necessarily different from that of any natural narrative. Joyce Carol Oates, for example, alters the physical layout of the standard printed page to create a "simultaneity effect" by using two parallel columns to disclose the simultaneous thoughts of separate individuals in her story "The Turn of the Screw."

Milorad Pavić's *Landscape Painted with Tea* is a novel that mimics the form of a crossword puzzle. After an opening section, the reader is offered two possible syuzhets, a linear one that corresponds to the "across" pattern of a crossword puzzle, and another that imitates its "down" sequence and leaps across independent sections of the text as the reader follows separate plot lines in isolation from each other. The narrator reflects on both kinds of reading as he asks rhetorically: "Why now introduce a new way of reading a book, instead of one that moves, like life, from beginning to end, from birth to death?" He continues, "because any new way of reading that goes against the matrix of time, which pulls us toward death, is a futile but honest effort to resist this inexorability of one's fate, in literature at least, if not in reality" (185–86). Hélène Cixous' narrative *Partie* (1976) has yet another kind of syuzhet. The book is physically composed of two parts that are superimposed on one another, as each portion is upside down in relation to the other. The reader may start in either direction; the two texts come together on page 66 (99). Another example of this practice is Carol Shields's *Happenstance: Two Novels in One about a Marriage in Transition* (1991). The book has two covers, two beginnings, two dedications. One must physically flip the book over to get what is literally the other side of this story. The format of this text ensures that the reader processes it very differently from a realist novel or an oral story. Even though the fabulas of Oates and Shields are entirely mimetic, the way they are presented produces an unfixed syuzhet whose reading partially resembles that of a hypertext and thus an unnatural reading experience.

A more extreme example of a variable syuzhet is B. S. Johnson's "novel-in-a-box," *The Unfortunates* (1969), which is composed of individually bound chapters that may be read in any sequence (though one chapter is to be read first and another, last). Readers are informed that the sections appear in a random order; if they don't like the arrangement, they are invited to place the segments in their own random sequence. The text describes the sensations and memories of a sports reporter who revisits the town where a close friend of his had died some time before. Each chapter primarily records one of two sets of events: poignant memories from the past or the meaningless events in the reporter's day. A few sections combine both temporal frameworks, but for the most part they situate themselves in one or the other period, each indicated by a different tense of narration, the past tense for the memories, and the present tense for the current day's account. What is interesting is that nearly all the chapters in the two sets can be situated within the earlier or later chronological sequence—there are no iterative accounts (e.g., "Year after year, we would . . .") and surprisingly little *achrony,* or temporally indeterminate events. Like a bound modernist novel, most of these segments can be placed within a normal fabula; the question that arises is, why does Johnson forgo sequencing his syuzhet? The answer lies, I believe, in the irrelevance of any possible sequence to the grieving narrator. It does not matter where he situates the account of his lunch, or where he places his memory of hitchhiking with his friend. The former event is utterly unimportant, and so is its placement; the latter event can appear anywhere, just as it will appear in a different setting when it is remembered again.

The metaphor of the deck of cards is made literal in Robert Coover's story

"Heart Suit" (2005), which is printed on thirteen oversized, glossy playing cards. The author states that the cards may be shuffled and read in any order, though the introductory card is to be read first and the Joker is to be read last. Each card begins with the continuation of a sentence that describes the adventures of an individual, who is never named. Each card ends with a new sentence beginning with the name of an individual. Thus, the Five of Hearts card begins with the words "... pent up with self-righteous anger, burst in upon the King of Hearts, who has fallen fast asleep on a kitchen maid, to complain that someone has penned a scurrilous accusation against him in the latrine." The construction of the work (as well as the kingdom) indicates that this statement could be made of any of the male principals. This kind of variability of identities is particularly problematic when one reaches the Three of Hearts card, which begins, "... is the thief who actually stole the tarts," a statement that can be predicated of any of the characters but proved of none, since in every possible arrangement the evidence will be inconclusive and, of course, the deck can always be shuffled again.

4. Beginnings and Endings

In a natural or conventional narrative, beginnings and endings are essential for demarcating the extent of the story itself, for framing it, for introducing and then resolving instabilities. Many unnatural narratives problematize these narrative boundaries. Samuel Beckett is particularly keen on deconstructing such artificial limits, beginning many works with an evocation of the ending: *Endgame* starts with the lines "Finished, it's finished, nearly finished, it must be finished" (1), while Fizzle 8 begins "For to end yet again skull alone in a dark place" (*Prose* 243). The idea of a single, definitive starting point is regularly mocked: Flann O'Brien's narrator brags about having three beginnings to *At Swim-Two-Birds* (as Brian McHale notes, he actually has four [109]), and Raymond Federman's *Double or Nothing* (1971) begins with the statement "THIS IS NOT THE BEGINNING." Italo Calvino's *If on a winter's night a traveler* is a single text largely composed of the beginning chapters of several different novels. The narrator longs for the pure state of possibility at the beginning of every narrative; he "would like to write a book that is only an incipit, that maintains for its whole duration the potentiality of the beginning" (6). Many hyperfictions offer the user several different possible starting points; at the end of the section "Begin" at the start of Michael Joyce's *afternoon: a story* the text asks, "Do you want to hear about it?" and offers two different narrative paths, depending on whether the reader clicks on "yes" or "no."

The ending of a traditional or natural narrative is generally expected to wrap up the plot, reveal all the mysteries, provide some sort of poetic justice, and resolve the major problems that generated the story in the first place. In fact, according to Peter Brooks and a number of other theorists, "only the end can finally determine meaning.... The end writes the beginning and shapes the middle" (22). Many modernist novels, by contrast, refuse to provide any definitive closure to the events out of a conviction that life never comes to convenient conclusions; their meanings must be determined differently. Unnatural authors go much further. As already noted, there is the ending that returns, Ouroboros-like, to the beginning of the story as the last sentence merges with the first (*Finnegans Wake*) and the ending that depends on which textual sequence was selected by the reader (*The Mixquiahuala Letters*). More outrageous is the ending that negates itself and presents another equally possible ending (John Fowles's *The French Lieutenant's Woman*). Michael Joyce explains his theory and practice in the module "work in progress" in *afternoon*: "closure is, as in any fiction, a suspect quality, although here it is made manifest. When the story no longer progresses, or when it cycles, or when you tire of the paths, the experience of reading ends."

Then there is the multiple ending that offers several possible conclusions. Malcolm Bradbury's "Composition" (1976) tells the story of a new teaching assistant at a Midwestern university during the Vietnam War. After completing his course on composition (but before turning in the final grades), he is invited to party with two of his female students. The evening itself is fairly innocent, though some extremely compromising photos are taken. The next morning, the instructor receives a sample Polaroid and a request for a higher grade for another student who has neglected composition in order to more fully engage in political struggles; he has to decide what to do, knowing that if the pictures get circulated he is sure to lose his position. The earlier sections of the work are numbered 1 through 4; the final section offers three different resolutions, designated 5A, 5B, and 5C. In the first option, the instructor quietly raises the grade and saves his job. In the second, he corrects the grammar of the letter, sends it back to the blackmailers, and defiantly turns in the correct grade. In the third, he agrees with the student that grades are crap and all words are inadequate; he destroys the grade sheet and abandons academic drudgery in order to move on and devote himself to life and love. The text offers no indication of which of these possibilities will be (or has been) actualized; each option has a certain plausibility. I don't see this as a hermeneutic test in which the reader needs to determine which is the most likely decision as much as the demonstration of a series of options from which the reader is implicitly invited to choose. As the instructor is informed by one of the other characters, "You have to write your own ending" (141). Here we have a fabula that forks into multiple incompatible directions at its end.

5. Narrative(s)

Continuing with the Bradbury example even as we circle back to the point where this essay began, we now need to consider how to theorize multiple versions of the same narrative when they are presented together. Here our primary example will be the German film *Lola rennt* (1998), by Tom Tykwer. The film begins with the dilemma: Lola must obtain 100,000 marks in the next twenty minutes or her boyfriend will be killed. Lola starts to run. The film then provides three different versions of the same basic story, though in each case a slight alteration in a minor event, the dodging of a dog in a stairway, produces a radically different final scenario. In the first, Lola can't get the money, she runs to be with her boyfriend who is trying to rob a bank, and she is unintentionally shot dead by the police. In the next version, she robs a bank, gets the money to her boyfriend, but he is then accidentally hit by an ambulance and dies. In the last variation, Lola wins the money at roulette, and she and her boyfriend stroll contentedly off into the future.

The viewer is challenged to make sense out of this sequence that seems to rewrite the story and then rewrite it again. One possible answer is that, according to the cultural logic that the latest version is the superior one, we may view the last one as the definitive or "real" story, the others being as it were "rough drafts" of the final, successful version. This would also accord with the logic of comedy (it is hard to imagine the versions being sequenced in a different order) and would thus imply a kind of teleological progression of the different scenarios. As the narrator of *The French Lieutenant's Woman* described this situation, "I cannot give both versions at once, yet whichever is the second will seem, so strong is the tyranny of the last chapter, the final, the 'real' version" (318). But such a move concerning *Lola* seems a facile way to partially naturalize this radical work, and there is nothing in the film to warrant this assumption. I prefer to see the film as simply three possible versions of a single set of events, unhierarchized and without ontological primacy being given to any one version. In a series of paintings of the same object, we don't struggle to establish the primacy of one canvas and the consequent subordination of the others to it; all are equally variations of a scene. Perhaps more pertinently, it resembles a video game that is played several times, with no single instance having any priority over the others: each playing is equally real.

6. Conclusion

Narrative theory, in order to be comprehensive, needs to be able to account for the distinctive practices of unnatural narratives. To do so, it requires a flexible definition of narrative that will be able both to include unnatural experiments and to provide a limit that allows us to articulate just how a given text challenges or plays with narrativity itself. We also badly need a greatly expanded concept of fabula. Most important is to go beyond the unilinear fabula and to add the concept of a multilinear fabula, a fabula with one or numerous forkings leading to different possible chains of events. As Jukka Tyrkkö explains, such narratives offer "alternative paths of access to events or episodes, leaving the construction of the plot up to the choices of the reader" (286; see also Ryan, esp. 242–70). Each resulting story is internally consistent; what is unnatural is that the reader is allowed to determine the course of events from those possibilities preselected by the author. This practice violates the conventional retrospective nature of narration, in which an event is related after it has occurred, and thus cannot possibly be selected from a list of options. Porter Abbott explains that narrative "is something that always *seems*" to come after the events it depicts; "to be a *re*-presentation" of them (36); it is the violation of this sense of the pastness of the narrative events that is foregrounded by multilinear fabulas. Many of the examples adduced in this essay employ multilinearity in one form or another, whether to determine the ending (Bradbury), the main parameters of the story (Castillo, Tykwer), or numerous narrative possibilities throughout the text (Queneau, many hyperfictions).

We also need an expanded framework to account for other kinds of unnatural stories, including infinite fabulas; dual or multiple storylines with inconsistent chronologies; inherently vague and unknowable fabulas; internally contradictory fabulas; denarrated fabulas; and repeated, multiple versions of the same essential story. The notion of syuzhet also needs to be enlarged to include partially and entirely variable syuzhet patterns. By greatly expanding our concepts of fabula and syuzhet, we will be able to do justice to the kinds of texts that seek to transform and extend the traditional practices that are readily embraced by those terms.

Finally, we may use these examples to help better understand the curious nature of unnatural narratives. All works of literature have mimetic and artificial aspects; literary realism attempts to hide its artifices; antimimetic texts flaunt them. We can imagine a kind of spectrum with the most mimetic works such as Richard Ford's photorealist *Independence Day* on one end and Beckett's *The Unnamable* at the other extreme. Close to Ford would be the characteristic works of canonical realists such as Tolstoy; close to Beckett would be slightly less extreme postmodern works, and beside them, absurdist dramas and the more outrageous plays of Aristophanes. There is obviously a lot of room in the middle, and many ways for a text to lean toward, partake of, or fully instantiate the antimimetic. An unresolved ending can be offered in the name of verisimilitude (Nadine Gordimer's *The Late Bourgeois World*); it can be a minor literary jest at the end of an otherwise largely mimetic text (David Lodge's *Changing Places*); or it may be part of a sustained, postmodern rejection of conventional narrative norms (Thomas Pynchon's *The Crying of Lot 49*). An unnatural ending may be closely integrated into other antimimetic practices as in the case of Pynchon, or it may violate the mimetic conventions of the rest of the work and thereby produce a powerful leap into the antimimetic that can generally be expected to upset those more traditional readers who feel that an implicit mimetic contract between author and audience has suddenly been ruptured (*The French Lieutenant's Woman*). In general, we may say that the more repeated, insistent, global, or compelling an antimimetic strategy is, the more unnatural the narrative becomes. Since the time of Aristotle, narrative theory has gravitated almost exclusively toward the mimetic aspect of narrative fiction; it is now time to explore and conceptualize the other half of the history of literature. The ignored antimimetic components of ostensibly mimetic fiction need to be identified and examined, a task begun in the essays by Nielsen, Mäkelä, and Phelan in this volume; and the unnatural poetics of antimimetic narratives needs to continue to be explored, documented, and theorized.

Works Cited

Abbott, H. Porter. *The Cambridge Introduction to Narrative*. 2nd ed. Cambridge: Cambridge University Press, 2008.
Ballard, J. G. *War Fever*. New York: Farrar, Straus, Giroux, 1990.
Beckett, Samuel. *The Complete Short Prose, 1929–1989*. New York: Grove, 1995.
———. *Endgame*. New York: Grove, 1958.
Boully, Jenny. "The Body." In *The Next American Essay*, ed. John D'Agata. St. Paul, MN: Graywolf, 2003. 435–66.
Bradbury, Malcolm. *Who Do You Think You Are? Stories and Parodies*. 1976. New York: Penguin, 1993.
Brooks, Peter. *Reading for the Plot*. Cambridge, MA: Harvard University Press, 1984.
Calvino, Italo. *If on a winter's night a traveler*. Trans. William Weaver. New York: Harcourt Brace Jovanovich, 1981.
Castillo, Ana. *The Mixquiahuala Letters*. New York: Doubleday, 1992.
Coover, Robert. "Heart Suit." Appended to *A Child Again*. San Francisco: McSweeney's, 2005.

DelConte, Matt. "Why *You* Can't Speak: Second Person Narration, Voice, and a New Model for Understanding Narrative." *Style* 37.2 (2003): 204–19.
Federman, Raymond. *Double or Nothing*. Chicago: Swallow, 1971.
Fludernik, Monika. *Towards a "Natural" Narratology*. London and New York: Routledge, 1996.
Fowles, John. *The French Lieutenant's Woman*. 1969. New York: Signet, 1970.
Heise, Ursula. *Chronoschisms: Time, Narrative, and Postmodernism*. Cambridge: Cambridge University Press, 1997.
Johnson, B. S. *The Unfortunates*. New York: New Diretions, 2009.
Joyce, Michael. *afternoon: a story*. Hypertext. Eastgate Systems, 1990.
Knowlson, James, and John Pilling. *Frescoes of the Skull: The Later Prose and Drama of Samuel Beckett*. New York: Grove, 1980.
McHale, Brian. *Postmodernist Fiction*. New York: Methuen, 1987.
Moody, Rick. *The Ring of Brightest Stars Around Heaven*. New York: Time-Warner, 1995.
Moore, Lorrie. *Self-Help*. New York: New American Library, 1986.
Pavić, Milorad. *Landscape Painted with Tea*. Trans. Christina Pribićević-Zorić. New York: Knopf, 1990.
Richardson, Brian. "Beyond Story and Discourse: Narrative Time in Postmodern and Non-mimetic Fiction." In *Narrative Dynamics: Essays on Time, Plot, Closure, and Frames*, ed. Brian Richardson. Columbus: The Ohio State University Press, 2002. 47–63.
———. "Beyond the Poetics of Plot: Alternative Forms of Narrative Progression and the Multiple Trajectories of *Ulysses*." In *A Companion to Narrative Theory*, ed. James Phelan and Peter Rabinowitz. Malden, MA: Blackwell, 2005. 167–80.
———. "'Time Is Out of Joint': Narrative Models and the Temporality of the Drama." *Poetics Today* 8.2 (1987): 299–310.
———. *Unnatural Voices: Extreme Narration in Modern and Contemporary Fiction*. Columbus: The Ohio State University Press, 2006.
Rimmon-Kenan, Shlomith. *Narrative Fiction: Contemporary Poetics*. New York: Methuen, 1983.
Robbe-Grillet, Alain. *For a New Novel: Essays on Fiction*. Trans. Richard Howard. New York: Grove, 1965.
"The Secret Room," In *Snapshots*. Trans. Bruce Morrissette. New York: Grove, 1968. 65–72.
———. *Two Novels by Robbe-Grillet: Jealousy and In the Labyrinth*. Trans. Richard Howard. New York: Grove, 1965.
Ryan, Marie-Laure. *Narrative as Virtual Reality: Immersion and Interactivity in Literature and Electronic Media*. Baltimore: Johns Hopkins University Press, 2001.
Shields, David. "Life Story." In *Remote*. Madison: University of Wisconsin Press, 1996. 15–17.
Sternberg, Meir. "Ordering the Unordered: Space, Time, and Descriptive Coherence." *Yale French Studies* 61 (1981): 60–88.
Tyrkkö, Jukka. "'Kaleidoscope' Novels and the Act of Reading." In *Theorizing Narrativity*, ed. John Pier and José Ángel García Landa. Berlin: de Gruyter, 2008. 277–306.

The Whirligig of Time

Toward a Poetics of Unnatural Temporality

RÜDIGER HEINZE

TIME is a fundamental concept of human experience, and of narrative. Paul Ricoeur begins his monumental *Time and Narrative* with the argument that "time becomes human time to the extent that it is organized after the manner of a narrative; narrative, in turn, is meaningful to the extent that it portrays the features of temporal experience" (3). Most narratologists follow suit. For Shlomith Rimmon-Kenan, time is "one of the most basic categories of human experience" (43); Porter Abbott bases his introduction to narrative on the assumption that "*narrative is the principal way in which our species organizes its understanding of time*" (3; emphasis in the original) and that, contrary to "mechanical time" and temporal measuring grids, narrative allows "*the events themselves to create the order of time*" (3–4; emphasis in the original). Time and narrative, then, appear to be both fundamental and inherently inseparable and interdependent concepts.

And yet time is also a highly enigmatic and complex concept. For one, we do not really know what time is. Most lay definitions are tautological: time is something that passes at a certain speed, but that passing of course would have to be measured in time. Physicists regularly commence their discussion of the physics of time by averring that it is hard, if not impossible, to define (Deutsch; Nahin; Greene). Brian Greene, for example, opens his chapter on "time and experience" by writing: "Time is among the most familiar yet least understood concepts that humanity has ever encountered. [. . .] Even the everyday experience of time taps into some of the universe's thorniest conundrums" (127). Most physical laws are time-symmetric, in other words, they have no temporal arrow, which gives rise to all sorts of problems and paradoxes. Also, many of our commonsense intuitions about time are scientifically untenable, while what science tells us about the actual nature of temporality is frighteningly counterintuitive. Especially the latter fact has been taken up in a number of narratives about extraordinary temporal scenarios such as diverging timelines or time travel through wormholes.

Second, it is no coincidence that many narratological discussions of time begin with anachrony, that is, the discordance between story and discourse. As Genette, Metz, and many others have noted, narrative is characterized by a doubly temporal sequence, "the time of the thing told and the time of the narrative" (Metz 18). "This duality not only renders possible all the temporal distortions that are commonplaces in narratives [. . .]. More basically, it invites us to consider that one of the functions of narrative is to invent one time scheme in terms of another time scheme" (18). In other words, not only is the "existence of literary narratives embodying the full spectrum of temporal, modal, and aspectual options" a fact (Margolin 159), and, judging by the number of examples that Brian Richardson or Marie-Laure Ryan adduce, quite a common fact at that;[1] it is actually the "various types of discordance between the two orderings of story and narrative" (Genette 35–36) and the resulting temporal complexity that are commonplace, while narratives veering in the

---

1. In his book *Unnatural Voices* Brian Richardson discusses a host of examples that confound commonsense notions of logic, causality, order, and so forth and the more rigid models of narratology. One of the terms he introduces is "denarration," which refers to "narrative negation in which a narrator denies significant aspects of his or her narrative that had earlier been presented as given" (87); such narratives (many by Beckett) render "causal and temporal relations [. . .] dubious" (87). His term is intentionally close to Gerald Prince's concept of "disnarration," which refers to events that are referred to but remain unactualized (88). In his essay "Beyond Story and Discourse: Narrative Time in Postmodern and Nonmimetic Fiction," Richardson concretizes "six kinds of temporal reconstruction that stand out as sufficiently distinctive" (48) in their violation of the mimetic contract: *circular* (in which the end leads right back to the beginning: *Finnegans Wake*); *contradictory* (temporalities that are impossible in the real world: Robert Coover's "The Babysitter"); *antinomic* (narratives that move backwards in time: Harold Pinter's *Betrayal*); *differential* (fictional worlds that combine two or more different temporalities in one fictional world, for example when one character ages faster than her surroundings: Caryl Churchill's *Cloud Nine*); *conflated* (the reciprocal "contamination" or spilling over of different temporalities into each other, as in Ishmael Reed's *Flight to Canada*); and *dual/multiple* (where different "times" pass for a different set of characters or place or world, as in the enchanted forest of Shakespeare's *Midsummer Night's Dream*) (48–51). As Richardson generally reminds us, not all texts have a consistent story that is retrievable or deducible from the text. Marie-Laure Ryan also mentions a host of quite varied examples of temporal paradoxes in narrative.

direction of isochrony are unusual, complete isochrony being hard to imagine. Also, as Abbott points out, "narrative time is not necessarily any length at all" (5). If we no longer take notice of the many possible temporal disjunctions and complexities of narrative (e.g., analepsis, prolepsis, ellipsis, summary, stretch), it is because many of them have become relatively easy to naturalize and narrativize for any but the most inexperienced reader. As a consequence, for an unnatural narratology of time to be productive, it has to make a number of important distinctions. In what follows, I will introduce and discuss these distinctions; I will also shortly discuss a number of examples.

If we follow Jan Alber in defining "unnatural" (with reference to Doležel) as "physically impossible scenarios and events, that is, impossible by the known laws governing the physical world, as well as logically impossible ones, that is, impossible by accepted principles of logic" (80), then it becomes clear that, first of all, with regard to time, we have to distinguish between what we *assume* are the physical laws governing time in the actual world and the *actual* physical laws. As Marie-Laure Ryan points out, we possess four intuitive and commonsense axioms about time: (1) time flows in a fixed direction at a relatively stable speed, (2) you cannot go back in time against this flow, (3) causes precede their effects, and (4) the past is unchangeable (142–43).[2] Consequently, narratives that subvert one or more of these axioms are almost inevitably situated in the realm of the physically and logically impossible by readers.[3] However, once we take a closer look at the actual physics, it turns out that these assumptions do not necessarily have a correlative expression in physical laws. In fact, modern physics and the rather bizarre consequences of the—experimentally verified—propositions of quantum mechanics and relativity have given the lie to at least two of these intuitive assumptions about time. First of all, it does not flow, nor does it have a speed, because that would be measured by distance over time; also, the division between past, present, and future is arbitrary, the future not being any more malleable than the past.[4]

   2. Ryan points out that the temporal arrow can actually be subdivided into more arrows such as a biological, cognitive, or intentional one, all of which may be subverted.
   3. It should be noted that while these axioms generally apply, there are situations (mostly extreme and/or traumatic) in which people may experience temporality as much more flexible and unstable than the axioms imply.
   4. One of the consequences of Einstein's special and general theory of relativity is that we should actually conceive of all of time as a kind of bread loaf. All of time is continuously extant: past, present, and future. In fact, the distinction between past, present, and future is physically untenable and seems to exist only in our minds. In this conception of time, the past and the future are always already present and unchanging. What we consider the future is already past from another perspective. Discussions about this missing temporal arrow frequently resort to the second law of thermodynamics about entropy in order to point out that there is change and temporal progression, that we can tell "before" from "after" by the degree of entropy. This

Second, under certain conditions, and with the right experimental setup, it is possible to demonstrate that events in the present can determine the past.[5] As a consequence, narratives with reverse causality, for example, do have a basis in physical reality, at least on the elemental particle level, and therefore should be called "unnatural" with this in mind.[6]

Nevertheless: even though we should keep in mind the distinction between *assumed* natural laws and *actual* natural laws, ultimately, the assumptions readers bring to the text will determine their assessment of it as unnatural. Our commonsense axioms about time determine our experience of the world and of life to such a degree that it is nonsensical to insist that temporality really functions quite differently. If readers insist that time flows, is linear and monodirectional, then a narrative that breaks with these assumptions will be considered unnatural regardless of the fact that it might actually be true to physical law.

An important distinction that has already been made above but that has to be repeated and kept in mind for what follows is the one between story and discourse. A narrative may depict an unnatural temporal scenario on the story level, for example time travel as in *The Time Machine* (2003) or *The Time Traveler's Wife* (2005), or a reversed temporal order as in *Time's Arrow* (2003), but do so in quite an unobtrusive manner on the level of discourse. Inversely, a narrative may tell a story with no temporal complication at all, but do so in an unnatural manner, for example episodically reversed as in *Memento* (2000) or *Irréversible* (2002), or simply fragmented and nonlinear as

---

argument, though common, is based on a facile understanding of entropy. Basically, entropy is a measure of energy, and thus of order and information. Changes in systems with relatively low entropy (and thus *high* order, e.g., the loose but ordered pages of a 600-page novel) are easily noticed (there are many more ways in which the pages can be out of order than in order); changes in systems with a high degree of entropy (and thus *low* order, e.g., 600 randomly typed pages with no particular order) are less obviously noticed. Black holes, for example, emit no energy and thus no information; therefore, they can be said to have total entropy (and even here there are exceptions, as Stephen Hawking has shown). The misunderstanding that entropy is a reliable measure of the progression of time (entropy tends to increase with time in closed systems) is based on the limited cases of isolated systems. As soon as one works with open and dynamic systems (as is most often the case, since very few systems are or can be entirely isolated), the issue becomes much more complicated. How else could one explain the existence of solar systems, which are highly ordered, or the aggregate of molecules called human being? For entropy to make sense as a temporal concept, it has to be considered cosmically. This in turn makes it problematic as a reliable concept for temporality in narratives.

5. This has been shown by John Wheeler in his so-called delayed-choice experiment.

6. Even certain forms of time travel appear to be possible, albeit only theoretically and very hypothetically (Deutsch; Deutsch and Lockwood). For one of the first—and still definitive—books on time travel, see Paul Nahin; for a survey essay on the real and seeming paradoxa of time travel, see Richard Hanley. Joe Haldeman's novel *The Forever War* (2009) is one of the few narratives to make use of the only kind of time travel possible already today: time dilation.

in *21 Grams* (2003).⁷ Obviously, narratives may also do both. As narratologists reflexively—and correctly—point out, the doubly temporal order inherent in narrative has been amply exploited to create all kinds of temporal complications and complexities, with the result that discordance, that is, anachrony, is the rule, not the exception.⁸ Put more bluntly, a certain degree of temporal complication is "natural" in narrative.

Many of these complications on the level of story as well as on the level of discourse have become so commonplace and conventional that we no longer notice them; in other words, we have naturalized (Jonathan Culler) and narrativized (Monika Fludernik) them. As Jan Alber points out, we also have at our disposal a variety of cognitive reading strategies to come to terms with unnatural scenarios, for example by reading them as symbolic, metaphorical, or oneiric, or by blending and/or enriching preexisting frames, scripts, and encyclopedias.⁹

Although this division between story and discourse has long proved a useful heuristic, it does have its shortcomings, which have been noted by a number of critics. In many narratives—particularly those about traumatic events—the division and thus the temporality of the text is blurred, for example, in Art Spiegelman's *Maus* (2003). As David Herman insists, we should allow for "fuzzy" or indeterminate temporality, for narratives to be multivalent and polychronic rather than just "doubly" ordered (212).¹⁰ In a similar vein,

---

7. Brian Richardson calls reverse narratives "antinomic" narratives ("Beyond"); Chatman distinguishes "sustained episodic reversals" (reversed sequential order of events) from "sustained continuous reversals" (reversed normal temporal progression of chronology). Per Krogh Hansen has written an extensive essay on reverse narratives in film in a collection of essays on unnatural narratives edited by Jan Alber and myself.

8. Even narratives in naturally occurring oral-storytelling situations are far more complicated than often assumed. The opposition between "complex written narrative" and "simple oral narrative" is misleading and untenable.

9. For an elaboration of cognitive reading strategies of "unnatural" scenarios, see Jan Alber's essay on impossible storyworlds as well as his contribution to this volume.

10. As will have become clear by now, this essay is based on the binary heuristic framework of unnatural/natural that is itself conspicuously open to various angles of attack. Readers familiar with the history of narratology will know that in addition to expansions and augmentations such as David Herman's, Brian Richardson's, or Peter Rabinowitz's, the division between story and discourse and the underlying notion of temporality has been fundamentally criticized and deconstructed for some time. However, if I work with the framework introduced here, it is because I find it highly productive, especially if adapted to the respective analytic purposes at hand, while I find many of the fundamental critiques of binary frameworks somewhat less than productive, even if their basic criticism has its merit. For example, when Mark Currie claims in his otherwise illuminating book that "narrative linearity is in itself a form which represses difference" (79) he ignores, first of all, that strict narrative linearity is impossible and that, second, this pronouncement itself represses the differential potential that narrative linearity may have. Andrew Gibson's Deleuzian division between open and closed conceptions of time (aion

Peter Rabinowitz argues for the supplementation of a third term, *path*, to the story/discourse distinction in order to allow for the fact that "a character's order of experience may conform to neither the story order nor the discourse order" (183).[11] And Brian Richardson generally reminds us that not all texts have a consistent story that is retrievable or deducible from the text ("Beyond" 51).

The fact that many narrative complications have become naturalized and narrativized and that we have a number of reading strategies to deal with them necessitates another important distinction between unnatural and unconventional. Science fiction and fantasy narratives regularly contain unnatural temporal scenarios that by now are quite conventional to the genres. As mentioned above, Genette describes all kinds of temporal complications on the level of discourse that have become conventional. Thus we may have narratives that are, strictly speaking, unnatural, but conventional (zero focalization). On the other hand, many naturally occurring oral-storytelling situations will appear quite unconventional when transcribed and printed on the page as a result of the many overlaps, interruptions, and incomplete clauses typical of oral storytelling.

The distinction between unnatural and unconventional is also significantly a question of medium and genre. Time travel such as in Wells's *The Time Machine* is entirely "naturalized" as science fiction, but might still be perceived as unnatural in narratives that otherwise indicate their adherence to the tradition of realism, as is the case in Audrey Niffenegger's *The Time Traveler's Wife*. Each genre has its own encyclopedia and scripts, which determine just what kind of parameters and rules readers may expect to govern that genre, which in turn affects the assessment of unnatural versus natural. Were the time traveler in *The Time Machine* to stumble across speaking animals or witches, readers would in all likelihood be much more confounded, whereas it is accepted that the animals in Orwell's *Animal Farm* can speak but not fly.

As an interesting sideline perhaps worthy of a more elaborate discussion in another context, note that the conventional unnatural temporalities in fantasy and science fiction are actualized almost exclusively on the level of story, and only rarely on the level of discourse (in the occasional short story by Philip K. Dick or Stanisław Lem). On the other hand, the temporal complications so

---

and chronos) is philosophically interesting, but highly metaphorical. The open conception of time is defined as independent of matter, a "time of pure becoming," a "continuum," with time as "limitless capacity." For analyzing literary texts, this metaphorization is not helpful (180). For a lucid discussion of postmodern variations of time and narrative, see Ursula Heise's book *Chronoschisms: Time, Narrative, Postmodernism* (1997).

11. Rabinowitz makes this argument in the context of an interesting discussion of temporal arrangement in Wells's *The Time Machine*.

typical of many postmodern narratives often occur on the level of discourse, to the degree that sometimes there is no retrievable coherent story, as has been pointed out above. One could venture the—very tentative—speculation that unnatural temporalities are more easily conventionalized if they occur on the level of story, and that relatively clearly defined generic scripts such as in fantasy and science fiction also facilitate further conventionalization.

Similar conditionals pertain to the specific medium. Johannes Fehrle argues in an essay on the unnatural in comics that

> there are many instances in which comics do not represent a natural (i.e. physically possible or realist) scenario, but instead follow a medial convention which is so established and expected that it does not cause estrangement. [. . .] [T]he breaking of one of these conventions, even though it might technically re-establish the physically natural, may in some cases seem "less right," and more estranging to a reader. (231)

In one of the screen adaptations, Superman turns the earth against its usual rotation at such speed that he manages to turn back time. This is definitely an unnatural scenario; however, were he to openly use a device to fly, this would be "far more upsetting to a viewer—despite being more natural in the above sense—and the viewer would certainly search for an explanation for this transgression of the laws of the storyworld" (Fehrle 231).[12] Therefore, evaluations of unnatural temporal scenarios also have to consider the conventions and rules of the particular medium and genre of the narrative in question. This also means that, according to Hansen, a poetics of the unnatural

> brings into focus [. . .] not only fictional worlds governed by alternative "natural" laws, but worlds which foreground a disruption of their own (im- or explicit) laws and logic—that is scenarios or events which demand the reader to actively intervene through an act of "naturalization." (165)

Last but not least, we have to consider the cultural context. Although the same physical laws govern our planet as a whole, their universal applicability is not universally accepted. It is conceivable that in other storytelling traditions, an alternative set of "physical laws" is believed to govern the actual world, either as a complement or even as an exclusive alternative to the physical laws widely accepted by the scholarly community. Though this should admittedly be rare, it is somewhat more likely that even if the actual laws

---

12. I have borrowed the entire example from the same essay by Johannes Fehrle.

remain untouched, the axioms that Ryan calls "intuitive and common sense" may be context- and culture-sensitive, for example regarding the "passing" and "speed" of time, or regarding the past being unchangeable. Also, and perhaps most immediately conceivable, story logic is context- and culture-sensitive. As Andrea Moll shows for oral-storytelling traditions in aboriginal New South Wales, Australia, scenarios and events considered logically impossible in predominantly Western narrative traditions would definitely be considered possible in other cultural contexts, for example the elimination of the distinction between past and present events, past and present persons, or a mythical person and the narrator. We can provisionally summarize these distinctions in figure 2.1.[13]

A poetics of unnatural temporality, hence, needs to consider (1) the particular axioms of time of a given cultural context of the narrative in question, (2) the specific traditions and rules of the medium and genre, and (3) the particular conjunction of story/discourse with unnatural/natural and unconventional/conventional. Obviously, this is a programmatic proposition. In many practical instances, it will be close to impossible to equally consider all aspects and conjunctions, especially if the analytic interest is diachronic and the selection of narratives exemplary. And while attention should be paid to the fact that notions of temporality are culture-sensitive, it will not be possible in all instances to grasp culturally inflected traditions and conceptions in all their complexity. In what follows, I will try to venture some generalizations about the consequences and functions of unnatural temporality with the help of specific examples.

Generally, although there exists a great variety of unnatural temporal scenarios, there seems to be a preponderance of a relatively limited number of certain scenarios on the levels of both story and discourse. On the level of story, unnatural temporality most often occurs in scenarios of time travel (Wells's *The Time Machine* [2003], Zemeckis's *Back to the Future* [1985]), time loops (Vonnegut's *Timequake* [1998], Ramis's *Groundhog Day* [1993]), time reversals (Amis's *Time's Arrow* [2003], Dick's *Counter-Clock World* [2002]), and diverging/alternative timelines (Tykwer's *Lola Rennt* [1998], Howitt's *Sliding Doors* [1998]). On the level of discourse, the most frequent scenarios employ temporal reversals of some kind or other (most often sustained episodic reversals as in Nolan's *Memento* [2000] or Noé's *Irréversible* [2002]), non-linearity/fragmentation (Iñárritu's *21 Grams* [2003], Marcks's *11:14* [2003]), future tense (seldom throughout an entire narrative, as in Moody's "The Grid"

---

13. Caveat: the interdependencies of these factors are difficult to visualize. Even though it might visually suggest so, the scheme depicted in figure 2.1 *does not* propose a hierarchy. Generic scripts, for example, cut across media, as in superhero narratives.

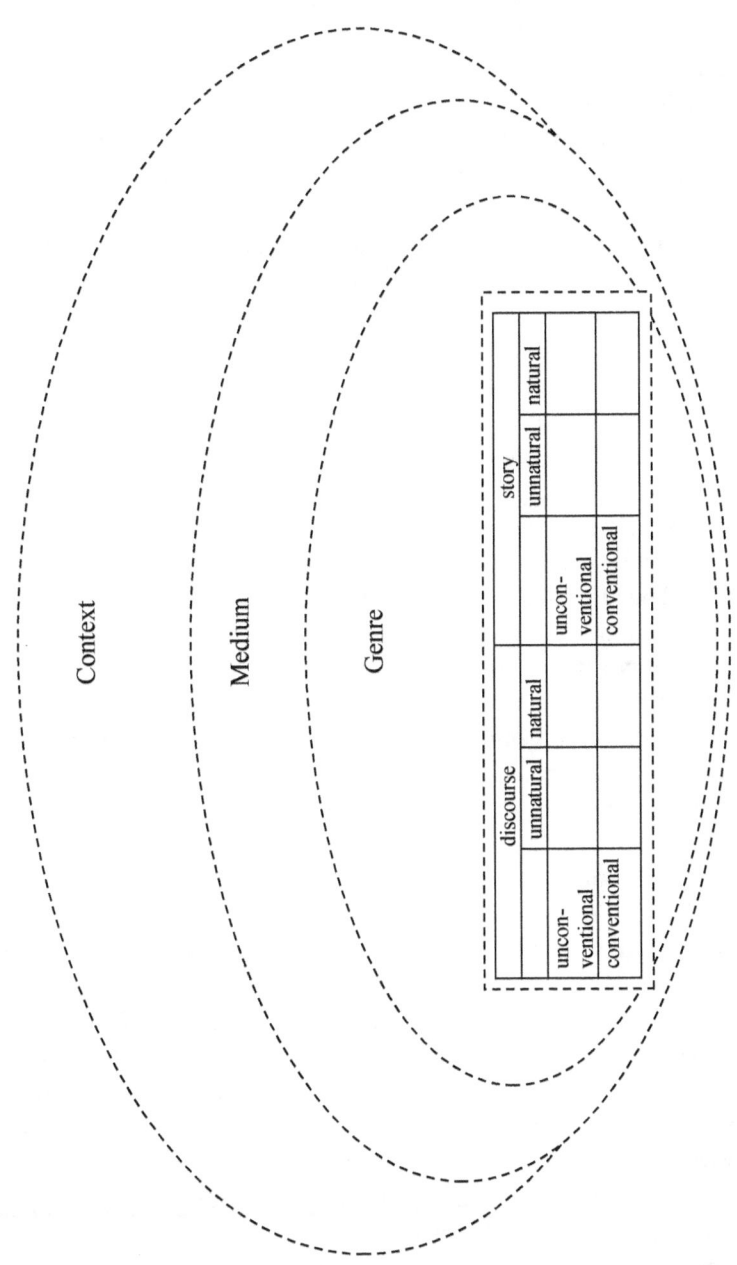

FIGURE 2.1

[2002], more often in chapters or paragraphs, as in Alvarez's *How the Garcia Girls Lost Their Accent* [1992] or Obejas's *We Came All the Way From Cuba So You Could Dress Like This?* [1994]), and denarration (Beckett's *Molloy* [1955] or Ellis's *Glamorama* [1999]). Interestingly, if we rearrange these examples in accordance with the distinctions introduced by Brian Richardson (note 1), the majority of unnatural temporalities on the level of *both* story and discourse tend to employ only three broad temporal complications, though in considerably numerous variations: contradictory (occasionally to the point of being nonreconstructable), antinomic (this might arguably include future tense), and differential (which I will take to include timeline divergences and parallelisms). It might be a rewarding speculation from a cognitive perspective whether these come closest to capturing our most common confounding experiences with, and perhaps contemplations about, time.

It is worth noting once more at this point that entire media and genres display a high propensity towards unnatural temporality in general. For example, due to the systematic arrangement and interplay of panels and gutters in order to create movement and time, the principally static medium of comics tends to allow for, and make use of, a significantly more flexible temporality, what David Herman calls multivalent or polychronic. In comics, thus, unnatural temporality actually occurs quite frequently on both the discourse and the story levels, for example, in Spiegelman's *Maus*, or Ware's *Jimmy Corrigan* (2000). Of course, the entire genre of superhero comics is based on physically (and often enough logically) impossible scenarios. To repeat Hansen, we should pay special attention to those narratives that break their own laws and logic.

More well-known examples such as Martin Amis's *Time's Arrow* or Christopher Nolan's *Memento* have been discussed in detail. I would therefore like to shortly address some lesser known, but no less instructive examples on the levels of story and discourse.[14] Terry Gilliam's movie *Time Bandits* (1981) is a good case in point. The protagonists, a young boy and several dwarves, use a stolen map of all temporal fractures of the cosmos to travel through time in order to steal valuable artifacts. This in itself is entirely within the conventions of time-travel films and fantasy. However, not only do the temporal fractures/gateways occur in randomly different forms (holes, doors, whirls, mirrors) while the protagonists seem to have precious little control over them but, more importantly, the protagonists also travel to legendary time (Agamemnon, who is incorrectly shown as killing the Minotaur), to fairy-tale time (a giant with

---

14. Even though my examples are relatively recent, there are numerous narratives from earlier centuries that display an unnatural temporality.

a boat on his head), and to some place beyond time where evil resides, and is defeated. At the end of the movie the boy wakes up in his bed with the house on fire, from which he is rescued by a fireman who is played by the same actor who plays Agamemnon (Sean Connery). While one might shortly entertain the explanation that the whole narrative was a dream of the boy, in the very end a little remaining "piece of evil" kills his parents. The movie does not even pretend to temporal logic and consistency, not even within the conventions of time-travel narratives, which usually offer at least a flimsy though not always convincing explanation for paradoxes and inconsistencies.[15]

Another example before I offer an explanation: in Rick Moody's (very) short story "The Grid," a first-person narrative begins in the present tense at a certain point in time, from which the narrative develops along a temporal line in will-future tense; towards the end, the narrative "circles around" and returns to the beginning. The narrative reads like the prediction of a storyteller, with the difference that it does not address a *you* but appears to make rock-bottom declarations about what will occur in the future: "Later, for example, she will believe that her lips yielded too easily" (30) or "In the bar, in fact, she will be having a first kiss" (31). Character function and narrator function could be separated for as long as it is unclear that the "I" as narrator and the "I" as character are simultaneously present—which is not long at all. The future tense and the force of the predictions might suggest someone who knows what is going to happen. The present tense then is merely an illusion, because there is a narrator who looks back at events as they happened in the past but chooses to tell them in present tense. But that does not explain anything, nor is there anything in the text to suggest this.[16]

Now, if we want to take these narratives and unnatural temporal scenarios in general seriously, we should consider one of Tamar Yacobi's "integration mechanisms," the functional design: "such peculiarities serve as a pointer, if not as a key, to the work's functional design" (117). "Whatever looks odd—about the characters, the ideas, the structure—can be motivated by the work's purpose, local or overall, literary or otherwise" (111). Even if not mentioned explicitly in her essay, it is this assumption that underlies Ryan's excellent summary of the function of temporal paradoxes: "temporal paradoxes do not completely block the construction of a fictional world, but rather, invite the reader to imagine a 'Swiss cheese' world in which contradictions occupy well-delimited holes of irrationality surrounded by solid areas about which the

15. Considering this, it is only a minor point that the two-dimensional map they use is supposed to show four-dimensional time holes.

16. For a lucid discussion of the consequences of present-tense narration for mimesis and unnaturalness, see James Phelan.

reader remains able to make logical inferences" (162). Such narratives then allow readers a "glance into the vertiginous philosophical abyss of the nature of time" (162) and "some aspect of human experience" (162); we may thus deal with unnatural temporal scenarios "logically by putting them in quarantine, so that they will not infect the entire fictional world"; "philosophically, by regarding them as thought experiments aimed at destabilizing common-sense conceptions of time"; "imaginatively, by putting ourselves in the skin of the characters whose life is being invaded by the irrational" (162).

For *Time Bandits,* this means that the irritating flouting of temporal logic and consistency is not a flaw in the script but is rather the point: an indication that time is not quite as stable as we tend to assume; that legendary, mythical, and historical past are not so far removed from each other; that even though the narrative does not make sense logically, it might adequately portray the occasionally puzzling and irrational *human experience* of time. Time-travel narratives in general tend to toy with the alluring but altogether unnatural idea that the past might be as malleable as the future seems to be and the future as foreseeable as the past seems to be with the wisdom of hindsight.

For "The Grid," this means that the title may be taken literally: the narrative unfolds a grid of how the moment of commencement in the present tense develops into various directions for different characters, who are all linked by that one moment, or in other words: in all four dimensions. If this is taken as the functional design, then the story could be read as a clever comment on the temporal and spatial relatedness of all human life, on the network of our communal existence. As Uri Margolin notes about prospective narratives in general, they give witness to a fascination with the virtual, speculation, and counterfactuals (163), all of which are basic ingredients of human storytelling. No wonder, really, that a small but relevant number of migration narratives seem to include passages in the future tense to counter the uncertainties of migration with the apparent certainty of prediction.

Among the greatest strengths and appeals of narrative fiction is that it can construct/contain/project a virtually endless variation of worlds and scenarios, a unique testing ground for thought experiments, with tremendous aesthetic and experiential "fringe benefits." Fictional narratives with unnatural temporalities offer one substantial way of compounding these pleasures by playing through a variation of temporal scenarios that are not strictly bound by the constraints of physical laws and logic and thus may capture aspects of human experience that, while strictly speaking unnatural, are actually quite "natural."[17]

---

17. As David Richter's essay on aspects of biblical narratology neatly shows, there are even

Works Cited

11:14. Dir. Greg Marcks. MDP Worldwide, 2003.
21 Grams. Dir. Alejandro González Iñárritu. This Is That Productions, 2003.
Abbott, H. Porter. *The Cambridge Introduction to Narrative.* Cambridge: Cambridge University Press, 2002.
Alber, Jan. "Impossible Storyworlds—And What to Do with Them." *Storyworlds* 1 (2009): 79-96.
Alber, Jan, and Rüdiger Heinze, eds. *Unnatural Narratives, Unnatural Narratology.* Berlin and New York: de Gruyter, 2011.
Alvarez, Julia. *How the Garcia Girls Lost Their Accents.* New York: Plume, 1992.
Amis, Martin. *Time's Arrow.* New York: Vintage, 2003.
Back to the Future. Dir. Robert Zemeckis. Universal, 1985.
Beckett, Samuel. *Molloy.* New York: Grove, 1955.
Chatman, Seymour. "Backwards." *Narrative* 17.1 (2009): 31-55.
Currie, Mark. *Postmodern Narrative Theory.* New York: St. Martin's, 1998.
Deutsch, David. *The Fabric of Reality.* New York: Penguin, 1997.
Deutsch, David, and Michael Lockwood. "The Quantum Physics of Time Travel." *Scientific American* 3 (1994): 50-56.
Dick, Philip K. *Counter-Clock World.* New York: Vintage, 2002.
Doležel, Lubomír. *Heterocosmica: Fiction and Possible Worlds.* Baltimore and London: Johns Hopkins University Press, 1998.
Ellis, Bret Easton. *Glamorama.* New York: Knopf, 1999.
Fehrle, Johannes. "Unnatural Worlds and Unnatural Narration in Comics? A Critical Examination." In Alber and Heinze, *Unnatural Narratives, Unnatural Narratology,* 210-45.
Genette, Gérard. *Narrative Discourse.* Ithaca, NY: Cornell University Press, 1980.
Gibson, Andrew. *Towards a Postmodern Theory of Narrative.* Edinburgh: Edinburgh University Press, 1996.
Greene, Brian. *The Fabric of the Cosmos.* New York: Penguin, 2005.
Groundhog Day. Dir. Harold Ramis. Columbia Pictures Corporation, 1993.
Haldeman, Joe. *The Forever War.* New York: St. Martin's, 2009.
Hanley, Richard. "No End in Sight: Causal Loops in Philosophy, Physics and Fiction." *Synthese* 141.1 (2004): 123-52.
Hansen, Per Krogh. "Backmasked Messages: On the Fabula Construction in Episodically Reversed Narratives." In Alber and Heinze, *Unnatural Narratives, Unnatural Narratology,* 162-85.
Heise, Ursula K. *Chronoschisms: Time, Narrative, Postmodernism.* Cambridge: Cambridge University Press, 1997.
Herman, David. *Story Logic: Problems and Possibilities of Narrative.* Lincoln: University of Nebraska Press, 2002.
Irréversible. Dir. Gaspar Noé. 120 Films, 2002.
Lola rennt. Dir. Tom Tykwer. X-Filme Creative Pool, 1998.
Margolin, Uri. "Of What Is Past, Passing, or To Come: Temporality, Aspectuality, Modality, and the Nature of Literary Narrative." In *Narratologies,* ed. David Herman. Columbus: The Ohio State University Press, 1999. 142-66.

---

texts that, if read strictly with an eye to the consistency of temporal order, would render quite disconcerting results (291-92).

Memento. Dir. Christopher Nolan. Newmarket Capital Group, 2000.
Metz, Christian. *Film Language: A Semiotics of the Cinema.* New York: Oxford University Press, 1974.
Moll, Andrea. "Natural or Unnatural? Linguistic Deep Level Structures in AbE: A Case Study of New South Wales Aboriginal English." In Alber and Heinze, *Unnatural Narratives, Unnatural Narratology,* 246–68.
Moody, Rick. "The Grid." *The Ring of Brightest Angels Around Heaven.* Boston: Little, Brown, 2002. 29–37.
Nahin, Paul. *Time Machines.* New York: Springer, 1999.
Niffenegger, Audrey. *The Time Traveler's Wife.* London: Vintage, 2005.
Obejas, Achy. *We Came All the Way From Cuba So You Could Dress Like This?* New York: Cleis, 1994.
Phelan, James. "Present Tense Narration, Mimesis, the Narrative Norm, and the Positioning of the Reader in *Waiting for the Barbarians.*" In *Understanding Narrative,* ed. James Phelan and Peter J. Rabinowitz. Columbus: The Ohio State University Press, 1994. 222–45.
Rabinowitz, Peter J. "They Shoot Tigers, Don't They? Path and Counterpoint in *The Long Goodbye.*" In *A Companion to Narrative Theory,* ed. James Phelan and Peter J. Rabinowitz. Malden, MA: Blackwell, 2008. 181–91.
Richardson, Brian. "Beyond Story and Discourse: Narrative Time in Postmodern and Nonmimetic Fiction." In *Narrative Dynamics: Essays on Time, Plot, Closure, and Frames,* ed. Brian Richardson. Columbus: The Ohio State University Press, 2002. 47–63.
———. *Unnatural Voices: Extreme Narration in Modern and Contemporary Fiction.* Columbus: The Ohio State University Press, 2006.
Richter, David. "Genre, Repetition, Temporal Order: Some Aspects of Biblical Narratology." In *A Companion to Narrative Theory,* ed. James Phelan and Peter J. Rabinowitz. Malden, MA: Blackwell, 2005. 285–98.
Ricoeur, Paul. *Time and Narrative.* Vol. 1. Chicago: University of Chicago Press, 1984.
Rimmon-Kenan, Shlomith. *Narrative Fiction.* 2nd ed. London and New York: Routledge, 2002.
Ryan, Marie-Laure. "Temporal Paradoxes in Narrative." *Style* 43.2 (2009): 142–64.
Sliding Doors. Dir. Peter Howitt. Intermedia Films, 1998.
Spiegelman, Art. *The Complete Maus.* New York: Penguin, 2003.
Time Bandits. Dir. Terry Gilliam. Handmade Films, 1981.
Vonnegut, Kurt. *Timequake.* New York: Vintage, 1998.
Ware, Chris. *Jimmy Corrigan: The Smartest Kid on Earth.* New York: Pantheon, 2000.
Wells, Herbert George. *The Time Machine.* New York: Bantam, 2003.
Yacobi, Tamar. "Authorial Rhetoric: Narratorial (Un)Reliability, Divergent Readings: Tolstoy's *Kreutzer Sonata.*" In *A Companion to Narrative Theory,* ed. James Phelan and Peter J. Rabinowitz. Malden, MA: Blackwell, 2005. 108–23.

Unnatural Spaces and Narrative Worlds

3

JAN ALBER

MANFRED JAHN and Sabine Buchholz define narrative space in terms of "the environment in which story-internal characters move about and live" (552). Similarly, in my usage, the term denotes the WHERE of narrative, that is, the demarcated space of the represented storyworld, including objects (such as houses, tables, chairs) or other entities (such as fog) that are part of the setting and that do not belong to one of the characters.

Narrative space has traditionally been considered to be much less important than narrative time. For example, in the eighteenth century, Gotthold Ephraim Lessing defined narrative literature as an art of time rather than space (102–15), and Gérard Genette was also much more interested in investigating temporal progression than issues of spatial organization in narrative. Furthermore, E. M. Forster's notorious example of a minimal plot ("The king died and then the queen died of grief" [130]) does not contain any reference to space, and we are presumably all familiar with bare stages in the theater that do not really obstruct our understanding of the play's represented action.

Other narratologists, however, have dealt with the representation of narrative space and its potential significance in greater detail. Already in the 1920s, Mikhail Bakhtin developed the concept of the "chronotope" or "time space," which highlights "the intrinsic connectedness of temporal and spatial relationships that are artistically expressed in literature" (84). Furthermore, Sey-

45

mour Chatman (96–97) distinguishes not only between story time (*erzählte Zeit*) and discourse time (*Erzählzeit*) but also between *story space* (the spatial parameters of the represented action) and *discourse space* (the immediate environment of the narrator or narrative discourse).

In *The Poetics of Space,* the French philosopher Gaston Bachelard shows that "inhabited space transcends geometrical space" (47). He semanticizes architectural structures (such as houses, drawers, wardrobes, corners, and so forth) by developing the concept of 'lived space' (*espace vécu*), that is, humanly experienced space, and addresses the question of what space means to its inhabitants. The notion of 'lived space' "indicates that human . . . conceptions of space always include a subject who is affected by (and in turn affects) space, a subject who experiences and reacts to space in a bodily way, a subject who 'feels' space through existential living conditions, mood, and atmosphere" (Jahn and Buchholz 553). Gerhard Hoffmann also deals with the multifarious functions of narrative space as experiential space (3–7). More specifically, on the basis of a comprehensive diachronic outlook, he shows how narratives semanticize domains of space and, among other things, discriminates between comic, fantastic, grotesque, uncanny, visionary, and mythic spaces (112–266).

Other theoreticians—such as Algirdas-Julien Greimas and Joseph Courtés; Gabriel Zoran; Ruth Ronen; Holly Taylor and Barbara Tversky ("Spatial Mental Models" and "Perspective"); David Herman ("Spatial Reference" and *Story Logic* 263–99); and Marie-Laure Ryan ("Cognitive Maps" and "From Parallel Universes")—have shown that narrative comprehension closely correlates with an understanding of the narrative's spatial organization.[1] In the words of David Herman, narratives necessitate "modeling, and enabling others to model, an emergent constellation of spatially related entities" ("Spatial Reference" 534). Similarly, Marie-Laure Ryan argues that "the reader's imagination needs a mental model of space to simulate the narrative action" ("Cognitive Maps" 237).

According to Holly Taylor and Barbara Tversky, we use spatial concepts to organize "space hierarchically, by salience or functional significance, and by describing elements at the top of the hierarchy prior to those lower in the hierarchy" ("Perspective" 389). At issue are "deictic expressions such as 'here,' 'there,' 'left,' 'right,' etc." (Jahn and Buchholz 552) as well as "locative adverbs (*forward, together, sideways*) and prepositions (*beyond, with, over*), which convey information about the geometric character of located and reference

---

1. In recent years, some critics have even begun to speak of a 'spatial turn' in literary studies (see Döring and Thielmann, for instance).

objects (volumes, surfaces, points, and lines)" (Herman, *Story Logic* 274–75; see also Dennerlein 75–84).

The aim of this essay is to further our understanding of narrative space by determining the potential functions of unnatural (i.e., physically or logically impossible) simulations of space in narrative fiction. Narrative spaces can be physically impossible (if they defy the laws of nature) or logically impossible (if they violate the principle of noncontradiction).² In this paper, I focus on the former. An example of a physically impossible setting can be found in Bret Easton Ellis's novel *Lunar Park,* in which the first-person narrator informs us that his house was "actually scarring on its own accord. Nothing was helping it. The paint was simply peeling off in a fine white shower, revealing more of the pink stucco underneath. It was doing this without any assistance" (222). Both physically and logically impossible spaces can be found in Mark Z. Danielewski's novel *House of Leaves*. When Will Navidson and his family return from a trip to Seattle in early June 1990, they realize that their new house has transformed itself: a dark, cold hallway (called "The Five and a Half Minute Hallway") has developed in the living room wall, and it even exists at two places at the same time. At first, we learn that the hallway has developed "on the north wall" (4), but later on, we are told that it is located "in the west wall" (57; see footnote 68, which explicitly comments on this logical impossibility).³

In a first step, I show in what ways narratives denaturalize space. I measure the unnaturalness of these spaces against the foil of the natural, that is, cognitive parameters derived from our real-world experience of space (Fludernik 10–11). In this context, Lubomír Doležel argues that

> in order to reconstruct and interpret a fictional world, the reader has to *reorient his cognitive stance* to agree with the world's encyclopedia. In other words, knowledge of the fictional encyclopedia is absolutely necessary for the reader to comprehend a fictional world. *The actual-world encyclopedia might be useful, but it is by no means universally sufficient; for many fictional worlds it is misleading, it provides not comprehension but misreading.* (181; my italics, J.A.)

---

2. Katrin Dennerlein also discusses a few ways in which narrated spaces may deviate from our real-world understandings of space (67–68).

3. Even though I focus on physical impossibilities, the unnatural in my sense also comprises human impossibilities, that is, scenarios that transcend standard limitations of knowledge. Examples would be Saleem Sinai, the telepathic first-person narrator in Rushdie's *Midnight's Children,* or the impossibly eloquent child narrator in John Hawkes's *Virginie: Her Two Lives.*

All of the cases that I discuss are *utopias* in the etymological sense of the word; they are 'no-places' that do not exist anywhere because they can only exist in the world of fiction.

In a second step, I then build on Bachelard's concept of 'lived space' by positing a human experiencer to address the significance, that is, the purpose or point, of representations of impossible space. I assume that unnatural spaces fulfill determinable functions and exist for particular reasons; they are not just ornamental or a form of art for art's sake. With regard to readers' ways of coping with impossible spaces, I would like to suggest the following reading strategies or navigational tools, which readers may follow in order to determine the functions of unnatural spaces (see also Yacobi; Ryan "From Parallel Universes"; and Alber).

1. *Blending/frame enrichment:* the processes of blending (see Fauconnier and Turner *The Way We Think* and Turner "Double-Scope Stories") and "frame enrichment" (Herman, *Story Logic* 108) play a role in all unnatural scenarios. Since the unnatural is by definition physically or logically impossible, it always urges us to create new frames (such as the shapeshifting house or the burning lake) by recombining, extending, or otherwise altering preexisting cognitive parameters.[4]
2. Readers may account for impossible spaces by identifying them as belonging to particular **literary genres** and **generic conventions** (such as the realm of the supernatural or magic [in epics, romances, or later fantasy narratives], or science fiction).[5]
3. We can explain some impossible spaces by attributing them to somebody's **interiority**.
4. Alternatively, unnatural spaces may be seen as exemplifications of particular **themes** that the narrative addresses.[6]

---

4. In an experiment, Mante S. Nieuwland and Jos J. A. van Berkum show that subjects try to make sense of narratives that contain unnatural entities (such as an amorous peanut or a crying yacht) through the blending of frames. They report that the subjects need "to construct and gradually update their situation model of the story to the point that they project human characteristics onto inanimate objects. . . . This process of projecting human properties (behavior, emotions, appearance) onto an inanimate object comes close to what has been called 'conceptual blending,' the ability to assemble new and vital relations from diverse scenarios" (1109).

5. In such cases, the unnatural has been conventionalized, in other words, turned into a basic cognitive frame.

6. In this context, the term 'theme' refers to "a specific representational component that recurs several times in the [narrative, J.A.], in different variations—our quest for the theme or themes *of* a story is always a quest for something that is not unique to this specific work" (Brinker 33). Since "anything written in meaningful language has a theme" (Tomashevsky 63),

5. Narratives can use impossible spaces to satirize, mock, or ridicule certain states of affairs. The most important feature of *satire* is critique through exaggeration, and the grotesque images of humiliation or ridicule may occasionally merge with the unnatural.
6. Readers may also see unnatural spaces as parts of *allegories* that say something about the human condition or the world in general (as opposed to particular individuals).[7]
7. Sometimes we can make sense of spatial impossibilities by assuming they are part of a *transcendental realm* such as purgatory or hell.

These reading strategies, which might overlap in actual analyses, cut across Lubomír Doležel's distinction between "world construction" and "meaning production" (165; 160) because the cognitive reconstruction of a storyworld always already involves a process of interpretation. Nevertheless, I feel that (1) and (2), that is, my first two strategies, correlate with cognitive processes that are closer to the pole of world-making, whereas the others are closer to the pole of meaning-making.

With the exception of my third reading strategy, which naturalizes the unnatural by revealing the seemingly unnatural to be entirely natural, namely somebody's fantasy, all of my proposals involve the accepting of the unnatural as an objective constituent of the projected storyworld. And once we have accepted the narratives' deviations from real-world frames, we can speculate about the potential consequences for us and our being in the world. In what follows, I will first determine the unnatural spatial parameters. In a second step, I will then suggest provisional ways of making sense of these impossible spaces.

1. *The Third Policeman:* Hallucination or Vision of the Narrator's Afterlife?

Flann O'Brien's novel *The Third Policeman* can be read as a vision of the narrator's afterlife (reading strategy 7) or as a hallucination (reading strategy 3). The narrative projects a storyworld that differs radically from the real world.

---

this reading strategy plays a role in most (if not all) cases in which we try to come to terms with the unnatural.

7. For me, a distinction can be drawn between modes (such as allegory and satire) and proper literary genres such as the science fiction novel. In principle, one could try reading any text allegorically (or satirically), and therefore I base separate reading strategies on the concepts of allegory and satire.

At the beginning, the unnamed first-person narrator informs us that he, along with John Divney, robbed and killed old Philip Mathers. More specifically, Mathers was "felled by an iron bicycle pump, hacked to death with a heavy spade and then securely buried in a field" (23). The stolen money is supposed to help the narrator publish his "De Selby Index" (11).[8] When the narrator reaches out for a black box, which supposedly contains the loot, everything becomes different "with *unnatural* suddenness" (20; my italics, J.A.), and he travels to a "mysterious townland" (40) of bizarrely shaped police barracks and gigantic policemen. Interestingly, the narrator repeatedly comments on this otherworld by using the term 'unnatural.' For instance, at some point, he informs us that he "had never seen with [his] eyes ever in [his] life before anything so *unnatural* and appalling" (55; my italics, J.A.). Also, throughout the novel, he does not manage to rid himself of "a very disquieting impression of *unnaturalness*" (57; my italics, J.A.).

Indeed, the spatial and temporal parameters of this world are unnatural in the sense in which I am using the term. For instance, the projected storyworld contains a two-dimensional police station that can become three-dimensional. When he first sees the house, the narrator describes it as follows: "It looked as if it were painted like an advertisement on a board on the roadside and indeed very poorly painted. It looked completely false and unconvincing. It did not have any depth or breadth and looked as if it would not deceive a child." A few lines later, we learn that the house can transform itself into a three-dimensional entity:

> As I approached, the house seemed to change its appearance. At first, it did nothing to reconcile itself with the shape of an ordinary house but it became uncertain in outline like a thing glimpsed under ruffled water. Then it became clear again and I saw that it began to have some back to it, some small space for rooms behind the frontage. (55–56)

The mysterious townland also contains buildings of impossible architecture (206), and it is populated with characters who have already died (such as old Mathers) (21–23) and semihuman bicycles (90–91).[9]

---

8. De Selby is a weird theoretician, and we learn about his thoughts about the world in both the running text and in footnotes. Among other things, de Selby believes that the earth is sausage-shaped rather than spherical (104).

9. The temporal setup of this world is equally bizarre. For example, when the narrator meets the dead Mathers, "years or minutes could be swallowed up with equal ease in that indescribable and unaccountable interval" (22). Also, at some point, the narrator reaches a timeless part "where it [is] always five o'clock in the afternoon" (87). At a different point, the narrator and a Sergeant take a "lift" (146) to reach "the entrance to . . . eternity" (139–42). The Sergeant

How can we explain the novel's unnatural spaces and its other impossibilities? Toward the end of the novel, we learn that John Divney booby-trapped the black box with explosives to make sure that the narrator does not get the loot (20–21, 214). That is to say that after the explosion, the narrator is dying. From this perspective, the story about the mysterious townland that follows the explosion can be seen as a fantasy or hallucination that details the narrator's attempts to come to terms with the crime and his feelings of guilt: the psychotic world of *The Third Policeman* can be explained as the result of the dying narrator's thought processes. In this context, David Herman argues that "the narrator's guilty conscience and fear of reprisal by the authorities may account for the otherworld's being populated chiefly by policemen" (*Story Logic* 287). Indeed, the first-person narrator's guilt might also explain why he permanently meets the dead Mathers, who, at one point, even appears as a policeman. It is of course rather unlikely that the narrator conceptualizes a story as complex and as long as *The Third Policeman* in the split second of his own death. However, it is also possible to assume that the narrator dies during a longer period of time, during which he imagines the story we read.

Alternatively, one can explain the spatiotemporal oddities in *The Third Policeman* by assuming that the narrator has already died and that the novel confronts us with a vision of his afterlife. The narrator might find himself trapped in a transcendental world in which he is punished for his sins. For David Herman, "the narrator's punishment is . . . to be perpetually unable to adjust, because of basic and general structures of cognition, to the spatiotemporal makeup of the world as de Selby theorized it" (*Story Logic* 289). One might argue that the narrator of *The Third Policeman* has already reached hell and is undergoing some kind of punishment there, which has to do with a state of cognitive disorientation.

2. Magical Spaces and Settings in Science Fiction

We can also explain unnatural spaces by seeing them in the context of certain literary genres (reading strategy 2). In such cases, impossibilities have been conventionalized, that is, turned into basic cognitive categories; the unnatural has become an important element of the conventions of genres such as epics, romances, fantasy novels, or science fiction narratives. Indeed, in the experi-

---

explains that "you don't grow old here. When you leave here you will be the same age as you were coming in and the same stature and latitude" (149). Furthermore, we learn that eternity "has no size at all . . . because there is no difference anywhere in it and we have no conception of the extent of its unchanging coequality" (149).

ment mentioned earlier, Nieuwland and Berkum showed that subjects typically process impossible entities (such as amorous peanuts) by seeing them "as actual 'cartoon-like entities' (i.e., a peanut that walks and talks like a human, having emotions and possibly even arms, legs and a face)." The two scientists thus assume that "the acceptability of a crying yacht or amorous peanut is not merely induced by repeated specific instances of such unusual feature combinations, but somehow also—perhaps even critically—by the *literary genre* . . . that such instances suggest" (1109; italics in original). That is to say, the evocation of a particular genre, in other words, the construction of a supportive context, helps us come to terms with unnatural entities such as an amorous peanut, and this is obviously also true of impossible settings.

For example, in the Old English epic *Beowulf*, the warrior hero Beowulf jumps into a mere to fight Grendel's mother, a monster. This mere is not only infested with other monsters such as sea-dragons ("sæ-dracan" [98, 1. 1426]); it also (impossibly) burns at night: "þær mæg nihta gehwæm nið-wundor sēon, / fȳr on flōde" (94, 11. 1365–66). Hence, Richard Butts speaks of the "highly *unnatural* character of the landscape" (113; my italics, J.A.). We can explain this physically impossible mere because we know that supernatural forces and settings are important ingredients of epics, which typically deal with "heroes performing impressive deeds usually in interaction with gods" (De Jong 138). More specifically, the brave hero here has to enter a supernatural realm that defies the laws of nature and then serves as the stage for an archetypal fight between the forces of good (Beowulf) and evil (Grendel's mother).

We can also easily cope with physically impossible settings in romances, which are "a species of magical narrative" (Heng 4). For instance, we can explain the insubstantiality of the splendid castle in the fourteenth-century romance *Sir Gawain and the Green Knight*, which seemed pared out of paper ("pared out of papure purely" [23, 1. 802]), as a form of magic once we know that it was conjured up by the witch Morgan le Fay in the context of her overall plan to test the Knights of the Round Table, drive Sir Gawain mad, and frighten Queen Guinevere to death (68, 11. 2459–60).

The animate door to Gryffindor Tower, one of the towers of the Hogwarts School of Witchcraft and Wizardry in J. K. Rowling's *Harry Potter* series, is another physical impossibility that can be explained as a part of a supernatural setting. This door is the portrait of the so-called Fat Lady, who opens the door only if the students give her the correct password. We can cope with such a living door because it is part of an institution for wizards and witches who are capable of magic.

Finally, we may attribute impossible spaces to the far and technologically advanced future depicted in science fiction narratives. An example would be

Arrakis, the setting of Frank Herbert's science fiction novel *Dune*. Arrakis is a desert planet without any natural precipitation and full of monstrous sandworms. However, in the novel the planet is "carefully structured as a coherent ecological unit" (Kneale 156). We can accept such a planet by seeing it in the context of the generic conventions of science fiction narratives, in other words, as an aspect of a potential future.

3. Foregrounding the Thematic in Borges and Davenport

Other unnatural spaces can be approached from a thematic angle (reading strategy 4). An example can be found in Jorge Luis Borges's short story "The Aleph," which confronts us with a rather extreme version of unnatural space, namely a vision of the infinite universe. In this narrative, the first-person narrator (called Borges) visits Carlos Daneri Argentino, who is a rival writer and the cousin of the deceased Beatriz Viterbo, loved by Borges. When the two descend to Argentino's cellar, the narrator views "the Aleph" (26), or, more specifically, a small point that projects a vision of "the unimaginable universe" (28). The writer-narrator describes what he sees as follows:

> How, then, can I translate into words the limitless Aleph, which my floundering mind can scarcely encompass? . . . Really, what I want to do is impossible, for any listing of an endless series is doomed to be infinitesimal. In that single gigantic instant I saw millions of acts both delightful and awful; not one of them amazed me more than the fact that all of them occupied the same point in space, without overlapping or transparency. . . . The Aleph's diameter was probably little more than an inch, but all space was there, actual and undiminished. Each thing (a mirror's face, let us say) was infinite things, since I distinctly saw it from every angle of the universe. (26–27)

The realism of the beginning and the ending of the story contrasts sharply with the unnaturalness of the Aleph, a vision of spatial infinity that is similar to the vision of eternity in Flann O'Brien's *The Third Policeman*.[10] In the words of Thomas Pavel, "this impossible object is not composed of parts; within it part and whole meet, including everything past and present within a unifying perception" (96). From a different perspective, Lisa Block de Behar argues that

---

10. According to Borges, an object such as the Aleph "could not exist because if it did, it would completely transform our idea of time, astronomy, mathematics, and space" (as quoted in De Behar 13).

Borges's narrator "describes a planetary voyage without moving" (11). In any case, the Aleph involves an impossible vision, namely an image of the total sum of the spatial universe.

How can we make sense of this impossible object? One might read "The Aleph" as accentuating that both absolute transcendence and total knowledge are impossible and irrelevant because neither of them can ever be achieved. Furthermore, absolute transcendence and/or total knowledge cannot be properly represented either. The narrator immediately realizes that, in contrast to Argentino's transgressive "attempt to fixate the infinite universe in the finite form of a poem" (Kluge 293), it is impossible to depict the Aleph in verbal art. In this context, Sophie Kluge argues that the two writers stand for two radically different approaches to literary representation:

> Whereas Argentino is confident that the tireless reworkings of the representational structures will eventually pave the way for a mimetic representation of the infinite in literature, Borges essentially denies the possibility of this project, emphasizing the necessity of perspective and the inability of literature ever to be more than language signifying itself. (297)

Indeed, after the incident, Borges haltingly describes the Aleph as "one hell of a—yes one hell of a," while later on, he simply refuses "to discuss the Aleph" (28).

At the same time, the short story suggests that the so-called total vision of the universe is relevant insofar as the narrator recognizes himself and his problems in the Aleph. Borges notably sees "unbelievable, obscene, detailed letters, which [his beloved, J.A.] Beatriz had written to Carlos Argentino" (27), and presumably due to his feelings of jealousy, he declares the Aleph to be "a false Aleph" (30).[11] The unnatural universe of the Aleph might be seen as highlighting the common human desire to think the unthinkable, represent the unrepresentable, or represent infinity in finite form. However, it also illustrates that even the most unnatural scenario ultimately takes us back to ourselves, that is, to the nature of the human mind and our problems in the actual world, and this is interestingly also one of the major claims of this article. In other words, what matters to the narrator is not "the Aleph," the first letter of the Hebrew alphabet, "which in Kabbalistic lore stands for and mysteriously participates in the infinity of the godhead" (Calinescu 4), but his hopeless love for Beatriz, whose name occurs in the narrative's first sentence and is also the short story's final word.

11. Earlier on, he notably addresses Beatriz's portrait—in a "seizure of tenderness"—as follows: "Beatriz, Beatriz Elena, Beatriz Elena Viterbo, darling Beatriz, Beatriz gone forever, it's me, it's Borges" (26).

The unnatural geography of Guy Davenport's short story "The Haile Selassie Funeral Train" can also be explained as a thematic occurrence. In this narrative, an unnamed narrator tells art critic "James Johnson Sweeney" (1900–1986) about a train ride through a geographically impossible version of Europe. More specifically, the train travels along the following itinerary: from Deauville in Normandy (108), it passes through Barcelona (110), along the Dalmatian coast (111), through Genoa (112), Madrid, Odessa, Atlanta (Georgia, USA), and back to Deauville (113).[12]

This narrative dispenses with real-world notions of space, and it also deconstructs our real-world notions of time and temporal progression: we learn that the train ride took place "in 1936" (108–9) even though the train is the funeral train of Haile Selassie (Ras Taffari), the last emperor of Ethiopia (1892–1975). Also, the train includes an odd collection of passengers such as James Joyce (1882–1941), Guillaume Apollinaire (1880–1918), "ambassadors, professors from the Sorbonne and Oxford, at least one Chinese field marshal, and the entire staff of *La Prensa*" (109). With regard to the narrative's temporality, it is worth noting that Guillaume Apollinaire died in 1918 (so he cannot possibly be there in 1936), while Haile Selassie, the "Lion of Judah" (111), died in 1975 (rather than in 1936). Hence, the short story fuses the narrative's present (the year 1936) with the narrative's past (the period before 1918, when Guillaume Apollinaire was still alive) and the narrative's future (the period after the death of Haile Selassie in 1975).

Davenport's short story revives Guillaume Apollinaire, "one of the first to have conceived of modern Europe as a heterotopian zone" (McHale 46),[13] while simultaneously killing Haile Selassie, "the last emperor of a three-thousand-year-old monarchy in Ethiopia" (Olsen 157). The short story thus argues in favor of the end of the totalizing and hierarchical monarchy system and the simultaneous development of a more open or hybrid Europe, and the collagelike spatiotemporal oddities and impossibilities serve to underline this argument. In this context, it is worth noting that the unnamed narrator, who is of American origin, is clearly fascinated by Apollinaire, who can be characterized in terms of hybridity as well: Apollinaire was actually called Wilhelm Albert Włodzimierz Apolinary Kostrowicki, and he was a French poet of Italian-Polish decent. At one point, the narrator tells us that "a bearded little

---

12. Other impossible geographies exist. For example, Guy Davenport's short story "The Invention of Photography in Toledo" fuses Toledo, Spain, with Toledo, Ohio, in a "disorienting double-vision" (McHale 47), while Walter Abish's novel *Alphabetical Africa* (1974) transforms the landlocked Republic of Chad in such a way that it suddenly has beaches.

13. The concept of the heterotopia was developed by Michel Foucault: "The heterotopia is capable of juxtaposing in a single real place several spaces, several sites that are in themselves incompatible" (25).

man in pince-nez must have seen with *what awe I was watching Apollinaire*, for he got out of his seat and came and put his hand on my arm" (109; my italics, J.A.), while at another time, he highlights "the compassion [he] felt for the wounded poet" (109).

4. Satires and Allegories: Abbott, Carter, and Danielewski

Other spatial impossibilities become meaningful as parts of satires (reading strategy 5) or allegories (reading strategy 6). For instance, the two-dimensional world of Edwin A. Abbott's novel *Flatland: A Romance of Many Dimensions* can be read as a satire on the limited perspective of representatives of the class system in Victorian England. The projected world is described as follows:

> Imagine a vast sheet of paper on which straight Lines, Triangles, Squares, Pentagons, Hexagons, and other figures, instead of remaining fixed in their places, move freely about, on or in the surface, but without the power of rising above or sinking below it, very much like shadows—only hard and with luminous edges—and you will then have a pretty correct notion of my country and countrymen. (3)

"A Square," the first-person narrator, informs us, the inhabitants of a three-dimensional world, that since the citizens of *Flatland* are not familiar with the third dimension, they "cannot distinguish one figure from another. Nothing was visible, to us, except Straight Lines" (4). Even though the individual citizens cannot be distinguished from one another, the society of *Flatland* is strictly hierarchical. That is to say, the novel's hierarchies are purely imaginary insofar as they are not really based on observable features. Nevertheless, the narrator differentiates between the individual classes as follows:

> Our Women are straight Lines. Our Soldiers and Lowest Classes of Workmen are Triangles with two equal sides, each about eleven inches long.... Our Middle Class consist of Equilateral or Equal-Sided Triangles. Our Professional Men and Gentlemen are Squares ... and Five-Sided Figures or Pentagons. Next above these come the Nobility, of whom there are several degrees, beginning at Six-Sided Figures, or Hexagons, and from thence rising in the number of their sides till they receive the honourable title of Polygonal, or many-sided. Finally, when the number of the sides

becomes so numerous, and the sides themselves so small, that the figure cannot be distinguished from a circle, he is included in the Circular or Priestly order; and this is the highest class of all. (8)

In this context, Andrea Henderson argues that "although Flatlanders believe that to know each other's shape is to know each other's essence, we as readers are urged to question this faith" (461). Indeed, the point of the well-ordered two-dimensional world of Flatland, which is both rainy and foggy (6; 22), seems to be to mock or ridicule the hierarchically ordered society of Victorian Britain. In the words of Elliott L. Gilbert "the satire . . . of an essentialist British class system in the late nineteenth century is clear enough" (396). *Flatland* can be read as a social satire that critiques the limited perspective of advocates of the class system of the nineteenth century, and in particular the general disrespect for women: the idea that women can make themselves "practically invisible at will" (11) mocks the Victorian ideal of women as quasi-invisible angels in the house.

In a second step, Abbott's narrative extends this critique of nineteenth-century Britain by showing that other societies suffer from limited perspectives as well. At one point, the narrator has a vision of Lineland, a one-dimensional world (53–63), and he is introduced to Pointland, "the Abyss of No dimensions" (92), where a miserable being exists as a voice in some kind of nowhere. We learn about this creature that

> He is himself his own World, his own Universe; of any other than himself he can form no conception; he knows not Length, nor Breadth, nor Height, for he has had no experience of them; he has no cognizance even of the number Two; nor has he a thought of Plurality; for he is himself his One and All, being really Nothing. (92–93)

Furthermore, the narrator encounters a visitor from the three-dimensional world of Spaceland (64) and he even visits Spaceland himself (78). The interesting thing is that, due to their limited perspectives, the inhabitants of these numerous worlds can never imagine what the other worlds might potentially look like. The following dialogue between Square, an inhabitant of a two-dimensional world, and the King of Lineland, a one-dimensional world, nicely illustrates this point:

> *I:* Besides your motion of Northward and Southward, there is another motion which I call from right to left.
> *King:* Exhibit to me, if you please, this motion from left to right.

>   *I:* Nay, that I cannot do, unless you could step out of your Line altogether.
>   *King:* Out of my Line? Do you mean out of the world? Out of Space?
>   *I:* Well, yes. Out of *your* world. Out of *your* space. For your Space is not the true Space. True Space is a Plane; but your Space is only a Line.
>   *King:* If you cannot indicate this motion from left to right by yourself moving in it, then I beg you to describe it to me in words.
>   *I:* If you cannot tell your right from your left, I fear that no words of mine can make my meaning clear to you. But surely you cannot be ignorant of so simple a distinction.
>   *King:* I do not in the least understand you. (61; italics in original)

The fact that the King of Lineland is the king of a one-dimensional world (in which one can only move along a line) renders the very idea of being king *ad absurdum*. Also, with regard to the miserable creature in Pointland we learn that "to be self-contented is to be vile and ignorant, and that to aspire is better than to be blindly and impotently happy" (93). Furthermore, *Flatland* highlights the limited perspective of Spaceland in the attempt to visualize space beyond the three dimensions we are familiar with (the "land of Four Dimensions" [87]). The general point that I am trying to make here is that readers can cope with the two-, one-, or nondimensional worlds of *Flatland* and their limitations when they see them in the context of common satirical strategies (such as parody, travesty, burlesque, exaggeration, or analogy) that seek to critique certain features of society.[14]

Sometimes readers can also make sense of unnatural spaces by reading them in the context of allegories. The unnatural spaces in Angela Carter's magical-realist novel *The Infernal Desire Machines of Doctor Hoffman*, for example, can be explicated as parts of an allegorical structure. In this novel, the diabolical Dr Hoffman wages a massive campaign against reason, and he uses reality-modifying machines to expand the dimensions of time and space. Desiderio, the first-person narrator, informs us that

>   Dr Hoffman's gigantic generators sent out a series of seismic vibrations which made great cracks in the hitherto immutable surface of the time and space equation we had informally formulated in order to realize our city and, out of these cracks, well—nobody knew what would come next. (17)

As we learn later on, Dr Hoffman seeks to liberate the unconscious and to

---

14. Similarly, the flying island of Laputa in Part III of Jonathan Swift's novel *Gulliver's Travels* can be explained as ridiculing the period's new institutions and schools of learning, in particular the inapplicability of the learned subjects.

objectify desire, and his machines use the secretions of numerous copulating couples in mesh cubicles to do so (208–14). The doctor's machines manage to turn the novel's storyworld into a physically impossible phantasmagoria that is reminiscent of an LSD trip or the paintings by the surrealist Salvador Dalí:

> Cloud palaces erected themselves then silently toppled to reveal for a moment the familiar warehouse beneath them until they were replaced by some fresh audacity. A group of chanting pillars exploded in the middle of a mantra and lo! they were once again street lamps until, with night, they changed to silent flowers. Giant heads in helmets of conquistadors sailed up like sad, painted kites over the giggling chimney pots. Hardly anything remained the same for more than one second and the city was no longer the conscious production of humanity; it had become the arbitrary realm of dream.... The sense of space was powerfully affected so that sometimes the proportions of buildings and townscapes swelled to enormous, ominous sizes or repeated themselves over and over again in a fretting infinity. (18–19)

In this novel, internal desires become externalized and materialize as entities in the storyworld. Later on, the projected world reaches another phase, called "Nebulous Time" (166), which carries Dr Hoffman's epistemological revolution to an extreme. During this phase, Desiderio meets a Lithuanian count, and his slave Lafleur, who turns out to be Albertina, Dr Hoffman's beautiful daughter, with whom Desiderio falls helplessly in love. Desiderio and the count then visit a brothel whose interior is physically impossible because its furniture is actually alive:

> They had employed a taxidermist instead of an upholsterer and sent him a pride of lions with instructions to make a sofa out of each pair. At both ends of the sofas, flamboyantly gothic arm-rests, were the gigantically maned heads of these lions. Their rheumy, golden eyes seeped gum and their cavernous, red mouths hung sleepily ajar, gaping wider, now and then, in a sleepy yawn or to let out a low, rumbling growl. The serviceable armchairs were brown bears who squatted on their haunches with the melancholy of all the Russias in their liquid eyes. When a girl sat on his shaggy lap, the bear grunted, leaned back and spread her legs out wide apart with his blunt forepaws. The occasional tables ran about, yelping obsequiously; they were toadying hyenas and on their brindled backs were strapped silver trays containing glasses, decanters, bowls of salted nuts and dishes of stuffed olives. (131–32)

Readers can make sense of the impossible spaces in *The Infernal Desire Machines of Doctor Hoffman* by seeing them as parts of an allegorical (or mythical) confrontation between diametrically opposed ideas such as Apollo versus Dionysus, the Freudian reality principle versus the pleasure principle, order versus freedom, conformism versus individualism, mimeticism versus imagination, the natural versus the unnatural. In this conflict, the drab Minister of Determination (who loves empirical reality, logic, and stasis) represents the former ideas, while the crazy sadist Dr Hoffman stands for the latter ones.

Furthermore, the novel illustrates that, taken to an extreme, every idea (including the idea of freedom) may possibly lead to the establishing of hierarchies and thus to a state of domination. Hence, we should take not only one's ideas but also one's attitude toward these ideas into consideration. For example, Dr Hoffman's former physics professor (who now works as blind peep-show proprietor) believes that

> when the sensual world unconditionally surrenders to the intermittency of mutability, man will be freed from the tyranny of a single present. And we will live on as many layers of consciousness as we can, all at the same time. After the Doctor liberates us, that is. Only after that. (100)

However, as the novel shows, Dr Hoffman's yearning for "*absolute* authority to establish a regime of *total* liberation" (38; my italics, J.A.) implies tyranny, subjection, and confinement just like the Minister's vulgar logical positivism and sense of order. *The Infernal Desire Machines of Doctor Hoffman* is structured around a rather static dichotomy or binary opposition that does not allow its two poles to merge, interact, or reach a state of equilibrium. At the end of the novel, Desiderio feels caught between two alternatives that cannot "possibly co-exist": while the Minister's attitudes lead to "a barren yet harmonious calm," Dr Hoffman's attitudes imply "a fertile yet cacophonous tempest" (207). Desiderio must choose between desire (Dr Hoffman wants to lock him up in a cubicle with his daughter Albertina) and reality. He finally opts in favor of restoring reality and kills both Dr Hoffman and his daughter Albertina (216–17).

The architecturally impossible house in Mark Z. Danielewski's novel *House of Leaves* can also be explained as an allegorical setting. This novel deals with *The Navidson Record*, a book written by an author called Zampanò on the basis of film footage about Will Navidson and his family (Karen Green, his wife, and their children Chad and Daisy). The Navidson house on Ash Tree Lane is interesting because it permanently transforms itself. For instance, at the beginning, Navidson and his family discover a new "white door with a glass knob" that leads to a "walk-in closet" and a "second door," which "opens up into the children's bedroom" (28). Furthermore, when Navidson begins to investigate this phenomenon, he discovers that the house's inside is bigger than its outside: "the width of the house inside" (impossibly) exceeds "the width of the house as measured from the outside by 1/4''" (30). In addition to that, a dark, cold hallway (called "The Five and a Half Minute Hallway") has developed, and this hallway also changes its size: it can both shrink (60) and grow (61). When Navidson inspects the hallway, he realizes that it has expanded into some kind of labyrinth of seemingly infinite dimensions: "a constant stream of corners and walls, all of them unreadable and perfectly smooth" (64). Inside the hallway, spatial orientation is impossible (68), and compasses refuse to settle on any one direction (90).

Like Will Slocombe, I think that one can explain the unnatural spatial parameters of this house by reading them as signifying the nothingness that potentially pervades all human relations. The house's labyrinth puts an end to Karen's and Navidson's otherwise thriving sex life (62), and it also leads to "impatience, frustration, and increasing familial alienation" (103). In other words, the domestic family home gradually gives way to a nihilist space of disorientation. From this perspective, the house becomes a version of the hostile world that systematically undermines successful interactions with others, and the novel becomes an allegory that makes a general point about our existence in the world.

However, Danielewski's novel does not only describe the problem of the nothingness of our existence; rather, it also presents a solution to this problem, and this solution has to do with love, or, more generally, the confrontation with others. *House of Leaves* frequently contrasts the nothingness of the house with the relationship between Karen and Navidson. For example, Karen produces a film called "A Brief History of Who I Love," which

> serves as the perfect *counterpoint* to that infinite stretch of hallways, rooms, and stairs. The house is *empty,* her piece is *full.* The house is *dark,* her film *glows.* A *growl* haunts that place, her place is *blessed by Charlie Parker.* On Ash Tree Lane stands a house of *darkness, cold,* and *emptiness.* In 16mm stands a house of *light, love,* and *color.* By following her heart, Karen made sense of what that place is not. (368; my italics, J.A.)

The production of this film enables Karen to rediscover "the longing and tenderness he [i.e., Navidson, J.A.] felt toward her and their children" (368). Furthermore, when Navidson is trapped inside the hallway in a state of total despair, his thoughts turn to his wife: "'Light,' Navidson croaks. 'Can't. Be. I see light. Care—'" (488). Sophia Blynn, one of Zampanò's many quoted 'critics,' argues that "it's commonly assumed his last word was 'care' or the start of 'careful.'" However, she believes that "this utterance is really just the first syllable of the very name on which his mind and heart had finally come to rest. His only hope, his only meaning: 'Karen'" (523). Once Karen and Navidson reunite, the house notably dissolves and they find themselves on the beautiful lawn of their "front yard" (524). According to Natalie Hamilton, "the novel implies that their love for each other brings them safely out of their individual labyrinths." For her, "each level of Danielewski's text involves characters attempting to navigate the maze of the self, and these attempts are in turn echoed in the structure of the text" (7; 5).

5. Conclusion

Numerous narratives openly and deliberately deconstruct our real-world notions of space and spatial organization. As I have shown, in the world of fiction we may encounter shapeshifting locations; burning lakes; insubstantial castles; impossible planets; visions of the infinite universe; unnatural geographies; two-, one-, and nondimensional worlds; literal manifestations of internal processes; houses that are bigger on the inside than they are on the outside; and so forth. Furthermore, I have proposed the following reading strategies that readers may try out when they are confronted with unnatural spaces (they constitute options and are not intrinsically connected with specific examples):

1. the blending of scripts / frame enrichment
2. generification (evoking generic conventions from literary history)
3. subjectification (reading as internal states)
4. foregrounding the thematic
5. satirization
6. reading allegorically
7. positing a transcendental realm

I do not conceive of the mental operations of these reading strategies in terms of a chronological before-after sequence. Rather, I assume that several cognitive mechanisms are layered on top of each other simultaneously during the reading process.

Interpretations and readings are of course always a tricky issue. Poststructuralist critics, for example, assume that texts can never be mastered because they deconstruct themselves. Indeed, according to J. Hillis Miller, meaning is always already deferred because "the critic's attempt to untwist the elements in the texts he interprets only twists them up again in another place and leaves always a remnant of opacity, or an added opacity, as yet unraveled" (247). Critics such as Ann Wilson even consider the process of interpretation to be inherently evil. She argues that "mastery always involves domination (in the case of interpretation, of understanding fully the action and hence, being able to control and contain its effect)." For her, interpretative mastery is "a mode of social regulation and containment based on relations of power which are, by definition, hierarchical and potentially oppressive" (187). From my perspective, these two approaches lead to a critical impasse insofar as they imply that the only thing that can still be said about literary texts is that ultimately nothing can be said.

My own approach differs from both of these critical perspectives. I am aware of the ultimate meaninglessness of our desperate attempts to create significance, and I appreciate this assumption as a necessary footnote to everything we do. Nevertheless, without trying to *master* literary texts once and for all, I attempt to enrich the polysemic makeup of fictional narratives by presenting interpretations that use unnatural spaces as their starting points. My readings are provisional explanations that primarily serve to illustrate that the unnatural is not completely alien to our thinking. Since, as I have shown, we can in fact engage productively with impossible spaces, they do not paralyze our interpretive faculties.[15]

For me, fiction is interesting and special because physically or logically impossible scenarios and events can be projected only in the world of fiction. Having said that, I refuse to see the unnatural as something transcendental or godly that we poor human beings cannot even begin to make sense of. Such an approach, which involves remaining in a state of "anxiety and wonder" (Abbott, "Unreadable Minds" 448), amounts to the monumentalization of the unnatural. The unnatural is created by human authors and should therefore be approached from the vantage point of our (human) world. Furthermore, we as readers are ultimately bound by our cognitive architecture (even when we try to make sense of the unnatural). Therefore, the only way we can possibly

    15. From my perspective, H. Porter Abbott's proposal "to rest in that peculiar combination of anxiety and wonder" (448), which is praised by Stefan Iversen in this volume, has nothing to do with the process of interpretation because it does not address the potential purpose of the unnatural at all. I think Abbott merely describes a preinterpretive state that calls for further elucidation and explanation. In her essay in this collection, Maria Mäkelä also follows what I call "the Zen way of reading" (Alber, "Impossible" 83–84) insofar as she repudiates cognitive explanations. I think this approach is challenging from a psychological perspective but I do not think it generates interesting readings of the unnatural, because we basically remain wondering.

respond to narratives of all sorts (including unnatural ones) is on the basis of cognitive frames and scripts. Hence, I emphatically argue in favor of a *cognitive* approach to the unnatural.[16]

Finally, I would like to thank David Herman and Peter Rabinowitz for suggesting that the unnatural might also figure prominently in new scientific theories. Indeed, Stephen Hawking and Leonard Mlodinow, for instance, claim that "it is possible to travel to the future" (*A Briefer History* 105), and that the universe consists of numerous subuniverses "with many different sets of physical laws" (*The Grand Design* 136). However, in contrast to fictional storyworlds, scientific theories are hypotheses which make predictions that can then be tested by observation. If they are not falsified (like Hawking's earlier theory that before the Big Bang, time had moved backward), such theories may ultimately lead to a renegotiation of the relationship between what we consider to be natural (or possible) and what we perceive as being unnatural (or impossible). It is only that, in order to actually influence our natural cognition of the world, that is, the cognitive parameters that we use to make sense of the real world, we will have to experience a journey into the future or see a universe with different sets of physical laws, and I think it might still take some time before this is technically possible—if it is possible at all.

Works Cited

Abbott, Edwin A. *Flatland: A Romance of Many Dimensions* [1884]. Oxford: Blackwell, 1974.
Abbott, H. Porter. "Unreadable Minds and the Captive Reader." *Style* 42.4 (2008): 448–70.
Alber, Jan. "Impossible Storyworlds—And What to Do with Them." *Storyworlds* 1 (2009): 79–96.
Bachelard, Gaston. *The Poetics of Space* [1958]. Trans. Maria Jolas. New York: Orion, 1964.
Bakhtin, Mikhail. "Forms of Time and the Chronotope in the Novel [1938–73]." In *The Dialogic Imagination: Four Essays*, ed. Michael Holquist. Austin: University of Texas Press, 1981. 84–258.
Borges, Jorge Luis. "The Aleph [1945]." In *The Aleph and Other Stories 1933–69*, ed. and trans. Norman Thomas di Giovanni. New York: Dutton, 1970. 15–30.
Brinker, Menachem. "Theme and Interpretation." In *Thematics: New Approaches*, ed. Claude Bremond, Joshua Landy, and Thomas Pavel. Albany: State University of New York Press, 1995. 33–44.

---

16. For an alternative perspective, see the essay by Henrik Skov Nielsen in this volume. From my vantage point, Nielsen does not actually present interpretations; rather, he shows that in certain cases, we have to accept the fact that narratives move beyond real-world frames. This is actually the first step ("world-making") in my model. In my model, this first step is then followed by a second one ("meaning-making") which addresses the potential point of such 'deviations,' that is, the question of why narratives might use the unnatural.

Butts, Richard. "The Analogical Mere: Landscape and Terror in *Beowulf.*" *English Studies* 2 (1987): 113–21.
Calinescu, Matei. *Rereading.* New Haven, CT, and London: Yale University Press, 1993.
Carter, Angela. *The Infernal Desire Machines of Doctor Hoffman* [1972]. New York: Penguin, 1985.
Chatman, Seymour. *Story and Discourse: Narrative Structure in Fiction and Film.* Ithaca, NY, and London: Cornell University Press, 1978.
Cox, Katharine. "What Has Made Me? Locating Mother in the Textual Labyrinth of Mark Z. Danielewski's *House of Leaves.*" *Critical Survey* 18.2 (2006): 4–15.
Danielewski, Mark Z. *House of Leaves.* New York: Pantheon, 2000.
Davenport, Guy. "The Haile Selassie Funeral Train [1975]." In *Da Vinci's Bicycle: Ten Stories by Guy Davenport.* Baltimore and London: Johns Hopkins University Press, 1979. 108–13.
De Behar, Lisa Block. "Borges, the Aleph, and Other Cardinal Points." *Review: Literature and Arts of the Americas* 38.1 (2005): 7–16.
De Jong, Irene J. F. "Epic." In *Routledge Encyclopedia of Narrative Theory,* ed. David Herman, Manfred Jahn, and Marie-Laure Ryan. London: Routledge, 2005. 138–40.
Dennerlein, Katrin. *Narratologie des Raumes.* Berlin and New York: de Gruyter, 2009.
Döring, Jörg, and Tristan Thielmann, eds. *Spatial Turn: Das Raumparadigma in den Kultur- und Sozialwissenschaften.* Bielefeld: Transcript, 2008.
Doležel, Lubomír. *Heterocosmica: Fiction and Possible Worlds.* Baltimore and London: Johns Hopkins University Press, 1998.
Ellis, Bret Easton. *Lunar Park.* New York: Vintage, 2005.
Fauconnier, Gilles, and Mark Turner. *The Way We Think: Conceptual Blending and the Mind's Hidden Complexities.* New York: Basic Books, 2002.
Fludernik, Monika. *Towards a "Natural" Narratology.* London and New York: Routledge, 1996.
Forster, E. M. *Aspects of the Novel* [1927]. London: Penguin, 1990.
Foucault, Michel. "Of Other Spaces." *Diacritics* 16 (1986): 22–27.
Genette, Gérard. *Narrative Discourse: An Essay in Method* [1972]. Trans. Jane E. Lewin. Ithaca, NY: Cornell University Press, 1980.
Gilbert, Elliott L. "'Upward, Not Northward': *Flatland* and the Quest for the New." *English Literature in Transition, 1880–1920* 34.4 (1991): 391–404.
Greimas, Algirdas-Julien, and Joseph Courtés. *Semiotics and Language: An Analytical Dictionary.* Trans. Larry Crist et al. Bloomington: Indiana University Press, 1983.
Hamilton, Natalie. "The A-Mazing House: The Labyrinth as Theme and Form in Mark Z. Danielewski's *House of Leaves.*" *Critique* 50.1 (2008): 3–15.
Hawking, Stephen, and Leonard Mlodinow. *A Briefer History of Time.* New York: Bantam Books, 2005.
———. *The Grand Design.* New York: Bantam Books, 2010.
Heaney, Seamus. *Beowulf: A New Verse Translation.* New York: Farrar, Straus and Giroux, 2000.
Henderson, Andrea. "Math for Math's Sake: Non-Euclidean Geometry, Aestheticism, and Flatland." *PMLA* 124.2 (2009): 455–71.
Heng, Geraldine. *Empire of Magic: Medieval Romance and the Politics of Cultural Fantasy.* New York: Columbia University Press, 2003.
Herman, David. "Spatial Reference in Narrative Domains." *Text* 21.4 (2001): 515–41.
———. *Story Logic: Problems and Possibilities of Narrative.* Lincoln: University of Nebraska Press, 2002.

Hoffmann, Gerhard. *Raum, Situation, erzählte Wirklichkeit: Poetologische und historische Studien zum englischen und amerikanischen Roman.* Stuttgart: Metzler, 1978.

Jahn, Manfred, and Sabine Buchholz. "Space in Narrative." In *The Routledge Encyclopedia of Narrative Theory,* ed. David Herman, Manfred Jahn, and Marie-Laure Ryan. London: Routledge, 2005. 551-55.

Kluge, Sofie. "The World in a Poem? Góngora versus Quevedo in Jorge Luis Borges' *El Aleph.*" *Orbis Litterarum* 60.4 (2005): 293-312.

Kneale, James. "Lost in Space? Exploring Impossible Geographies." In *Impossibility Fiction: Alternativity, Extrapolation, Speculation,* ed. Derek Littlewood and Peter Stockwell. Amsterdam: Rodopi, 1996. 147-62.

Lessing, Gotthold Ephraim. *Werke. Sechster Band. Kunsttheoretische und kunsthistorische Schriften.* Munich: Carl Hanser, 1974.

McHale, Brian. *Postmodernist Fiction.* New York and London: Methuen, 1987.

Miller, J. Hillis. "The Critic as Host." In *Deconstruction and Criticism,* ed. Harold Bloom. New York: Seabury, 1979. 217-53.

Nieuwland, Mante S., and Jos J. A. van Berkum. "When Peanuts Fall in Love: N400 Evidence for the Power of Discourse." *Journal of Cognitive Neuroscience* 18.7 (2006): 1098-111.

O'Brien, Flann. *The Third Policeman* [1967]. London: Flamingo, 2001.

Olsen, Lance. "A Guydebook to the Last Modernist: Davenport on Davenport and *Da Vinci's Bicycle.*" *Journal of Narrative Technique* 16.2 (1986): 148-61.

Pavel, Thomas. *Fictional Worlds.* Cambridge, MA: Harvard University Press, 1986.

Ronen, Ruth. "Space in Fiction." *Poetics Today* 7.3 (1986): 421-38.

Ryan, Marie-Laure. "Cognitive Maps and the Construction of Narrative Space." In *Narrative Theory and the Cognitive Sciences,* ed. David Herman. Stanford, CA: Center for the Study of Language and Information, 2003. 214-42.

———. "From Parallel Universes to Possible Worlds: Ontological Pluralism in Physics, Narratology, and Narrative." *Poetics Today* 27.4 (2006): 633-74.

Slocombe, Will. "'This Is Not for You': Nihilism and the House that Jacques Built." *Modern Fiction Studies* 51.1 (2005): 88-109.

Taylor, Holly A., and Barbara Tversky. "Perspective in Spatial Descriptions." *Journal of Memory and Language* 35.3 (1996): 371-91.

———. "Spatial Mental Models Derived from Survey and Route Descriptions." *Journal of Memory and Language* 31.2 (1992): 261-92.

Tolkien, J. R. R., and E. V. Gordon, eds. *Sir Gawain and the Green Knight.* 2nd ed. Rev. Norman Davis. Oxford: Clarendon, 1967.

Tomashevsky, Boris. "Thematics." In *Russian Formalist Criticism,* ed. Lee T. Lemon and Marion J. Reis. Lincoln: University of Nebraska Press, 1965. 61-95.

Turner, Mark. "Double-Scope Stories." In *Narrative Theory and the Cognitive Sciences,* ed. David Herman. Stanford, CA: Center for the Study of Language and Information, 2003. 117-42.

Wilson, Ann. "Failure and the Limits of Representation in *The Skriker.*" In *Essays on Caryl Churchill,* ed. Sheila Rabillard. Winnipeg and Buffalo, NY: Blizzard, 1998. 174-88.

Yacobi, Tamar. "Fictional Reliability as a Communicative Problem." *Poetics Today* 2.2 (1981): 113-26.

Zoran, Gabriel. "Toward a Theory of Space in Narrative." *Poetics Today* 5.2 (1984): 309-35.

Naturalizing and Unnaturalizing Reading Strategies

Focalization Revisited[1]

HENRIK SKOV NIELSEN

1. Aims of the Essay

In this essay I argue that applying the principles of unnatural narratology in the form of what I call unnaturalizing reading strategies to the interpretation of unnatural narratives is often a more appropriate choice than applying the principles of naturalization and familiarization. A main contention is that Genette's separation of voice and mood (who speaks and who perceives) and Genette's understanding of focalization as a restriction of access to point of view are more radical proposals than previous narratologists have recognized—and that they are in line with unnatural narratology and allow for unnaturalizing reading strategies.

The argument compels me to revisit some points from an early essay of mine called "The Impersonal Voice in First-Person Narrative Fiction" that played a role in the emergence of unnatural narratology along with work by Maria Mäkelä, Jan Alber, and Brian Richardson. In the essay I argue that in first-person narrative fiction, the limits of the protagonist's voice in such areas as knowledge, vocabulary, and memory are sometimes strikingly transgressed

---

1. I wish to thank Jan Alber, Stefan Iversen, Rolf Reitan, Brian Richardson, and Richard Walsh for their comments on an earlier version of this essay. Very special thanks go to Jim Phelan for invaluable support and help.

and that this is neither a mistake nor something foreign to the genre but, on the contrary, a matter of utilizing a possibility fundamental to it.

In the present essay I wish to take this one step further and to argue that what seemed to me and most other narrative theorists at the time to be a rare and strange type of narrative does in fact tell us much about character narration in general, and that character narration, in this view, in turn, tells us something about fictional narration in general. This is because these narrative types are all most fruitfully understood as different manifestations of a relationship between author and characters. In natural frameworks one would expect all character narrators to be internally focalized, since one would expect a character narrator to have access to his or her own thoughts and not to other people's thoughts. I argue that Genette's focalization theory is really a relational theory about the relation between characters and authors, and that it is an integral part of the system that an author can choose to combine any access or nonaccess to thoughts and knowledge with any kind of narration, including character narration, precisely because the system disconnects mood and voice.

Genette's insight into the disconnect between mood and voice in fiction explains why and how fiction can (but obviously need not) employ a range of unnatural mind representations in combinations such as homodiegetic narration with zero focalization (in the manner of Ishmael in *Moby-Dick*). Furthermore, this combinatory principle can even be expanded beyond Genette's own examples to include such unnatural combinations as you-narration with internal focalization, we-narration with external focalization, and so on. Therefore, it fits nicely with the discussions of strange and unnatural narratives in Brian Richardson's *Unnatural Voices*, in which chapter 2 covers second-person narration, chapter 3 covers we-narration, and the rest of the chapters cover other unusual narrative situations.

I argue further that the separation of mood and voice and the possible combinations that follow from it are connected to the no-narrator thesis. These combinations are attributable not to a fact-reporting narrator but rather to a fictional world–creating author. This attribution in turn emphasizes the difference between reading with the assumption that the storyworld is invented (fiction) and reading with the assumption that the storyworld is not invented (nonfiction). This understanding then logically leads to a choice between interpretations: If we interpret the words in a 300-page dialogue novel with a character narrator, or—on a smaller scale—the shorter rendering of a dialogue that took place 50 years ago[2] as only *appearing* to be verbatim accounts, we

---

2. Cf. Phelan on Poe's "The Cask of Amontillado" in the current volume.

make a legitimate but naturalizing choice. If we believe instead that they are part of the invented act of narration, we can also believe that the dialogues are verbatim accounts and can thus base interpretations on the characters saying some words rather than others. In making this equally legitimate choice we would also be following the principles of unnatural narratology because we would make an interpretational choice that is unnaturalizing in the sense that it is not limiting the narrative possibilities to what is mnemonically possible or plausible in real-world narration. In what follows I test these assumptions and argue in favor of unnaturalizing reading strategies in a range of examples before finally suggesting a simple, rhetorical model in which the real author rather than the narrator is the main agent of the telling, and in which not all narrative acts are representational.

2. Exceptionality, Similarity, and Unnatural Narratology

Much of the introduction to David Herman's impressive anthology *The Emergence of Mind* is based on a refutation of what he calls the exceptionality thesis. He directly connects this thesis to the question of unnatural narratology and to theorists such as Alber, Mäkelä, Richardson, and Skov Nielsen (11). Herman writes that "[. . .] the questioning of the exceptionality thesis is in a sense the starting point for all the approaches to fictional minds outlined by the chapters in this volume [. . .]" (18), and refers to almost every contributor in the volume as "anti-exceptionalist" (20, 21, 22). The exceptionality thesis, then, is the thesis that we approach fiction and nonfiction by means of different protocols for reasoning and with different interpretive strategies, and that, for example, "[. . .] readers' experiences of fictional minds are different in kind from their experiences of the minds they encounter outside the domain of narrative fiction [. . .]" (8), "[. . .] a thesis against which I think this volume militates," writes Herman (32). Interestingly, Herman explicitly notes his opposition to Richardson:

> Richardson describes as follows the conventions for representing minds in texts he characterizes as mimetic: "A first person narrator cannot know what is in the minds of others, and a third person narrator may perform this, and a few other such acts, but may not stray beyond the established conventions of depicting such perceptions: the thought of one character may not be lodged within the mind of another without any intervening plausible explanation" (6–7). I would argue by contrast that, in light of the research on folk psychology that I discuss in this section, the modes

of narration that Richardson characterizes as unnatural or "anti-mimetic" converge with present-day understandings of how minds actually work. (33–34)

Finally, I wish to mention a call to the exceptionalists that seems apt to me:

> Granted, fictional narratives have the power to stipulate as true reports about characters' mind-contents. But the onus is on Exceptionalists to demonstrate that readers have to use different interpretive protocols to make sense of such stipulated mental states and dispositions, in comparison with the protocols they use for construing actual minds. (33)

I agree with the latter quote, and, accordingly, I want to argue that it is *sometimes* necessary, *often* profitable, and *nearly always* possible to use different interpretive protocols when the mind-content of characters (other than of a character narrator herself/himself) is rendered. To make this argument, however, I need to engage in a reading of Genette's focalization theory. Genette is completely absent in Herman's introduction and in its voluminous list of references, and this is not surprising since the study of consciousness-representation in fiction has been almost totally separated from the study of focalization. I will argue, however, that they are two sides of the same coin. Before doing so, I will first define what I mean by unnatural narratives and unnatural narratology and clarify my intention, which is not to claim that all fictional narratives are unnatural.

3. Definitions

For me, the expression "unnatural narratives" first and foremost takes on meaning in relation to what it is not: natural narratives. By natural narratives I refer to narratives that have been designated as such by influential narrative theorists. Most prominently the term "natural" has been applied to narrative theory by Monika Fludernik in *Towards a "Natural" Narratology*. Here, she describes the term as follows:

> *Natural narrative* is a term that has come to define "naturally occurring" storytelling [...] What will be called *natural narrative* in this book includes, mainly, spontaneous conversational storytelling, a term which would be more appropriate but is rather unwieldy. (*Towards* 13)

This is the first and most important of three different meanings that feed into the term "natural narratology." Its source is Labov and linguistic discourse analysis. The second meaning of the term "natural" comes from "Natürlichkeitstheorie," which uses the term to "[...] designate aspects of language which appear to be regulated and motivated by cognitive parameters based on man's experience of embodiedness in a real-world context" (17). Whereas both of these two meanings function as descriptive denominators of a certain kind of narrative or language, the third one is on a completely different level and refers to the readers' *reaction* to certain types of narrative, literature, or discourse. It comes from Culler and his use of the term "naturalization" to designate readers' efforts to make the strange and deviant seem natural and thus to familiarize it: "Culler's naturalization in particular embraces the familiarization of the strange" (*Towards* 31). I do not disagree that natural narratives of the kind described by Fludernik exist, but an equally important point is one that Fludernik herself stresses in 2003: that we should not necessarily privilege these:

> Rather than privileging naturally occurring storytelling situations, Natural Narratology, by contrast, attempts to show how in the historical development of narratorial forms natural base frames are again and again being extended. [...] [O]nce an originally non-natural storytelling situation has become widely disseminated in fictional texts, it acquires a second-level "naturalness" from habituality, creating a cognitive frame [...] which readers subconsciously deploy in their textual processing. Even more paradoxically, fiction as a genre comes to represent precisely those impossible naturalized forms and to create readerly expectations along those lines. ("Natural Narratology" 255)

It is instructive to see explicitly stressed that such a thing as an "originally non-natural storytelling situation" exists. The question, though, is whether the reader will always try to naturalize anything—and if so, if it can always be done successfully.

In yet another text, this time from 2001, Fludernik writes: "When readers read narrative texts, they project real-life parameters into the reading process and, if at all possible, treat the text as a real-life instance of narrating" ("New Wine" 623). I think it is worth noting, first, that as a descriptive statement as opposed to a normative statement about what readers *should* do, it hardly covers all readers, nor all lay readers; and second, that even if this is what many readers tend to do, we are not obliged to repeat the projection at a methodological level. Familiarization, or what Culler calls naturalization and

Fludernik, narrativization, is a choice, and whether the choice is conscious or automatic, it remains a choice and not a necessity. A different choice in the form of unnaturalizing interpretation is equally legitimate and rewarding in many texts. Following from this, these are my answers to the "what?" and the "how?" of unnatural narratology:

- What are unnatural narratives? They are a subset of fictional narratives that—unlike many realistic and mimetic narratives—cue the reader to employ interpretational strategies that are different from those she employs in nonfictionalized, conversational storytelling situations. More specifically, such narratives may have temporalities, storyworlds, mind representations, or acts of narration that would have to be construed as physically, logically, mnemonically, or psychologically impossible or implausible in real-world storytelling situations, but that allow the reader to interpret them instead as reliable, possible, and/or authoritative by cueing her to change her interpretational strategies.
- What is unnatural narratology? The investigation of these strategies and their interpretational consequences and, more broadly, the effort to state the theoretical and interpretive principles relevant to such unnatural narratives. This means that for me all unnatural narratives are fictional but only some fictional narratives are unnatural. Only some fictional narratives cue the reader to interpret differently than real-life storytelling situations do, whereas scores of realistic and conventional fictional narratives do not do that. I do wish to stress, though, the unnaturalness also of some conventional forms,[3] such as, say, the use of zero focalization in traditional works of realism.

4. Genette's Focalization Theory

By rereading Genette in *Narrative Discourse* and *Narrative Discourse Revisited*, I will demonstrate how his distinction between "who sees?" and "who speaks?" is more radical and unnatural than has generally been acknowledged. Next I argue that even though the distinction between "who sees?" and "who speaks?" is indispensable, it is also problematic in several ways, among other things because narrative allows for a traffic between voices and for techniques such as free indirect discourse which mix voices that belong to different levels in Genette's system, and because it attributes incompatible fea-

---

3. See Maria Mäkelä's essay in the present volume.

tures to the narrator. This, however, does not destroy the system. On the contrary, it does, in a sense, strengthen it, by allowing for a system in which the author's voice is influenced and supplemented by character discourse instead of vice versa.

Let me begin this section by quoting two famous moments of postclassical and classical narratology respectively. Moment 1 is Fludernik's redefinition of narrativity in terms of experientiality instead of plot: in my model there can be narratives without plot, but there cannot be any narratives without a human (anthropomorphic) experiencer of some sort at some narrative level (*Towards* 13).

This approach has gained tremendous influence in a number of important definitions and conceptualizations of narrative, including Herman's in his *Basic Elements of Narrative,* in which "what it is like" (to experience events and disruptions) is one basic element. More generally, there seems to be a shift from plot-based to experience-based conceptions of narrativity.

Moment 2 is so famous that it is already a commonplace to say that it is so famous that it hardly needs quoting. It is from Genette's *Narrative Discourse:*

> However, to my mind most of the theoretical works on this subject [. . .] suffer from a regrettable confusion between what I call here *mood* and *voice,* a confusion between the question *who is the character whose point of view orients the narrative perspective?* and the very different question *who is the narrator?*—or, more simply, the question *who sees?* and the question *who speaks?* (186)

Even at first glance it is easy to see some of the differences between the two moments: Genette is interested in linguistic categories such as mood and voice. Fludernik is interested in cognition and human experience. Yet, how does Genette arrive at this distinction which is, although not unchallenged, so widely recognized today? What is truly original about Genette's insight and distinction here? In *Narrative Discourse Revisited,* Genette does his best to downplay the discovery. He says about his study of focalizations that it was just a reformulation:

> It was never anything but a reformulation, whose main advantage was to draw together and systematize such standard ideas as "narrative with an omniscient narrator" or "vision from behind" (zero focalization); "narrative with a point of view, reflector, selective omniscience, restriction of field" or "vision with" (internal focalization); or "objective, behaviorist technique" or "vision from without" (external focalization). (65–66)

To say that zero focalization is nothing more than a systematization of standard ideas such as that of the omniscient narrator is—it seems to me—at the same time far too modest and wildly imprecise. *Narrative Discourse Revisited* is striking in at least two ways.

First, the visits it pays to each of the chapters in *ND* are very, very far from equally long: in *ND* the first four of the five chapters comprise more than two hundred pages. These chapters are done away with in some twenty to thirty pages in *NDR*. Then, in revisiting the final chapter on voice and the intersection between mood and voice, *NDR* devotes close to one hundred pages to discussions of the questions in this chapter.

Second, in *ND* the long chapter on "Order" goes on for some fifty pages but does not lead (in *ND* or *NDR*) to any taxonomy or scheme for different kinds of narratives. The same holds true for the almost equally long chapter on "Duration" and the revisit, and for that of "Frequency" and its revisit. And ditto for "Mood." But then, when it comes to narrative situations and the considering of mood and voice jointly, schemes suddenly proliferate, resulting—among other things—in the famous six-box scheme, shown in figure 4.1.

Why exactly is it that this distinction (mood/voice, who sees/who speaks), which was "never anything but a reformulation," is the distinction on which Genette's narrative situations are based? Why does it seem much more useful to distinguish between types of narratives on the basis of different focalizations than on the basis of, say, frequency or order? To try to answer this, we have to examine what is, in *ND* and *NDR*, the insight about focalizations that actually does not just amount to a reformulation of earlier standard ideas. In *ND* Genette talks about a possible typology:

> It is certainly legitimate to envisage a typology of "narrative situations" that would take into account *both* mood and voice; what is not legitimate is to present such a classification under the single category of "point of view," or to draw up a list where the two determinations compete with each other on the basis of an obvious confusion. (188; my italics, H.S.N.)

This envisaged typology is not provided in *ND*, but in *NDR* it is provided in the form of the six-box scheme. This already tells us that not only is the classification not reducible to questions of omniscience or ratios of knowledge, but it is not even commensurable or compatible with these. What it does instead is take into account *both* mood and voice. Genette actually knows very well that the real question does not concern the ratio of knowledge:

> The narrator almost always "knows" more than the hero, even if he himself is the hero, and therefore for the narrator focalization through the hero is a

Narrating (Relation) \ Type (Focal.)	Authorial (Zero focal.)	Actorial (Internal focal.)	Neutral (External focal.)
Heterodiegetic	A *Tom Jones*	B *The Ambassadors*	C "The Killers"
Homodiegetic	D *Moby-Dick*	E *Hunger*	

FIGURE 4.1

restriction of field just as artificial in the first person as in the third. (*Narrative Discourse* 194)

The keyword here is "restriction." Genette describes and exemplifies but never actually precisely *defines* focalization. Yet, from his examples and discussions we may be able to extract a precise definition:

Focalization = restriction of access to point of view

Thus, in zero focalization there is no (zero) restriction of access to point of view. In internal focalization there is a restriction of access to the internal point of view of one or more characters. In external focalization there is a restriction of access to external points of view on the characters. The knowledge of the narrator in general is irrelevant compared with the choice of restriction. Omniscience and knowledge do not really play a role here. The choice of focalization is not a choice of knowledge. If it was, it could not be a choice anyway. How could a narrator choose to know more or less than he did? The choice of restriction, or nonrestriction, of access to point of view, on the other hand, makes perfect sense. But let us also remember that the visual metaphors are themselves too limited. Genette says in *NDR:*

> My only regret is that I used a purely visual, and hence overly narrow, formulation. [. . .] so obviously we must replace *who sees?* with the broader question of *who perceives?* (64)

There is a strong sense in which consciousness, perception, mind access, and experientiality are at the very center of Genette's focalization theory. The different ways in which narratives can give us access to minds are the very means by which narratives are typologized in Genette. Focalization is thus not dependent on knowledge in and of itself, and the narrator arguably always knows more than she tells, independent of whether the reader gets access to the thoughts of one, all, or none of the characters. Instead, focalization is dependent on the restriction or nonrestriction of access to characters' perception.

Genette's focalization theory is not essentially a theory about voice and certainly not one about vision. It is—in the way it is explicitly formulated by Genette—a relational theory about the *relation* between characters and narrator, but actually, as we will see, between authors and characters.[4] If the question "who sees?" is too purely visual and should—as indicated by Genette—be replaced by the question "who perceives?" then it is equally true that the question "who speaks?" is too purely verbal and should be replaced or at the very least supplemented by the question "who chooses the restriction or nonrestriction of access to this perceiving?" Together, the two rephrased questions allow us to ask: "To which character's/characters' experientiality (if any) does the narrator give access?" A narrative situation, in Genette's sense, then, results from the combination of restriction of access to the perception of one, all, or none of the characters with the presence or absence of the narrator as a character of whom mention is made. A short passage in which Genette reflects on the possibility of talking about a "focalizer" is extremely illuminating in this respect:

> [. . .] if *focalizer* applied to anyone, it could only be the person who *focalizes the narrative*—that is, the narrator, or, if one wanted to go outside the conventions of fiction, the *author* himself [. . .]. (*Narrative Discourse Revisited* 73)

It seems to me that this reveals a necessary feature of the theory. Focalization theory is really a theory about the relation between authors and characters. If we attribute the choice of restriction to a narrator, we encounter an aporia: for each of the six boxes in Genette's system two questions have to be asked and answered. For example, in the homodiegetic narration with zero focalization, the question "who speaks?" can be answered by "the first person narrator, Ishmael," and the question "who sees?" can be answered by "several characters including Ishmael, Starbuck, and Ahab" (this being the very reason that focalization is zero and not internal). The quite surprising lack of surprise on Genette's part toward this strange option is probably due to the fact and the paradox of Genette's focalization theory that not only is the choice of focalization contingent on the question of relation (the question of whether there is

---

4. In my view it is this relational nature that is lost all too often in accounts and applications of focalization theory where focalization is repeatedly conflated with one of its two subparts, that of point of view, and thus reduced to a matter of the question "Who sees?"

any mention of the narrator as a character in the storyworld or not); it simply disconnects this question of relation (narrating instance) from the question of type (focalization). In other words: the questions of the narrator as enunciator of the story and the narrator as responsible for the choice of focalization are never really brought to bear upon each other.[5] In fact, the narrator is assigned two completely distinct and incompatible roles, one inside and one outside the fictional world. And the idea of the narrator as the one who speaks and reports a story (e.g., as Ishmael does) is actually incompatible with the idea of the narrator choosing a type of focalization. This incompatibility is more hidden, but equally important, in third-person narration.

A merit of Genette's system is that its very premise is based on the assumption that fictional narratives can most usefully be categorized according to their employment or nonemployment of authoritative representation of minds. Neither temporal order, duration, frequency, nor above all thematics is used by Genette to typologize the narratives of the world. Instead the six boxes represent six different ways to mediate experientiality.

The very distinction upon which the system is built—the distinction between "who sees?" and "who speaks?"—is fundamental for fictional narration where the author can represent the experiences, thoughts, and perceptions of someone else whether or not this someone is referred to in the first or the third person. Again, focalization is essential to, whereas relation is contingent upon, fiction.

As soon as the complete disconnect between mood and voice in fiction is acknowledged, there is nothing particularly strange about, say, homodiegetic narration with zero focalization (though it certainly may be interpreted as unnatural).[6]

To sum up: Genette categorizes the narratives of the world on the basis of the different ways in which they do or do not give us access to minds. His approach is theoretical and deductive instead of empirical, to the degree that it includes both unconventional as well as conventional unnatural options (in the form of, respectively, heterodiegetic and homodiegetic narratives in zero focalization) and even leaves a box empty for the possible but not fully actualized homodiegetic narrative with external focalization.[7]

5. This may be one of the main reasons why Genette underestimates his own insights. I agree with what Phelan says in *Living to Tell About It* about Genette's getting sidetracked by the linguistic meaning of mood (110–19), and I think additionally that Genette would have had to revise his "obligatory narrator theory" if he had pursued the insight that the only viable candidate for "focalizing" in the sense of choosing focalization is the author. In *ND* and *NDR* this is clearly a revision he strongly wants to resist.

6. Obviously, it does not correlate with any real-world framework, but the same holds true for heterodiegetic narration with zero focalization.

7. Genette, of course, discusses several potential candidates, including Camus' *L'Étranger*,

Let me emphasize that for me what is unnatural about zero focalization has to do with interpretation rather than ontology. Thus I am not suggesting that sentences such as "He is missing his girlfriend" or "She blushed and felt ashamed of herself" are impossible in real life or are always fictional or unnatural. Rather, I propose that when interpreting zero focalization, it is very often possible and rewarding to interpret the mind representations in a way that is exactly "[. . .] different in kind from [. . .] experiences of the minds [we] encounter outside the domain of narrative fiction [. . .]" (Herman 8). In the next section I demonstrate how unnaturalizing approaches to certain texts may correspond to common sense and to how actual readers actually often tend to read.[8]

5. Four Examples of Unnaturalizing Reading Strategies

5.1. *Glamorama*

In *Recent Theories of Narrative* (1986), Martin Wallace writes "One telltale sign of omniscience [. . .]: comments on what a character did not think" (146). Several times in the first-person novel *Glamorama*, by Bret Easton Ellis, we are explicitly told what the protagonist Victor does not perceive:

> "Disarm" by the Smashing Pumpkins starts playing on the soundtrack and the music overlaps a shot of the club I was going to open in TriBeCa and I walk into that frame, *not noticing* the black limousine parked across the street [. . .]. (168; my italics, H.S.N.)

This strange feature presents the reader with the paradoxical situation that the narrator seems to be at once omniscient and ignorant. This paradox arises, however, only if we attribute the narrative act and the enunciation of the narrative as a whole to Victor—and in fact there is little evidence, aside from the use of the first-person pronoun, that we should do that. In the course of *Glamorama* there are numerous passages in which events and thoughts are related that the character, Victor, could not possibly know about—indeed, that

---

but does not find any of them completely satisfactory. I can think of only one perfect example myself: a Danish novel called *Tredje gang så ta'r vi ham* . . . by a favorite author of mine, Svend Åge Madsen. Here we find sentences such as these: "I am waiting at the entrance to the house. Maybe I am hoping for Djedja to regret and return, maybe I just can't make a decision"; and "Shortly after, however, I find myself on my way to the castle. Apparently I intend to ask for her there" (Madsen 22; my translation, H.S.N.).

8. For a similar point, see the last passages in Mäkelä's essay in the current volume.

no character narrator would be able to know about. Among the most striking examples is the rendering of the passengers' last thoughts in an exploding airplane (438–41), and of the sleeping Cloe's dream (43). One example from the exploding airplane—which no one survives, and where Victor is not present—reads like this:

> "Why me?" someone wonders uselessly. [. . .] Susan Goldman, who has [. . .] cancer, is partly thankful as she braces herself, but changes her mind as she's sprayed with burning jet fuel. (440)

What do we make of this? Victor is not on the plane. All the passengers die. This seems like a clear-cut case of homodiegetic narration with zero focalization.[9] Naturalizing readings will have to explain this peculiarity by searching for ways to naturalize it. Might Victor somehow have gained access to the thoughts represented? Naturalizing options also include but are not limited to assuming that Victor is outright lying or making up what he cannot know, that he is unreliable, has gone temporarily mad, is joking or being ironic, or even that he might have—as a character in the storyworld—the gift of telepathy. I am not going to argue against each one of these options, but I think they are all extremely unlikely and heavily contradicted by other parts of the text. It seems to me that **if** we make the interpretational choice of believing that we can trust that this is actually what the passengers are thinking, then this in and of itself entails an interpretation that does **not** "converge with present-day understandings of how minds actually work" (Herman 33–34) since surely it is not a present-day understanding of real minds to say that they are able to reliably render what dying persons isolated in a plane far away are thinking.

This has to do exactly with the disconnect between mood and voice. In natural frameworks one would expect all homodiegetic narratives to be internally focalized, since we would expect a first-person narrator to have access to his or her own thoughts as opposed to external focalization but not to other people's thoughts as opposed to zero focalization. However, if we assume, as a reading strategy, that mood and voice are disconnected, then we can also assume that the possibility of transgressing the limits of personal voice regarding knowledge, vocabulary, memory, and so forth, is present. Therefore, we

---

9. I prefer the description homodiegetic narration with zero focalization over descriptions such as first-person narrative with paralepsis. Insofar as "paralepsis" means "saying too much" in the sense of disclosing knowledge you could not possess, it is only a question of paralepsis in *Glamorama* and similar narratives if we still think of the first person as the source of the narration, and this is exactly the view I want to challenge. In this sense, "paralepsis" serves to naturalize the understanding in its own way by assuming that "I" must be the speaker, as in natural linguistics, only occasionally displaying information "I" could not have.

should not restrict our interpretations to what would be possible or plausible if mood and voice were connected, if the answer to "who speaks?" and "who sees?" was necessarily the same as in natural narration, and if, accordingly, the character, that is, Victor, had to the source of the narrative.

Without presenting a detailed analysis of the novel,[10] I wish to mention that this general conception has considerable interpretive consequences. The very feature of a voice that does not unambiguously belong to Victor referring to Victor in the first person greatly contributes to the effect of the uncanny and is deeply connected with the theme of the double, it being one of the many elements in the book that cause the narrative's words—and even the words "I," "me," and "my"—to be open for the intrusion of the double. The words "Who the fuck is Moi?" on the first page of the novel thus become the starting signal for a game of hide and seek in which the reader is invited to make a guess: "Who is 'I' now referring to?" *Glamorama* is in some respects a classic doppelganger narrative. The protagonist and first-person narrator Victor Ward apparently has a double, and gradually this double takes over his identity. In the end, one Victor—and everything seems to indicate that he is the one we have followed throughout most of the book—dies in Italy while the other Victor, his double, enjoys life in New York. The really odd and unnatural thing about *Glamorama*, however, is that not only does the double overtake the identity of the first-person narrator on the thematic level and in the narrated universe; he even becomes the new referent of the pronoun "I." He has intruded in Victor's life and even overtaken his pronoun. This phenomenon does not seem to correspond to any real-world, natural discourse. In my opinion, a natural linguistic conception in which "I" inevitably refers to the speaker would not be able to account for either the many passages with zero focalization or this pronominal takeover. Yet an understanding of the basic events and the storyline in *Glamorama* hinges crucially on understanding these.[11]

10. For a more developed reading of *Glamorama*, see Nielsen "Telling Doubles."
11. At the very beginning of the book the reader is warned, in Ellis's humoristic way, that there will be no unity of plot and no unity of character (that I is another, as Rimbaud put it) in the following two passages:

> "[. . .] I don't want a lot of description, just the story, streamlined, no frills, the lowdown: who, what, where, when and don't leave out why, though I'm getting the distinct expression by the looks on your sorry faces that *why* won't get answered—now, come on, goddamnit, what's the *story*?" (5)

> "Who the fuck is Moi?" I ask. "I have no fucking idea who this Moi is, baby," I exclaim. "Because I'm like shvitzing."
> "Moi is Peyton, Victor," JD says quietly.
> "I'm Moi," Peyton says, nodding. "Moi is, um, French." (5)

5.2. *Moby-Dick*

Chapter 37 of *Moby-Dick* begins as follows:

> The cabin; by the stern windows; Ahab sitting alone, and gazing out.
>
> I leave a white and turbid wake; pale waters, paler cheeks, where'er I sail. The envious billows sidelong swell to whelm my track; let them; but first I pass.
>
> Yonder, by ever-brimming goblet's rim, the warm waves blush like wine. The gold brow plumbs the blue. The diver sun—slow dived from noon—goes down; my soul mounts up! she wearies with her endless hill. Is, then, the crown too heavy that I wear? this Iron Crown of Lombardy. Yet is it bright with many a gem; I the wearer, see not its far flashings; but darkly feel that I wear that, that dazzlingly confounds. 'Tis iron—that I know—not gold. 'Tis split, too—that I feel; the jagged edge galls me so, my brain seems to beat against the solid metal; aye, steel skull, mine; the sort that needs no helmet in the most brain-battering fight!

The character narrator, Ishmael, is not present in the cabin; Ahab is alone, it says. Again, we have a similar range of naturalizing options at our disposal: Has Ishmael gone mad? Is he imagining things? Should we be careful to notice that the passage has to be clearly unreliable and therefore doubt that this is really happening?

A much simpler assumption is that we are invited to read Ahab's lonely thoughts in his cabin as authoritative and as true by stipulation even though the character, Ishmael, could not and does not know about them. This assumption is based on the idea that the invitation here is to conceive of the narrative as inventive in a way that does not **have to** assume that there are natural explanations for this transparency, which, in my view, seems to go well beyond any possible accessibility in the encounter with everyday minds. Tying back to the interpretation of Genette's system as a disconnect between mood and voice, this would mean that the person in the storyworld (let's again call him Ishmael) is relevant to the question of mood ("who sees?") but not to the question of voice[12] and access to thoughts. And surely few readers would attribute to Ishmael the character the gift of mindreading or telepathy. One could even think, conversely, of a homodiegetic narrative with internal focalization in which the protagonist is a mind reader who constantly provides the reader with access to other people's thoughts. In that case, focalization would still be

---

12. The exception is voice as idiom (cf. Walsh), but this question has to be addressed elsewhere.

internal, not zero, just as a story is not turned into a third-person narrative just because the character narrator refers to someone as "she."

The naturalizing suggestions all have in common that they explain the passage as if real-world limitations apply and thus work from the assumption that the rules and constraints of real-life narration have to be in place. Even if I believe that these interpretations are misguided, I do not want to claim that they are self-evidently wrong. On the contrary: naturalizing and unnaturalizing options will necessarily stand in an agonistic relationship to each other, so that it is always a matter of competing interpretations. This is not something to regret. Instead it is an opportunity to emphasize that naturalizing readings are options and interpretational choices as opposed to the idea that it is natural or necessary to naturalize.

In *Moby-Dick* one finds sentences and long passages in which the perspective of the "narrator" Ishmael is respected and entire chapters in which it is transgressed to a striking degree. In the chapters in which the breaks with the focalization through Ishmael are very distinct, they nevertheless take place with an ingenuity that causes them not to shock at first reading. Genette himself explicitly mentions *Moby-Dick* as belonging to the category of homodiegetic narratives with zero focalization. Another description of the narrative situation in *Moby-Dick* would be to simply state that Melville leaves Ishmael altogether in the relevant chapters. As Phelan reminded me, this also points to the crucial agency of the author. This reading finds support in the fact that after the transgressive chapters 37 through 40, we return to Ishmael in chapter 41 with the following words of reassurance: "I, Ishmael, was one of that crew."

No matter which description we prefer, what is important is that *Moby-Dick* shows us that an existential indexical continuity need not exist between the character referred to in the first person and the referring voice in first-person narrative fiction. This, in turn, makes it a particular subcase confirming the more general insight that mood and voice are separate in fictional narration in general.

5.3. *The Great Gatsby*

In a discussion of *The Great Gatsby* in *Narrative as Rhetoric,* Phelan observes that Fitzgerald does not even try to justify how the first-person narrator, Nick Carraway, is able to narrate what he could not possibly know. Phelan shows that Fitzgerald was rightly not concerned about providing any justification and that the reported scene is invested with full authority all the same (108–9). Similarly, in *Living to Tell About It,* Phelan exemplifies:

In chapter 8 of *The Great Gatsby*, Nick Carraway reports the scene at Wilson's garage involving Michaelis and Wilson as if he were a non-character narrator with the privilege of moving between his own focalization and that of Michaelis. What is curious here is not just that Nick narrates a scene at which he was not present but also that Fitzgerald does not try to justify how Nick came to know what Michaelis must have been thinking. (4)

In my opinion, the choice to think of the garage scene in *The Great Gatsby* as authoritatively represented—even though the narrator, Carraway, was not present—is a result of what I call an unnaturalizing interpretation strategy. This is especially because it does not try to justify itself by interpreting the passage as the possible guess of the character narrator. Nor does it claim that he must later have obtained this knowledge. Instead, one of the most important consequences is very nicely captured by Phelan in the following sentence—which in my view acknowledges the disconnect between mood and voice: "When the narratorial functions are operating independently of the character functions, then the narration will be reliable and authoritative" (*Narrative as Rhetoric* 112).

5.4. Watt

The fourth and final example is from Samuel Beckett's *Watt*, which seems to me paradigmatic in its inventionality as well as in its disconnect between person and voice. One example is when we read about Arsene on his way out: "Before leaving he made the following short statement" (37).[13] This "short statement" is then rendered word by word for some twenty-five pages. Shortly after, we learn about Watt himself, who is our only source for the words rendered for twenty-five pages:

> He had realized, to be sure, that Arsene was speaking, and in a sense to him, but something had prevented him, perhaps his fatigue, from paying attention to what was being said [. . .]. (77)

It seems to me quite clear that Watt cannot remember Arsene's words even though they are there in front of our eyes, and it seems equally clear that we are not invited to dismiss the content of the twenty-five pages. As a conse-

---

13. For a discussion of *Watt* and this and many of its other implausibilities with a different aim, cf. Walsh "Force."

quence there is an exceptionality thesis here, but not in the sense of exceptionality or distinction as a generic, ontological or categorical trait of fiction, literature, or unnatural narratives, but as an interpretational assumption.

The suggested unnaturalizing readings in the four examples possess different degrees of legitimacy, in the sense that it is more and more debatable which interpretation to choose. The examples are comparable to the situation in "The Cask of Amontillado," discussed by Phelan in the current volume, in which there is arguably even more room for naturalizing interpretational choices. The general point that goes beyond the specific examples is that the reader is faced with interpretational choices in narratives that can be interpreted as unnatural. In each case the options will be agonistic and negotiable, so it remains a question of interpretation how interpretation and understanding are maximized. This is the very reason why it is fruitful to discuss how and why and when natural and unnatural readings are useful or inappropriate.

The four works discussed here are interpreted as unnatural in the sense that they designate and refer to a character with the first-person pronoun "I" without *emanating* from that character. The narrating "voice" does not emanate from the character but invents and creates a world, including the first person and his knowledge or lack of knowledge. This means that they are interpreted here as structurally similar in that they are all homodiegetic narratives with zero focalization. This form can be interpreted as unusual, strange, or experimental, and yet I would claim that it is paradigmatic for an unnaturalness that we find even in some of the most traditional fictional first-person forms, such as, for example, the classic detective novel. Take, for instance, the following short excerpt from Chandler:

> The next morning was bright, clear and sunny. I woke up with a motorman's glove in my mouth, drank two cups of coffee and went through the morning papers. [...] I was shaking the wrinkles out of my damp suit when the phone rang. (40)

There is no zero focalization here and no transgressions of point of view. This prose is not experimental as regards narrative situation. Yet, what exactly is the relationship between mood and voice; between character and words? It seems equally unlikely that Marlowe should ever write, speak, or think exactly these words during or after the action. The reader would be hard-pressed to imagine that he thinks this to himself using the preterit tense while hungover. To imagine instead that Marlowe, in his old age, would occupy himself with autobiographical writings during quiet nights collides with the picture of

Marlowe provided. Thus, every time it says in the text, for example, "I walked," "I drank a whiskey," "I" refers to Marlowe, but Marlowe himself is not saying anything about what he did or drank. This, at least, is my contention. It is unnaturalizing in its assumption that a disconnect between mood and voice exists even here in internal focalization. It is an interpretational choice competing with other choices that might want to connect character and words and to ask—also in this case—about the occasion and purposes of the narration at the character's rather than the author's level.

Thus homodiegetic narration with zero focalization is just one of many unnatural narrative situations that Genette's system allows for (heterodiegetic narration with zero focalization being the conventionalized type and homodiegetic narration with external focalization being the absolute rarity). Below I will indicate how the combinatory logic of focalization can be extended beyond the limits of Genette's own system to include other unnatural forms and argue that these unnaturalizing options and readings hinge on an understanding of fiction as inventive (which sometimes, but not always, leads to fictional narratives being unnatural). Then I will connect this claim with the theoretical point that it is more theoretically sound to speak of the author than the narrator as the main agent of the telling. Finally, I will present the system that this leads to.

6. Inventing Authors

The peculiarities that allow for unnaturalizing interpretations do not mysteriously or inexplicably arise out of the blue. They result from two connected aspects of what we identified as integral parts of Genette's insight, and they exist because of the disconnect between mood and voice (and more generally the contingent relation between pronoun and access to perception) and because of the relational nature of focalization theory as a theory about the relation between inventing authors and perceiving and reporting characters.

If we assume that the thoughts of the passengers on the airplane and of Ahab in his cabin come to us as authoritative, and (to a lesser degree) if we believe the events in Wilson's garage are rendered precisely and that Arsene's monologue in *Watt* and the dialogue in "The Cask of Amontillado" come to us as sufficiently trustworthy for us to give weight to single words and phrases in an interpretation, then all of these assumptions rely on a deeper assumption that really the source of information in each instance is not the unknowing character but the world-creating author. In what follows I will sketch the kind of model of narrative transmission this assumption leads to.

In a banal and obvious sense, real authors narrate to real readers. They write books telling the stories that the reader reads. The reader likes some authors but not others because he rightly attributes to the authors the storytelling capacity he finds in the books. It is an equally self-evident fact that characters in the books often narrate to each other. Whether there are also narrators in addition to and as something *different from* authors and characters is more debatable for the good reason that they are not obviously present for all to see. A possible objection to this point could be that in first-person narration, the first-person narrator is obviously present, and certainly I would not disagree that Victor, Nick Carraway, and Ishmael all exist in their respective storyworlds. None of these cases, however, force us to think of a narrator as someone distinct from authors and characters, since all of the mentioned persons (insofar as they narrate at all) narrate in their capacity as characters. I will argue that we do not need the concept of narrators as something distinct from authors and characters to explain or understand fictionalized narration. All of the mentioned persons clearly exist as characters, but my contention is that they do not transmit the narrative to a narratee or a reader.

Positing a narrator to help understand a fictional narrative as a report about something that the narrator supposedly knows or sees or experiences and hence as a literal communicative act from the narrator (cf. Walsh, "Person" 39) amounts to assuming that someone, that is, the narrator, is telling a story that is not fictional and that can therefore, on its own level, be interpreted as if the rules of nonfiction were in play. It is, in a sense, a way of conceiving of fiction as framed nonfiction (cf. Walsh, *The Rhetoric of Fictionality* 69).By assuming instead that a narrative is the fictional invention of the author, the reader assumes that she is invited to interpret the story and the world as invented and contingent upon the real world.[14] If we interpret a narrative as fiction, we interpret it as creating (aspects of) a fictional world. This fictional world need not be like the real world. The author's statements, then, are interpreted not as statements about or as referring to the real world or any other preexisting world. Therefore, they are, as a rule, not subject to doubt. A reader who doubts time travel or UFOs in a science fiction novel that mentions the existence of these things is led astray. The author's narration of a fictional narrative is then considered inventional in the sense that it brings a fictional world into existence.

However, the author is not the only narrating agent in most works of fic-

---

14. Needless to say, readers can make different assumptions about these matters and may simply be wrong, just as we can disagree on the potential invitation to conceive of something as ironic.

tion. Characters often have conversations, thoughts, and ideas, and tell each other stories. As opposed to the author's narration, these thoughts and ideas and stories **do** refer to a storyworld that preexists them, which is the fictional world invented by the author. They may or may not therefore be true. So, in a psychological narrative about a mentally ill character, this character might wrongly assume that UFOs exist in the world he inhabits, and he may tell about this incorrect assumption.

One interpretational problem, then, is that the authoritative, undoubtable narration by the author and the personal, potentially unreliable narration by characters are not always clearly distinguishable. In character narration in the grammatical first person (homodiegetic narration), the narration by the character can be unreliable. And in third-person narration (heterodiegetic narration), the authorial narrative can lend idioms, worldviews, and mistaken thoughts from the characters via free indirect discourse and similar techniques. What we read in such instances is the **reliable** rendering of mistaken thoughts or beliefs. The author is still authoritatively inventing a world in which the reader should trust—including trusting that these mistaken beliefs exist in the world.

My argument against the narrator and for readings that are unnaturalizing in the sense that they resist applying real-world limitations to all narratives is thus not at all a move toward incomprehensiveness, mysteriousness, or noncommunication. Nor is it a move beyond rhetorical interests in the means, ends, purposes, and occasions of narratives. Instead, it is an attempt to reframe these very questions about communicational techniques, purposes, means, and ends and to attribute them to the appropriate agent in order to show the relevance of unnaturalizing readings and in order to not unnecessarily limit interpretations to what is possible in literal communicative acts and in representational models. In an unnatural framework we do not have to assume that there has to be a speaker at the same ontological level as the storyworld.

In effect, my proposals are completely compatible with rhetorical models such as James Phelan's and seem to me to be another step in a move that Phelan has begun toward revising standard models of narrative such as Chatman's (figure 4.2). Phelan rightly remarks that the model calls for a revision because "in Chatman's model, the implied author outsources just about everything to the narrator or to the nonnarrated mimesis" ("Rhetorical Literary Ethics"). Changing the emphasis exactly from narrator to author, Phelan ends his paper with the words "[. . .] it's all about a specific somebody, an implied author, telling to somebody else, an actual audience, for some purposes."

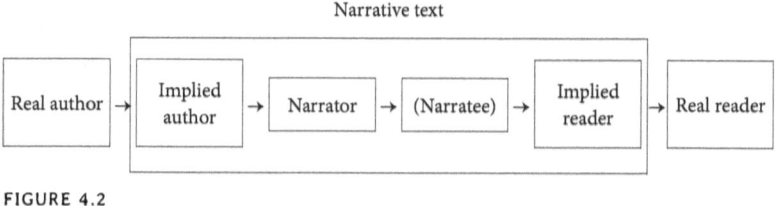

FIGURE 4.2

I would totally agree with this assessment. For me, though, it necessarily leads to the following model:

Real author → Narrative → Real reader

Or, if we want to acknowledge that the author is not the only narrating agent in many works of fiction and to include everything in the model:

Real author → Narrative (in which characters might narrate to other characters) → Real reader

In this model the author is the main storytelling agent, and character narration is conceived of as a means that an author can choose to employ. Characters are subordinated to authors in the model, and character discourse is not supplemented by author discourse but sometimes vice versa when an author invites the reader to see that what is invented is how a character perceives the universe, not necessarily the universe as it is. Fictional narration lends itself very well to a rhetorical model interested in examining (among other things) the means and ends and techniques by which an author successfully or unsuccessfully realizes or fails to realize his or her intentions. Likewise, the rhetorical model is very apt for describing at a character level why, how, and for what purposes someone is telling someone else that something happened, as Phelan has taught us. However, my argument is that we should not apply the rhetorical model to narrators when we can apply it directly to authors and characters. If we begin to ask about the occasion and purpose of the supposed narrator, we will either be led astray or led back to the author or to a character. This is because more often than not "the narrator" (if it is an extradiegetic narrator)[15] will have no identifiable or even imaginable occasion to tell to some narratee that the events happened. The communicational situation and occasion of

---

15. Intradiegetic narrators are characters; cf. Walsh, *The Rhetoric of Fictionality* 70–74.

author, on the other hand, is completely logical and well defined: he or she is telling the reader about a fictional universe. Take, for example, the words "Stately, plump Buck Mulligan came from the stairhead [. . .]." The place of these words in communication from author to reader is relatively straightforward. The author does not want the reader to believe that the described situation actually took place at some specific point in the real world but wants the reader to acknowledge that he *invents* a situation in which they do. As for the narrator, the situation is much less clear. The narrator must be conceived of either as someone who does not invent but tells what he or she knows to someone (the narratee) or as someone inventing a story for an audience. The problem with the former conception is that it is often thoroughly contradicted by the form and technique of the narration. The problem with the latter conception is that it amounts to an unnecessary doubling of agents, since the narrator is then only doing exactly what we already know the author is doing.[16]

The system I propose here is, I think, simple and consistent in that it always attributes narration to the author while allowing for the possibility of the author embedding narration in her representation and thus representing a character's narration. Its premise is that the invitation in fiction is to conceive of the narrative as inventive, and thus it does not have to assume about a case such as Melville's that there are natural explanations for diversions from nonfictionalized real-life frames, nor that it is a matter of accessibility in ways similar to encounters with everyday minds, nor that a character's or another narrator's account is supplemented because of the purposes and needs of the author. In this respect it is different from Phelan's rhetorical approach. For example, Phelan concludes his friendly reading of my interpretation of *Glamorama* with the following remark:

> The narration, after all, has so many features of standard character. In the sentence "I hand her a French tulip I happen to be holding," a character narrator, Victor, assumes that his narratee knows what a French tulip is but does not know that Victor is holding one and does not know what Victor is doing with it. (See James Phelan's essay in the present volume.)

I would tend to claim, instead, that "In the sentence 'I hand her a French tulip I happen to be holding,' the author, Ellis, assumes that the reader knows what a French tulip is but does not know that Victor is holding one and does

---

16. Unreliable narration in the first person is not really an exception to this, since we do not have to say that the author or the character wants something different from the narrator, but only that our interpretation of the narration as unreliable amounts to assuming that the character's narrative is an unreliable source for the facts of the narrated world.

not know what Victor is doing with it." The author refers to Victor with the pronoun "I" even when he narrates to the reader words that Victor never narrates to anyone. The similarity between Phelan's approach and mine is that they both have the immediate consequence for interpretation that we are allowed to trust narration that could not possibly be reliable real-world narration. The difference is that Phelan attributes the fictional discourse to a narrator whether or not this narrator is a character narrator and then assumes that narrator functions can, in turn, be supplemented by disclosure functions. Conversely, I attribute fictional discourse to the author and say that disclosure functions can, in turn, be supplemented by narrator functions in the sense that idioms, purposes, techniques, and so forth, that belong to one or more characters can influence the narration, as is the case in *Moby-Dick* when the idioms and thoughts of Ishmael, Ahab, and Starbuck are represented. What is unnatural and experimental in *Moby-Dick*, then, is not the character Ishmael, which would amount to creating an unnatural storyworld. The character is fairly natural. The experiment is to foreground the disconnection between voice and person.

Let me reiterate that this also goes to show that not all fiction is unnatural. Far from it, because only in some works of fiction will the author create temporalities, storyworlds or mind representations that would be impossible in the real world, and only in some works of fiction will anything be gained from assuming that the reliability of the narration should be judged by standards that are different from real-world narration (as is the case if we assume that what could not be a reliable report by a character narrator is an authoritative invention by the author), since an author will very often choose "to accept all the constraints and work scrupulously within them."[17]

As argued above, the real force of the combinatory logic behind Genette's system is not between characters inside fiction and narrators in- or outside, mentioned or not (homodiegetic and heterodiegetic). In fact, these two axes are incompatible. Instead, it is between characters always inside and authors always outside choosing the reader's restriction of access to these characters' minds and points of view. So far we have examined unnatural combinations within the system, but the reformulation allows us—as a final perspective—to extend the scope of possible combinations: The author chooses two things: (1) pronoun (or pronouns), and (2) restriction of access to thoughts (basically and typically all, one, or none). Only some of the resulting possible variants will look like real-life narratives—that is, heterodiegetic narration with external focalization and homodiegetic narration with internal focalization.

17. Cf. Phelan in the current volume.

But notice that in addition to Genette's dichotomy between homo- and heterodiegetic narration, the author can choose all kinds of pronouns to refer to characters. In principle as well as in reality, nothing rules out the choice of "odd" pronouns such as "we," "they," and "you," and each of these is, in turn, combinable with zero, internal, or external focalization.[18] Natural and unnatural readings will have different views on these narrative possibilities. From an unnatural point of view, these forms, like the works above, cue the reader to interpret in ways that differ from the interpretation of real-world acts of narration and of conversational storytelling. For example, you-narration is a comparatively odd form that lends itself well to unnatural interpretations. Rolf Reitan recently provided a thorough review of the field ("Second Person"), and in *Unnatural Voices* (2006), Brian Richardson makes a comprehensive list of second-person narratives, defining and delimiting the field so well that it does not include any narrative employing the second-person pronoun, since this pronoun is also used in several standard situations in which an author unambiguously addresses his reader, and in apostrophes. Richardson aptly writes, "We may define second person narrative as any narration other than an apostrophe that designates its protagonist by a second person pronoun" (19).

Notice that Richardson does not mention *addressing* the protagonist. He continues: "It is important to note that second person narration is an artificial mode that does not normally occur in natural narrative [. . .]" (19). I think Richardson is right, but would like to add a few words on why that is. We talk about and to each other using "you" all the time. Is it not true that second-person narratives are the most natural things in the world? To answer this, we have to remember, first, that using the "you" as a disguised form of "I" or "everybody,"[19] as in "you just get so mad in these kind of situations, don't you?" does not count as you-narration since it does not specifically designate the protagonist but rather designates the speaker as part of an imagined community. Second, the curious thing about most fictional second-person narratives (with Butor's *La modification* as a prominent and classical example) is that although the protagonist is *designated* by "you" throughout these narratives, nothing at all suggests that he/she feels in any way addressed. He is not hearing voices, does not feel he is being spoken to, and does not respond to the narrative.[20] In short: nothing except the very use of the second-person pro-

---

18. For an impressive and intriguing analysis of these kinds of narratives, see Brian Richardson in *Unnatural Voices*.

19. This is sometimes referred to as the "generalized you."

20. At least this is the case in what Richardson calls standard cases and what Reitan shows to be more or less the only "real fictional, second person" narratives. For the point I am making here it is not important whether it holds true for some or all fictional, second-person narratives.

noun suggests that he is being addressed.[21] So if in natural linguistics the first-person pronoun designates "the speaker," the third person "the one spoken about," and the second person "the one spoken to," then it seems that in many fictional second-person narratives the pronoun loses this functionality. The protagonist is referred to and designated, but not addressed, by the second-person pronoun. He is just as ignorant of being the center of a narrative as are the protagonists in third-person narratives. Outside fiction, then—in, say, conversational narratives—the referent of "you" is inevitably addressed, and obviously not created by the pronoun. In most fictional second-person narratives, the referent of "you" is inevitably created and obviously not addressed by the pronoun. Looping back to first-person narratives, my argument above suggests that this line of reasoning can even be extended to first-person narratives in which "I" often does not refer to "the speaker" and in which, accordingly, even the first-person protagonist (Marlowe, Victor, etc.) may well be just as ignorant as third-person characters about being the center of a narrative.

From an unnatural point of view, we need not impose real-world necessities on all fictional narratives. We need not put all narratives into communicational models based on real-life storytelling situations. Common to the interpretations of the mentioned first-person and second-person narratives is that they read the stories as transgressing real-world communicational situations. Completely unlike what is possible in standard interpretations of "natural narratives," the reader can assume about some unnatural first-person narratives that the protagonist is designated by the pronoun "I" but not enunciating it, and about some unnatural second-person narratives that the protagonist is designated by the pronoun "you" but not addressed by it. By doing this the reader effectively (1) attributes narration to the author, and (2) reads it as inventional and (3) as transgressing linguistic understandings of real-world language. One consequence is that the reader can interpret mind representations as authoritatively rendered in a way that distinguishes them from any representation of real minds and that foregrounds the difference between invented and reported storyworlds and minds.

What connects the *unconventional* and unnatural first-person and second-person narratives mentioned in this essay with *conventional*, unnatural third-person with zero focalization is that the relation between inventing authors and perceiving and reporting characters allows the reader to make interpretational choices that are unnaturalizing in the sense that she can trust as authoritative and reliable what would in real life be impossible, implausible, or, at the very least, subject to doubt.

21. Cf. Reitan: "Summing up: [...] Only category C [*Narrative you referring to protagonist, but not used as address*] covers proper second person narratives [...]" (153).

Works Cited

Alber, Jan. "Impossible Storyworlds—And What to Do with Them." *Storyworlds* 1 (2009): 79–96.
Beckett, Samuel. *Watt*. London: Calder & Boyars, 1972 [1953].
Chandler, Raymond. *The Big Sleep*. London and New York: Hamish Hamilton, 1973.
Ellis, Bret Easton. *Glamorama*. New York: Knopf, 1999.
Fludernik, Monika. "Natural Narratology and Cognitive Parameters." In *Narrative Theory and the Cognitive Sciences*, ed. David Herman. Stanford, CA: Center for the Study of Language and Information, 2003. 243–67.
———. "New Wine in Old Bottles? Voice, Focalization, and New Writing." *New Literary History* 32 (2001): 619–38.
———. *Towards a "Natural" Narratology*. London and New York: Routledge, 1996.
Genette, Gérard. *Narrative Discourse*. Ithaca, NY: Cornell University Press, 1980 [1972].
———. *Narrative Discourse Revisited*. Ithaca, NY: Cornell University Press, 1988 [1983].
Herman, David. "Introduction." In *The Emergence of Mind: Representations of Consciousness in Narrative Discourse in English*, ed. David Herman. Lincoln: University of Nebraska Press, 2011. 1–40.
Madsen, Svend Åge. *Tredje gang så ta'r vi ham . . .* København: Gyldendal, 1969.
Melville, Herman. *Moby-Dick or The Whale*. Evanston and Chicago: Northwestern University Press, 1988 [1851].
Nielsen, Henrik Skov. "The Impersonal Voice in First-Person Narrative Fiction." *Narrative* 12.2 (May 2004): 133–50.
———. "Telling Doubles and Literal Minded Reading in Bret Easton Ellis's *Glamorama*." In *Novels of the Contemporary Extreme*, ed. Naomi Mandel and Alain-Philippe Durand. London and New York: Continuum, 2006. 20–30.
———. "Unnatural Narratology, Impersonal Voices, Real Authors, and Non-Communicative Narration." In *Unnatural Narratives, Unnatural Narratology*, ed. Jan Alber and Rüdiger Heinze. Berlin and Boston: De Gruyter, 2011. 71–88.
Phelan, James. *Living to Tell About It: A Rhetoric and Ethics of Character Narration*. Ithaca, NY: Cornell University Press, 2005.
———. *Narrative as Rhetoric: Technique, Audiences, Ethics, Ideology*. Columbus: The Ohio State University Press, 1996
———. "Rhetorical Literary Ethics: Or, Authors, Audiences, and the Resources of Narrative" (forthcoming).
Reitan, Rolf. "Theorizing Second-Person Narratives: A Backwater Project?" In *Strange Voices in Narrative Fiction*, ed. Per Krogh Hansen, Stefan Iversen, Henrik Skov Nielsen, and Rolf Reitan. Berlin and Boston: de Gruyter, 2011. 147–74.
Richardson, Brian. *Unnatural Voices*. Columbus: The Ohio State University Press, 2006.
Wallace, Martin. *Recent Theories of Narrative*. Ithaca, NY: Cornell University Press, 1986.
Walsh, Richard. "The Force of Fictions." In *Why Study Literature*, ed. Jan Alber et al. Aarhus: Aarhus University Press, 2011. 235–52.
———. "Person, Level, Voice: A Rhetorical Consideration." In *Postclassical Narratology*, ed. Jan Alber and Monika Fludernik. Columbus: The Ohio State University Press, 2010. 35–57.
———. *The Rhetoric of Fictionality*. Columbus: The Ohio State University Press, 2007.

Unnatural Minds

5

STEFAN IVERSEN

THE GOAL of this essay is twofold. First, in taking certain types of subversive, arresting, strange, and odd minds that one encounters in narratives as my primary target, I aim to propose a definition of such narrative phenomena as *unnatural minds* and illustrate how they might be constructed and interpreted in a concrete narrative. Second, in order to situate this definition in the current postnarratological landscape, I want to discuss some of the promising and problematic aspects of the tools developed by cognitive narratology for dealing with presentations of consciousness in narrative. Seen as a whole, the essay thus attempts to highlight a specific type of unnatural textual phenomena and to negotiate the usefulness and validity of several of the key concepts in the previous decade's massive influx of works dealing with minds in narratives. In order to try to steer clear of what might be considered either/or reactions to the solutions and tools offered by cognitive narratology, the approach attempts to navigate between these offerings, suggesting ways to learn from them without subscribing to all their underlying assumptions.

The essay is divided into four parts. Before presenting my definition of the unnatural mind I will in what remains of this introduction present the position this essay aims to take in the field of unnatural narratology. For the reason stated above I will do so with special regard to the ways in which approaches within unnatural narratology have related to work done in cognitive narratology. The second part of the essay contains my definition. In the third part I will explore some of the possible implications of recent work that questions the validity of the so-called Theory of Mind thesis. Turning, in the fourth part, to unnatural minds, I have chosen not to present a catalogue or typology but rather to put my arguments to the test by analyzing a case of an unnatural mind in the guise of the metamorphosed mind in modern narrative fiction, as exemplified by the *Pig Tales* of Marie Darrieussecq. In the fifth and final part I draw some conclusions and outline some perspectives for further work.

One way of outlining the field of unnatural narratology is to say that what unites the researchers who consider themselves part of this paradigm is, first, an interest in narratives that "defy, flaunt, mock, play, and experiment with some (or all) of [the anthropomorphic] core assumptions about narrative" (Alber, Iversen, Nielsen, and Richardson 114) and, second, a skepticism toward theories of narrative that rely solely on mimetic models for understanding how narratives function. Inside this shared frame, however, several rather substantial differences reside, the source of some of those being the acceptance of or rejection of the tools, concepts, and basic assumptions developed by cognitive narratology. I would like to briefly highlight two of these differences, one related to the choice of methodology, one related to questions of interpretation.

The question of methodology is the question of how to work with unnatural narratives. Jan Alber has argued in favor of using tools developed by cognitive narratology in that he advocates using "the cognitive-narratological work to clarify how some literary texts not only rely on but also aggressively challenge the mind's fundamental sense-making capabilities" (80). In contrast to this position Brian Richardson and Henrik Skov Nielsen have, with different means and goals, argued in favor of the development of post- or post-poststructuralist concepts. According to Richardson, "we will be most effective as narrative theorists if we reject models that, based on categories derived from linguistics or natural narrative, insist on firm distinctions, binary oppositions, fixed hierarchies, or impermeable categories" (139), while Nielsen in his essay "The Impersonal Voice in First-Person Narrative Fiction" (2004) extends Genettean vocabulary beyond the scope and framework of linguistically based structuralist narratology.

The question of interpretation, then, is the question not of how to work with these narratives but of what sense to make of them. Again the cognitive approach is represented by Alber, who aims at making "strange narratives more readable" (82). According to such an interpretive strategy, the job of both the layman and the professional reader is to renaturalize or translate the odd and strange matters of the unnatural narratives into statements about the way humans experience and make sense of the world, by applying what Alber calls allegorical, script-blending, or frame-enriching techniques of interpretation. In contrast, what one might call nonnaturalizing readings leave open the possibility that unnatural narratives contain or produce effects and emotions that are not easily (if at all) explainable or resolvable with reference to everyday phenomena. According to Nielsen, when a reader faces unnatural narratives, she "will not be able to optimize relevance and understanding by applying the same rules of interpretation as normally applied to everyday, conversational narratives and real-world reports" ("Fictional Voices?" 79). Along the same lines, in the context of a discussion of unreadable minds, Porter Abbott claims that unreadable minds "work best when we allow ourselves to rest in that peculiar combination of anxiety and wonder that is aroused when an unreadable mind is accepted as unreadable. In this regard, my stance is at odds with efforts to make sense of the unreadable, as, for example, Jan Alber's effort" (448).

I am now able to more precisely designate the position suggested in this essay: I agree with most of Alber's points on the level of methodology, while I agree with Abbott and Nielsen when they disagree with Alber on the level of interpretation. Like Alber, I find it useful to engage with cognitive narratology's importation of knowledge about how actual minds function, knowledge developed by fields such as philosophy of mind, cognitive linguistics, and cognitive psychology. However, in contrast to Alber's unreserved embrace of cognitive narratology, I approach the field with a good deal of skepticism, a skepticism which is to some degree shared by research in the very fields cognitive narratology attempts to learn from. I will treat this issue in more detail shortly. On an interpretational level, I object to Alber's insistence on the relevance of always aiming for renaturalizations or translations. Narrative fiction, and perhaps narrative as such, is capable of both constructing and probing unnaturalness in ways that not only evoke paradoxical and/or sublime feelings, insights, and horrors but at the same time question these very feelings and insights, which produces what Abbott refers to as states of "anxiety and wonder" (448). As I see it, one major limitation inherent in a full-blown cognitive approach to narrative, with an insistence on fully renaturalizing or recognizing the haunting and wondrous otherworldly visions of minds, events, and scenarios that some narratives manage to capture, is that it runs the risk of reducing the affective power and resonance of such narratives.

1. Definition

Say I read a story about a man who wakes and finds himself transformed into a giant bug but still in possession of a human mind—and then have the end of the story tell me it all took place in a dream. Or say I read a story about a brilliant but gentle and fragile scientist turning into a giant green thing who beats up supervillains when he gets really angry. Or say I read a story about a man situated in a possible world that looks very much like my own who wakes up as a giant bug with a human mind and stays like that while trying, to the best of his newfound physical abilities, to act in accordance with what is expected of him as the human he no longer is, at least not in his physical appearance.

These three examples are alike in that they all present the reader with combinations of physical and mental attributes that are impossible in my world, but they differ because they prompt rather different readings. As I see it, the mind in the first case is naturalized by the fact that the transformation takes place in a dream, in the sense that it doesn't really happen. A slightly different logic can be applied to case two. Here, the transformed mind is unnatural in the sense that it is impossible in a real-world scenario, but the mind may be conventionalized with the help of my knowledge of the genre in which it appears: in certain action-hero comic books, fragile but brilliant scientists are known to transform into raging beasts. In the third case, however, I am unable to naturalize or conventionalize the consciousness resulting from the physically impossible metamorphosis.[1] This monstrous irregularity cannot be exterminated in the name of sense-making with the aid of text-external cues such as knowledge of how actual minds typically work ("this happens all the time to central-European salespeople"), knowledge of genre or literary conventions ("this type of text is easily resolved with recourse to an allegorical reading"), or text-internal cues.

The third human/bug, who might go by the name Gregor Samsa, is an example of what I propose to call the unnatural mind, which I define as follows: an unnatural mind is a presented consciousness that in its functions or realizations violates the rules governing the possible world it is part of in a way that resists naturalization or conventionalization. Compared with Alber's definition of the unnatural narrative as containing logically or physically impossible elements or scenarios,[2] this definition operates with the looser "violates"

---

1. This division draws upon a matrix suggested by Henrik Skov Nielsen, who "distinguishes between four categories by combining the natural/unnatural dichotomy with the conventional/unconventional dichotomy" ("Unnatural Narratology" 85).

2. The definition of the 'unnatural' as an impossible scenario has been suggested by Jan Alber: "The term *unnatural* denotes physically impossible scenarios and events, that is, impossible by the known laws governing the physical world, as well as logically impossible ones, that is, impossible by accepted principles of logic" (80). The arguments put forth in this essay share a fundamental premise behind Alber's definition of unnatural narratives, in that I view them as narratives that exhibit physically or logically impossible scenarios or events—although, as I will argue, they are heavily influenced by notions of genre and convention. The main advantage of this definition is that it radically limits the number of unnatural narratives, which heightens the

rather than the strong "impossible" while linking the determination of something as unnatural to notions of convention and genre: the unnatural is unnatural compared with the naturalness set forth by the specific narrative, not compared with some sort of global naturalness, whatever that might be.

Unnatural minds come in a wide range of shapes and sizes, often but not exclusively in the context of experimental fiction. My goal here is not to suggest a taxonomy but rather to focus on one example of an unnatural mind in the form of the metamorphosed mind. Before detailing my approach to the poetics and pragmatics of such minds, it is necessary to dwell on the notion of mind and the understanding of the minds of others and oneself: what does it mean to naturalize or conventionalize a mind? I have two reasons for elaborating on this question. First, it is crucial to a discussion of the role that cognitive narratology can or should play in dealing with unnatural narratives. Second, researchers from different positions inside the field of philosophy of mind have recently presented a string of convincing arguments against the very basic assumptions underlining the core ideas of mindreading. Since these ideas also form the core of major aspects of the methodological development done by cognitive narratology during the last decade, addressing these challenges is of vital importance for anyone wishing to use or criticize the concepts and tools brought forth by cognitive narratology.

2. Mindreading

In this part of the essay I will first provide a brief look at the current state of cognitive narratology's import of the notion of mindreading before examining some of the key points of the critique of mindreading outside the field of narratology. Finally, I will discuss some of the implications that can be drawn from this critique, especially as this relates to unnatural minds in narratives.

Alan Palmer argues that "novel reading is mind-reading" ("Attribution" 83). This sentence contains perhaps the shortest formulation of the basic premise behind cognitive narratology's effort to bring insights from philosophy of mind, developmental psychology, and cognitive linguistics to bear on the theories of how and why narratives work. When we read narrative fiction, we read minds; we perform mindreading, so the basic argument goes. The notion of *mindreading* (also known as *mentalizing*) has been a cornerstone of most of the work on what is known as commonsense psychology or folk

---

explanatory power and precision of the definition as compared with a definition of all fiction as unnatural.

psychology. Folk psychology, in the words of Hutto, is typically understood as "our everyday practice of making sense of intentional actions (i.e. our own and those of others) in terms of reasons, where this implies having a capacity for the competent invocation of propositional attitude talk" ("Folk Psychology" 10). Baron-Cohen's *Mindblindness: An Essay on Autism and Theory of Mind,* one of the classic contributions to the concept of mindreading, puts it as follows: "We mindread all the time, effortlessly, automatically, and mostly unconsciously . . . In the words of Sperber, 'attribution of mental states is to humans as echolocation is to the bat.' It is our natural way of understanding the social environment" (3–4).

Without the ability to read the minds of others by ascribing beliefs and desires to them, Baron-Cohen claims, we would be unable to understand the doings and intentions of other people—we would suffer from mindblindness, which is Baron-Cohen's way of describing the psychological and social reality of the psychopathological condition of autism. We are able to perform these attributions because we have a theory of the mind of the other; this is what is known as the Theory of Mind (ToM) explanation of our fairly formidable though not always perfect social cognition skills.

Two different models of how this attribution actually happens have fought for primacy. The so-called Theory Theory (TT) claims that we draw our inferences about the beliefs and desires of others with recourse to our own folk psychological theory, while the so-called Simulation Theory (ST) claims that "simulation is the primitive, root form of interpersonal mentalization" (Goldman 8). In other words, rather than theorizing about what the other is thinking, we put ourselves in the position of the other, trying to understand the beliefs and desires of the other by simulating their state of mind.

Palmer's statement—"novel reading is mind-reading"—might appear to be a truism (as in: "well of course we read minds when we read fiction"). In fact it is anything but a truism. The consequences of subscribing to Palmer's statement and the approach it epitomizes are substantial. By positioning mindreading as ToM-informed, cognitive narratology envisions it as both the purpose and essence of reading narrative fiction. Palmer's approach thus asserts claims about what it means to read as well as claims about what narrative theory should be able to account for.

The most important of the first set of claims is what we might call the Similarity Thesis[3] regarding the distinction between our understanding of the

3. This claim is put forth most strongly by David Herman, who suggests using the term "Exceptionality Thesis" to describe the opposite claim that "fictional minds are different in kind from their experiences of the minds they encounter outside the domain of narrative fiction" ("Introduction" 17).

attribution of mental processes to fictive minds and attributions of mental processes to actual minds. For David Herman, "a unified picture of mind representations of all sorts, fictional and other" ("Introduction" 12) is the desirable and reachable goal made possible by drawing upon ToM when working with narrative fiction. The second set of claims has to do with theoretical and methodological ramifications, and there are several important new insights to be gained here. Central among these is the intention to demonstrate and to try to remedy the fact that classical narratology has always treated minds, especially understood as social phenomena, as tangential to character, to narrator, or to focalization, if treated at all: "there is a hole in literary theory between the analysis of consciousness, characterization and focalization. Oddly, as I hope to have shown, a good deal of fictional discourse is situated precisely within this analytical gap" (Palmer, *Fictional Minds* 186).

Taking Cohn's *Transparent Minds* as his point of departure, Palmer shows the limitations of Cohn's concepts: they deal only with the linguistically based mind, and they deal with the mind as an inner phenomenon. In contrast to this, Palmer and others have convincingly argued that our understanding of fictional minds is based on much more data than Cohn's vocabulary can account for. Therefore, Palmer and other theorists import and refine tools to deal with this data, including concepts such as the social mind, attribution, intermental minds, metarepresentation, sociocognitive complexity, embedded narratives, and continued consciousness.

Furthermore, the ToM approaches are capable of simultaneously dealing with aspects of narratives that are normally kept apart because the mechanics structuring mindreading are operative on the level of narration (the narrator reads the mind of his characters), on the level of thematics (the characters read each other's minds), and on the level of reception (the reader reads the minds of the characters).

I will now turn my attention to the recent critique of the suppositions underlining the primacy given to the model of ToM in explanations of folk psychology. This critique, which has been put forth by various researchers in the fields of philosophy of mind and developmental psychology, has become substantiated in a series of essays, books, and special issues of journals during the last couple of years by researchers such as Shaun Gallagher and Daniel Hutto.[4]

---

4. Several of the key contributions to this critique are represented in the anthologies *Folk Psychology Re-Assessed* (2007), edited by Hutto and Ratcliffe, and *Against Theory of Mind* (2009), edited by Leudar and Costall, as well as in the 2008 special issue of *Philosophical Explorations* titled "Rethinking Folk-Psychology: Alternatives to Theories of Mind," edited by Slors and Macdonald.

In "Inference or Interaction: Social Cognition without Precursors" (2008), Gallagher summarizes what he sees as the pertinent challenges to ToM suppositions in the three points. First, there is the rejection of what Gallagher calls "the mentalizing supposition, that is, the Cartesian idea that other minds are hidden away and inaccessible" (164). In contrast to ToM approaches, which treat the beliefs and desires of others as something locked away inside the heads of others, Gallagher argues that "in many cases knowing the other person's intentions, emotions, and dispositions is simply a matter of perceiving their embodied behaviour in the situation" (164).

Second, Gallagher rejects what he calls "the spectatorial supposition" (164): "Our normal everyday stance toward the other person is not third-person, detached observation; it is second-person interaction" (164). Hutto argues along similar lines for the idea that "understanding others in normal contexts of interaction is not a spectator sport" (*Folk Psychological Narratives* 12). ToM, whether TT or ST, is based on what Gallagher and Hutto find to be a faulty assumption, that we make sense of other people in a detached, observational third-person context. What actually happens when we comprehend the actions of others as intentional and meaningful is something rather different: this typically takes place in the form of an interactive, involved second-person context.

From this rejection follows Gallagher's third rejection, the rejection of "the supposition of universality":

> Mentalizing or mindreading are, at best, specialized abilities that are relatively rarely employed, and they depend on more embodied and situated ways of perceiving and understanding others, which are more primary and pervasive. (164)

If we do undertake the massive amount of work needed in order to actually ascribe desires and beliefs to others from a purely spectatorial stance, it happens only rarely, argue Gallagher and Hutto. According to Hutto, this is because "we simply do not need to make such ascriptions in most everyday, second-person contexts" (*Folk Psychological Narratives* 6).[5]

---

5. While Gallagher and Hutto, and others with them, agree in their critique of basing folk psychological understanding on a ToM module, they offer fairly different alternatives to the TT and ST approaches. Gallagher ("Inference") highlights interaction as what enables our understanding of others. Hutto has put forth the fairly radical and potentially very consequential narrative practice hypothesis (NPH), claiming that we gain the ability to understand beliefs and desires of others through developmental (thus culturally situated) series of interactions with caregivers, interactions that center on discussing or practicing explanations of intentions and motivations as they appear in narratives (see *Journal of Consciousness Studies* 16: 6–8 (2009),

I will now move into the third and final part of this tour through the landscape of mindreading theory by turning my attention to what conclusions cognitive narratology—and narratology in general—can or must draw from these convincing refutations of ToM as folk psychology's universal means of understanding actual minds. As we have seen, the idea that we read actual minds is fundamental to different approaches inside cognitive narratology, whether the goal is to argue in favor of a unified approach to the representation and reception of consciousness in fiction and nonfiction (Herman) or to develop new tools for a more fine-grained analysis of narrative fiction (Palmer). These approaches are now facing critiques that challenge them to come up with either new or refined arguments in favor of ToM or new ways of anchoring their cognitive approach.

An interesting but not unproblematic take on this challenge is to be found in the introduction to *The Emergence of Mind: Representations of Consciousness in Narrative Discourse in English* (2011), an anthology edited by Herman. As mentioned, Herman argues in favor of a "unified picture of mind representations" (what I have suggested calling the Similarity Thesis), and he underscores not the fundamental incompatibility between the two approaches in folk psychology but rather the way in which both can be said to refute what Herman calls the Exceptionality Thesis, which is the idea that minds in fiction operate according to rules different from those governing actual minds.

According to Herman, from one direction, the insights of ToM can be used to refute the notion that fictional minds must be understood differently from actual minds:

> [. . .] dichotomous treatments of fictional and actual minds can be questioned via research suggesting that readers' knowledge of fictional minds is mediated by the same kinds of reasoning protocols [. . .] that mediate encounters with everyday minds. ("Introduction" 20)

From another direction, still according to Herman, "The Exceptionality Thesis" can *also* be refuted by using insights from theorists who *reject* ToM: "people do in fact experience others' minds, encountering the I-originarity of others in everyday settings as well as fictional narratives" ("Introduction"

---

especially the essay "Storied Minds: Narrative Scaffolding for Folk Psychology," by Herman, for possible applications, consequences, and problems in Hutto's ideas). Slors and Macdonald put the difference between Gallagher's and Hutto's approaches this way: "While Gallagher's criticism of ToM is that in a sense it does too much—we can understand most of our social interaction in more basic and epistemologically direct ways—the claim of Hutto's NPH can be interpreted as saying that when it comes to FP [folk psychology] or providing reasons for actions, ToMs do too little" (Slors and Macdonald 157).

20). This is a case of having one's cake and eating it too: seeing ToM and anti-ToM approaches as having "ultimately the same" ("Introduction" 21) force is possible only if one neglects the fact that they are mutually exclusive in their native domain.[6]

While ToM once seemed to guarantee that the understanding of actual and fictional minds followed the same rule, the rule of mindreading, the opposite situation now seems more plausible: in real life we rarely read minds, whereas in fiction we have no choice but to do so. In my view, the rejection of ToM as a universal means of making sense of actual minds carries different implications for different aspects of the practice of cognitive narratology. Since the ToM module is essential to a unified theory of consciousness representation, this aspect—along with the idea that understanding the minds of actual people and reading the paper minds of fiction amount to the same activity—is put into serious doubt. However, for methodological approaches that use the ToM module as one among many different modules imported from folk psychology or cognitive linguistics, the loss of ToM as the fundamental principle of sense-making in real life may be less crucial.

In the methodological aspects of both Palmer's and Herman's work, many of the key concepts rely on other aspects of folk psychology, and this is the main grounds for my own adaptations of cognitive narratology's work on minds in narratives; the arguments that minds are more to narratives and that there is more to minds in narratives than is dealt with in classical narratology still stand as valid. It is perfectly possible to agree with the rejection of real-life mind understanding as a spectator sport put forth by Gallagher, Hutto, and others while at the same time agreeing with Palmer that literary theory has paid too little attention to the role of consciousnesses in narrative.

Also, the cognitive-narratological idea that both writers and readers of fictive narratives initially draw upon their folk psychological knowledge of the workings of real minds when dealing with fictional minds appears convincing to me. These processes of meaning production normally happen effortlessly; but narratives that stray from or disrupt or subvert the norms or rules of our folk psychological competences pose an interesting methodological challenge. To my mind this is one of the sites in the current narratological landscape

6. A second problem lies in the way Herman presents the recent break with ToM. What Hamburger says about minds in fiction differs substantially from what philosophers such as Hutto, Dan Zahavi, and Gallagher say about actual minds in action. As Herman also notes, their critique of the ToM approach hinges on the idea that social cognition and interaction are guided not by observational, distanced reasoning (i.e., a theory) but rather by bodily, second-person involvement. Such involvement is clearly not present when we read, whether we are reading fiction or nonfiction, so when dealing with written minds, do we make sense of them as we make sense of (or engage with) actual minds?

at which methodological reflection and development are called for.[7] What, then, happens when these non-ToM aspects of cognitive narratology are set in motion with what I call unnatural minds?

3. The Metamorphosed Mind

As described earlier, unnatural minds occur in a wide range of narratives and they come in rather different shapes and sizes. One such shape is what Abbott convincingly suggests calling "unreadable minds." In a move similar to the one I am arguing for, Abbott places "a focus on fictional minds that cannot be read" (448), and he moves forward through readings of "characters that disallow the default reading of opaque stereotypes through lack of sufficient narrative action to release them from their unreadability" (448). These stereotypes are reading patterns capable of naturalizing the seemingly unreadable, and Abbott lists three: the insane (the strange mind read as a mad mind), the catalyst (the strange mind read as portraying another character), and the symbol (the strange mind read as a metaphor or allegory). The crucial aspect of Abbott's approach is that he insists on the existence of narrative minds that resist being naturalized by these three conventional reading patterns. Melville's Bartleby is one such mind who, according to Abbott, should not be turned readable but rather invites us to experience the unreadable as such (448).

In the following I will focus on another type of unnatural mind that I will call the impossible mind. The impossible mind is a mind that is biologically or logically impossible, such as a mindreading mind, a deceased mind, a radically metaleptic mind, or a mind running without the hardware that the human mind as we know it is nested in. Impossible minds are often conventionalized—the double consciousness of Bruce Banner / Hulk is conventionalized using knowledge of genre. I will focus on a type of impossible mind that is both unnatural and unconventionalizable: the mind of the metamorphosed human. In my discussion of this type of mind I will draw upon concepts from cognitive narratology, more specifically on the notions of attributions and the distinction between intermental and intramental minds as developed by Palmer.

7. This approach—taking the tools for describing our means of making sense of real people developed by cognitive studies to deal with the strange scenarios, the odd consciousnesses, and the logically impossible worlds presented to us by unnatural narratives, revising or supplementing these tools when needed—is what I aim to do in my section of Alber, Iversen, Nielsen, and Richardson and in "'In Flaming Flames': Crises of Experientiality in Non-Fictional Narratives." The concepts in question are Palmer's notion of continued consciousness and Fludernik's notion of experientiality.

Metamorphoses are fairly common in almost every existing oral and/or written storytelling tradition: from Ovid to myths to fairy tales to fantasy and science fiction. In the majority of these traditions, the metamorphoses are part of the rules set up by the possible world of the narrative. From frog to prince or from young beautiful lady to horse: these are metamorphoses that obey the rules of the narrative in which they appear. They might appear impossible according to the conventions of our world, but inside the world of their narrative they are expected. They are typically conventionalized using genre.

The kind of metamorphosis I would like to focus on, the human–animal transformation as described in the literary fiction of the last one hundred years, behaves differently. One canonized narrative is Kafka's "The Metamorphosis." Another example would be William S. Burroughs's *Naked Lunch*. A more recent example that has gathered a lot of attention is the *Pig Tales* of Marie Darrieussecq from 1996. In this context I will focus primarily on the unnaturalness of the metamorphosed mind in *Pig Tales*, but several of characteristics of this mind are found in Kafka's and Burroughs's work as well.

Pig Tales is set in a parallel universe around the year 2000. In this universe several major destructive events have taken place—among those apparently a giant war which has laid waste to most of the animal life on the planet—and the world is now a dystopian nightmare, ruled by a decadent, corrupt, and misogynous small group of completely ruthless men. Women are either giving birth or employed as prostitutes. Our knowledge of the world is filtered through the character narrator, a woman who is also a pig. The narrative structure resembles that of a memoir: the story told by the woman/pig is the story of how the woman metamorphosed from a young girl into a sow. The setting, as well as the protagonist's reaction to it, is captured in this passage in the beginning of the novel:

> So I was looking for work. I had interviews. And got nowhere. Until I filled out a *job application form* (words are coming back to me) for a big perfume and cosmetics chain. The director of the form sat me on his lap and pawed my right breast, obviously finding it marvelously elastic [. . .] The director had me get down on my knees in front of him, and while I was hard at work, I daydreamed about these beauty preparations, about how good I was going to smell, about the glowing complexion I'd have. (2–3)

"The Metamorphosis" and *Pig Tales* share several basic premises: a young protagonist's mind lives on after a metamorphosis from human form to animal form has taken place. While the transformations are primarily physical (human body to bug and pig, respectively), in both cases the desires and beliefs of the new bodies slowly start to intermingle with those remembered by the human brains. Gregor and the young woman both experience new urges, stemming from the needs and wants of their new bodies. To the woman in *Pig Tales* this includes things such as excessive eating of her own vomit and rolling in the mud. This intermingling of experiences from two radically different—and in a real-life scenario radically incompatible—types of embodiment is what justifies calling these minds impossible.

We might compare this kind of mind with one described by Abbott. In the case of what Abbott calls the unreadable mind we are dealing with no mind where there should have been one. In the case of these modern human-animal-metamorphosis minds we are dealing with the opposite: a human mind where there should have been none; a mind with the memory of the desires and beliefs of its former body as well as with new urges and experiences, brought forth by the new body. These two works also share the fact that the violations against the world they appear in are not easily resolvable with recourse to conventions such as genre or allegorical readings. The many discussions of how to read Kafka's story are well known, and the reception of *Pig Tales*, while still young, is characterized by similarly fundamental disagreements on the level of interpretation.[8]

There are also some important differences between the two texts, and while they are vital to a full reading of *Pig Tales*, as well as to a reading of its relationship to "The Metamorphosis," my aim here is more limited. What I would like to do is to focus on aspects of the way in which this unnatural mind is constructed by the narrative. I will do so by drawing upon Palmer's idea of the social mind. According to Palmer, traditional narratology deals with fictional consciousness as solely an inner phenomenon, employing what Palmer calls an internalist perspective on the mind which stresses those aspects that are hidden, solitary, mysterious, and detached: "As a result, the *social* nature of fictional thought has been neglected" (*Social Minds* 39). In contrast to this internalist view, Palmer argues in favor of an externalist view that sees the mind as something social as well as something private, a view that stresses the outer, active, public, social, behavioral, evident, embodied, and engaged aspects of the mind. Palmer introduces two concepts into narratology in order to better deal with the social mind: attributions and intermental minds. "*Attribution theory* is the study of how attributions of states of mind are made"

8. In her reading of the novel Katharine Swarbrick sums up the reception as follows: "the reception of *Truismes* was marked by anxiety: critics and the public faced with narratives devices which had all the familiarity of *Candide* and Kafka, of Orwell and *Arabian Nights*, described the effect provoked by Darrieussecq's production in terms of nauseous uncertainty" (58).

("Attributions" 293). In narrative fiction such attributions take place on several levels: on the level of the narrator, on the level of the characters, and on the level of the reader. Intermental minds or intermental thought "is joint, group, shared or collective thought, as opposed to intramental, or individual or private thought [. . .] It is also known as *socially distributed, situated or extended cognition,* and also as *intersubjectivity*" ("Attributions" 293).

In *Pig Tales,* the initial shocks delivered by the novel originate from the very elaborate descriptions of the actual physical transformation, of the becoming-a-pig. But the real horrors of the novel are to be found in the way the novel deals with the attribution of desires and beliefs; more specifically, with the protagonist's attribution of desires and beliefs to herself and the surrounding world's attribution of desires and beliefs to her. As she gains weight and changes color, her work as a prostitute changes as well. From what appears to be fairly standard, if deeply impersonal sessions the services she provides start to take on more and more extreme shapes, as does her body. The combination of the physical transformation and the degrading actions becomes too much even for her to handle:

> It wasn't a life any more. I could never be *in tune* with my body, yet the constant refrain of *Gilda Mag* and *My Beauty, My Health,* magazines I received at the boutique, was that if you didn't achieve this harmony with yourself, you risked getting cancer, an *anarchic growth of cells.* (35)

This passage mirrors the kind of intrusions her physical body is subjected to in her work as a prostitute on a semantic and mental level. To put it bluntly, while her clients and her boss have been inserting strange objects into her body, the language and logic of commercials have been inserted into her mind. And these semantic objects are not just supplements to the wordings of her soliloquies—they form the basic building blocks for the reconstruction and explanation of her own desires, beliefs, and emotions.

As the story continues so does the protagonist's transformation. Her boyfriend leaves her behind in the large amusement park Aqualand. The park closes with her trapped inside and she suddenly finds herself naked, in the middle of a large closed party for Edgar, the evil politician on the rise. After being submitted to severe abuse—they unleash dogs on her—she is about to be shot, when one of Edgar's assistants intervenes and brings her to Edgar. They decide to use her as the main model in his election campaign under the slogan "For a healthier world!" She then spends the entire night being photographed.

> The photographer sent me off with a wad of bills in my hand. I thought that was fair. The one thing I regretted was not having seen the end of the party at Aqualand, when I'd never in my whole life been invited to such a high-class affair. (56)

On the one hand, this passage displays the classical situation of a character's access to the content of her own mind: she has experienced something, has reacted to it, and is now reflecting on these experiences and reactions. The trouble for the reader, on the other hand, comes from the fact that her evaluation of the experience radically differs from what most would consider normal. As readers of her story we witness a series of massive violations of human dignity. But when she rereads these events in her mind, her thoughts are full of other peoples' words, other peoples' perspectives, other peoples' demands and wishes. As is the case with Kafka's Samsa, in the rendering of the metamorphosed mind in a tortured body we would expect hidden, detached introspection on the wrongs being done to her, but what we read is for the most part detached not from the perpetrators in the outer world but from the core of her inner world, a core that has been eradicated by the doxa of a society gone wrong.

I will now take up some examples of how the novel deals with the minds of others. I will restrict my focus to the attribution aspect of the social mind. The protagonist is in principle capable of attributing mental states to others, even though she often refrains from doing so. But what is striking about the novel's presentation of the social aspect of what constitutes a mind is that the story contains almost no passages in which others attribute desires or beliefs to the protagonist. What we are able to reconstruct from the narrator's tales of her interaction with others can be boiled down to the following: they either use her or are horrified by her bizarre looks. In the Perfume Plus she is treated solely as a commodity. The only customer who attributes a minimal amount of inner life to her is a mad preacher who calls her a sinner. I have previously mentioned some of the ways in which the politician Edgar puts her to use: as a model and as a spectacular freak. The horrified responses come from all sides: when she visits a doctor the doctor "exclaimed indignantly" (45). When she meets a woman with a child we hear that "the sight of me seemed to frighten the woman" (71). And when a policeman shortly after pursues her, he yells, "'It's monstrous!' [. . .] His hand shook as he drew his weapon—which is what saved me" (73).

After a long time in a prison cell, she becomes the center of attention at a huge New Year's Eve party at Edgar's place. She is brought in and received like a freak, and after she has eaten someone's vomit they begin throwing food at her and make her perform tricks for it. This episode is followed by a rare example of someone reacting to her as if she had actual desires and beliefs:

> Everyone was having lots of fun. I was getting dizzy from the champagne they were pouring into me and I started feeling sentimental, shedding tears of gratitude for all the food I was getting. One lady with a stunning dress of lazuré from Gilda flung her arms around me and kissed me on both cheeks, sobbing and babbling incoherently. I would have liked to understand what she was saying, while we were both rolling around on the floor. She seemed quite fond of me. It had been a long time since anyone had shown me such affection, and I was moved to fresh tears. "Look at that!" the lady stammered. "She's crying!" (93)

The passage may be read as both a demonstration and a parody of what Palmer refers to as the attribution of mental states on the basis of external signs. In this scene the external signs are tears, and they are produced by the protagonist and the lady in the stunning dress, respectively. The autodiegetic narration prevents the reader from insight into the intentions of the lady, but based on her tears and motions it is safe to assume that the lady reads the tears of the protagonist as tears of misery and sadness. But this rare example of someone actually attributing an inner life to the protagonist is undermined by the grotesque irony of the situation; the woman concludes from the tears that there is in fact a human being behind the mass of red flesh, but even so she totally misjudges her: the tears of the protagonist, so we are told by the narrator, are in fact tears of joy and gratitude, not of sorrow or pain.

Pig Tales holds one major exception to its otherwise complete lack of intermental units: at the end of the narrative, the protagonist enjoys a short and stormy love affair with a werewolf, the only other person in this world also capable of shifting from human to animal form. He is later hunted down and shot.

4. Conclusion

I have selected the modern human–animal metamorphosis narrative as an example of the possibilities as well as the limitations of drawing upon cognitive narratology because this form of narrative dislocates the distinction between the mind as an intramental phenomenon and the mind as a social phenomenon in an instructive way, especially with regard to the distinction between internal and external minds. Where we would expect to find inner thoughts, feelings, and motivation in these narratives, we instead encounter public language, common expressions, doxa, and vice versa: where we would expect to find a readable face, a set of decodable gestures and movements, we encounter fearful reactions to what are perceived as bizarre physical appearances. The uncanny effect of these narratives stems from precisely this double estrangement: the inside of the consciousness has been invaded by the truisms of the outside public sphere, while the outside appearance and hence the social interface with other minds have been disfigured beyond the human form.

On a theoretical and methodological level, the goal of this essay has been twofold: on the one hand, I have suggested ways of drawing upon insights and concepts from cognitive narratology in dealing with unnatural narratives. Classical narratological approaches to representations of consciousness, such as the one offered by Cohn in *Transparent Minds*, excel at dealing with the minds of narratives at an intramental level, as a set of linguistically based inner phenomena. As I hope to have indicated, and this is where I agree with several of the proposals made by Palmer's recent work, cognitive research on the enactive, social, and intermental aspects of the mind enables, when brought into narrative analysis, a more thorough and precise reading of the workings of the impossible and unnatural minds of the likes of Samsa and the woman-pig, even if these narratives affirm the conventions of the intramental by deliberately dissolving them.

On the other hand, I have stressed what I take to be some of the shortcomings of basing a unified theory of consciousness representation on ToM, a theory that now appears less convincing than the available alternatives.

As I see it, the tools of cognitive narratology offer invaluable help in explaining what happens on the level of structure and reception. Nonetheless (and this is where I disagree with Alber and agree with Abbott), cognitive concepts will not save us from the unknown, will not undo the haunting feelings some narratives produce. These narratives could be out to teach us something, but because of the current intellectual and emotional setup of humans this something continues to elude us. And while the new contributions to the theory of narrative offered by cognitive narratology can help shed light on what makes these narratives unnatural, their unnaturalness remains resistant to being fully translated, normalized, or recognized. That's why they read us while we read them.

Works Cited

Abbott, H. Porter. "Unreadable Minds and the Captive Reader." *Style* 42.4 (2008): 448-70.
Alber, Jan. "Impossible Storyworlds—And What to Do with Them." *Storyworlds* 1 (2009): 79-96.
Alber, Jan, Stefan Iversen, Henrik Skov Nielsen, and Brian Richardson. "Unnatural Narratives, Unnatural Narratology: Beyond Mimetic Models." *Narrative* 18.2 (2010): 113-36.
Baron-Cohen, Simon. *Mindblindness: An Essay on Autism and Theory of Mind.* Cambridge, MA: MIT Press, 1997.
Burroughs, William S. *Naked Lunch.* New York: Grove, 1966.
Cohn, Dorrit. *Transparent Minds: Narrative Modes for Presenting Consciousness in Fiction.* Princeton, NJ: Princeton University Press, 1978.
Darrieussecq, Marie. *Pig Tales: A Novel of Lust and Transformation.* Kent: New Press, 2003.
Gallagher, Shaun. "Inference or Interaction: Social Cognition without Precursors." *Philosophical Explorations* 11.3 (2008): 163-74.
Goldman, Alvin. "Simulation Theory and Mental Concepts." In *Simulation and Knowledge of Action,* ed. Jérôme Dokic and Joëlle Proust. Philadelphia: John Benjamins, 2002. 1-20.
Hansen, Per Krogh, Stefan Iversen, Henrik Skov Nielsen, and Rolf Reitan, eds. *Strange Voices in Narrative Fiction.* Berlin and New York: de Gruyter, 2011.
Herman, David. "Introduction." In *The Emergence of Mind: Representations of Consciousness in Narrative Discourse in English,* ed. David Herman. Lincoln: University of Nebraska Press, 2011. 1-40.
———. "Storied Minds: Narrative Scaffolding for Folk Psychology." *Journal of Consciousness Studies* 16.6-8 (2009): 40-68.
Hutto, Daniel D. "Folk Psychology as Narrative Practice." *Journal of Consciousness Studies* 16.6-8 (2009): 9-39.
———. *Folk Psychological Narratives: The Sociocultural Basis of Understanding Reasons.* Cambridge, MA: MIT Press, 2008.
Hutto, Daniel D., and Matthew Ratcliffe, eds. *Folk Psychology Re-Assessed.* Berlin: Springer, 2007.
Iversen, Stefan. "'In Flaming Flames': Crises of Experientiality in Non-Fictional Narratives." In *Unnatural Narratives, Unnatural Narratology,* ed. Jan Alber and Rüdiger Heinze. Berlin and New York: de Gruyter, 2011. 89-103.
———. "States of Exception: Decoupling, Metarepresentation, and Strange Voices in Narrative Fiction." In Hansen, Iversen, Nielsen, and Reitan, *Strange Voices in Narrative Fiction,* 127-46.
Kafka, Franz. *The Metamorphosis.* Trans. David Wyllie. Project Gutenberg ebook #5200, 2005.
Leudar, Ivan and Costal, Allan. *Against Theory of Mind.* London: Palgrave Macmillan, 2009.
Mäkelä, Maria. "Masters of Interiority: Figural Voices as Discursive Appropriators and as Loopholes in Narrative Communication." In Hansen, Iversen, Nielsen, and Reitan, *Strange Voices in Narrative Fiction,* 191-218.
———. "Possible Minds: Constructing—and Reading—Another Consciousness as Fiction." In *FREE Language INDIRECT Translation DISCOURSE Narratology: Linguistic, Translatological, and Literary-Theoretical Encounters,* ed. Pekka Tammi and Hannu Tommola. Tampere: Tampere University Press, 2006. 231-60.
Nielsen, Henrik Skov. "Fictional Voices? Strange Voices? Unnatural Voices?" In Hansen, Iversen, Nielsen, and Reitan, *Strange Voices in Narrative Fiction,* 55-82.

———. "The Impersonal Voice in First-Person Narrative Fiction." *Narrative* 12.2 (2004): 133–50.

———. "Unnatural Narratology, Impersonal Voices, Real Authors, and Non-Communicative Narration." In *Unnatural Narratives, Unnatural Narratology*, ed. Jan Alber and Rüdiger Heinze. Berlin and New York: de Gruyter, 2011. 71–88.

Palmer, Alan. "Attribution Theory: Action and Emotion in Dickens and Pynchon." In *Contemporary Stylistics*, ed. Marina Lambrou and Peter Stockwell. London: Continuum, 2007. 81–92.

———. "Attributions of Madness in Ian McEwan's Enduring Love." *Style* 43.3 (2009): 291–308.

———. *Fictional Minds*. Lincoln and London: University of Nebraska Press, 2004.

———. *Social Minds in the Novel*. Columbus: The Ohio State University Press, 2010.

Richardson, Brian. *Unnatural Voices: Extreme Narration in Modern and Contemporary Fiction*. Columbus: The Ohio State University Press, 2006.

Slors, Marc and Macdonald, Cynthia. "Rethinking Folk-Psychology: Alternatives to Theories of Mind." *Philosophical Explorations* 11.3 (2008): 153–61.

Swarbrick, Katharine. "Truismes and Truths." *Forum for Modern Language Studies* 46.1 (2009): 58–70.

Zunshine, Lisa. *Why We Read Fiction: Theory of Mind and the Novel*. Columbus: The Ohio State University Press, 2006.

'Unnatural' Metalepsis and Immersion

Necessarily Incompatible?[1]

WERNER WOLF

1. Introduction: Two Formally Similar Metalepses, Two Different Effects—and a Research Problem

Imagine the following two reception situations and narrative scenarios: one— you are watching a film that is set during the Great Depression in the United States. It starts out as the realistically described predicament of a frustrated woman who is unhappily married and has an uninteresting job. Her only relief from drab reality is to watch Hollywood films in the local cinema. In spite of several *mises en abyme* of films within the film that you are watching (which, given the story, are perfectly plausible and natural) you are gripped by the film. In fact it elicits in you a vivid feeling of being immersed in the fictional storyworld—that is, until a scene in which the heroine watches one of her favorite films for the fifth time and in which the protagonist *mis en abyme* steps down from the screen amid the confusion of the viewers assembled in the cinema and the protests of the characters on the screen.

---

1. I would like to thank Jutta Klobasek-Ladler, Ingrid Pfandl-Buchegger, and Nick Scott for proofreading this text and for technical support (Ingrid Pfandl-Buchegger and Daniel Schäbler also for the translation of non-English passages) as well as Evelyn Krummen and my former PhD student and expert on metalepsis, Jeff Thoss, for their valuable suggestions.

For the second scenario, imagine that you are listening to a rhapsode in ancient Greece who is just telling you and a fascinated audience the story of a sculptor who is frustrated about women in general but has the gift of producing exquisitely beautiful female statues. One of them is so charming that he falls in love with it and, abandoning his misogyny, prays to Aphrodite to give him a wife similar to the statue in question. The goddess grants him his wish and even more, as his statue appears to be suddenly endowed with life: his creation has risen to his own level of existence, so that creation and creator can even engender a child.

Both scenarios contain what can technically be classified as 'metalepses'; indeed, both stories even sport a classic case of this device, namely the confusion of different ontological levels—the level of represented 'reality' and the level of artifacts. These levels are short-circuited by what may be considered an 'unnatural,' physically impossible bottom-up border-crossing: a hypodiegetic artifact becoming a diegetic 'reality.' And yet both scenarios may arguably elicit different effects. These may even be so divergent that the second scenario would not necessarily appear as unnatural or impossible to its recipients. As a consequence, both scenarios will also differ in terms of immersion. The first scenario, taken from Woody Allen's film *The Purple Rose of Cairo* (1985), will doubtlessly destroy the credibility of the story, be it only for the moment, and thus endanger our immersion, while the second story, a version of the Pygmalion myth handed down to us by book X of Ovid's *Metamorphoseon libri* (1 B.C.–c. 10 A.D.),[2] may go without triggering at least his contemporaries' disbelief and can thus be seen to be (or have been) compatible with immersion. It appears that similar metaleptic devices can produce conspicuously different effects.[3]

> 2. For the sake of argument I have here somewhat anachronistically projected the myth as transmitted by Ovid in written form back to an earlier oral context. Actually, in these earlier times Pygmalion appears not to have been an artist as yet but a king of Cyprus (cf. Martin 631: "Der für die Rezeption des P[ygmalion]mythos verbindlichen Version von Ovid (Ov. met., 243–97) geht wohl eine reichere, aber nur noch in Umrissen greifbare [. . .] Stofftradition voraus: P. wird als König der Kyprer erwähnt [. . .]"). ("Ovid's text, which has been the accepted version for the reception of the Pygmalion myth, is probably preceded by the richer, but only partially accessible outlines of a plot tradition: P. is mentioned as a king of the Cypriots [. . .].")
>
> 3. The animation of an artifact in the myth of Pygmalion must be distinguished from the tradition of humanoid automata or artificial human beings, machines that are constructed with a lifelike animation in mind right from the start (such as the female automata created by Hephaistos, as narrated in book 18 of the *Iliad*). These contraptions are technical miracles but basically remain automata which only imitate life without actually becoming living beings in the full sense of the word. In contrast to them, Pygmalion's statue (which is not a machine) makes a truly ontological leap and becomes genuinely human, a metamorphosis that gives the narrated event a formally metaleptic quality. For the tradition of humanoid automata see LaGrandeur, in particular 408–11; for the cultural history of the 'Pygmalion effect' of aesthetic simulacra that "rever[t] the hierarchy between *model* and *copy*" see Stoichita 5.

Such a divergence of possible effects has, however, not sufficiently been taken into account by research: in discussions of metalepsis—including what I myself used to write on the subject—it is the first of the aforementioned effects, the disruption of immersion and aesthetic illusion, which has one-sidedly been stressed on the grounds of its 'unnatural' paradoxicality (cf. Wolf, *Ästhetische Illusion* 358; Wagner 239; Pier, "Métalepse" 253; Pier, "Metalepsis" 193; Döpp). Referring to Coleridge's well-known definition of aesthetic illusion, Genette, one of the first and foremost theoreticians of metalepsis, clearly states that metalepsis forms "une transgression qui ne peut que mettre à mal la fameuse 'suspension volontaire de l'incrédulité'" ("De la figure à la fiction" 30).[4] If one attributes 'unnaturalness' to all metalepses, as is done, for example, by Thoss ("Unnatural Narrative and Metalepsis" 189-190), the assumption of a tension between this device and immersion does not in fact come as a surprise, since, according to Jan Alber, "[a]ll instances of the unnatural have an estranging effect" ("Impossible Storyworlds" 80). Yet, arguably, such defamiliarization need not always occur, as Alber's own research on the 'naturalization' of unnatural, impossible storyworlds implies ("Impossible Storyworlds," "Unnatural Narratives," "The Diachronic Development of Unnaturalness"). Indeed, as the second of the aforementioned scenarios indicates, there are cases in which even the particularly strong variant of 'unnaturalness' embodied by metalepsis does not of necessity appear incompatible with one of the most frequent and powerful effects normally elicited by plausible, 'natural,' well-told or represented scenarios, namely immersion (aka, in certain contexts, aesthetic illusion).[5]

This may be clear enough, but what is less clear and has so far hardly ever been addressed as a research problem[6] is the question of what conditions precisely elicit such contrary effects. In the following I propose to inquire into

---

4. This translates as "a transgression which cannot but do harm to the famous 'willing suspension of disbelief.'"

5. For the relationship between 'aesthetic illusion' and 'immersion' see section 2 in this essay and Wolf, "Aesthetic Illusion."

6. As an exception I would like to mention Sonja Klimek's research on metalepsis (cf. "Metalepsis and Its (Anti-)Illusionist Effects" and *Paradoxes Erzählen*); I am grateful to her for having made me revise former, perhaps too apodictic, statements as formulated in my theory of aesthetic illusion and the breaking thereof (see Wolf, *Ästhetische Illusion und Illusionsdurchbrechung*, ch. 3.5.4). Nelles (94) also makes a brief remark on the possibility that metalepsis could produce an "effect of realism," suggesting that narrator and character thereby appear to share the same sphere of reality, but this claim may at best be limited to rhetorical metalepsis and remains unconvincing, since the alleged continuity between the worlds involved in metalepsis could also be interpreted as indicative of their sharing the same irreality or fictionality. Finally, Schaeffer must also be mentioned in this context, but his contention that metalepsis, far from being incompatible with immersion, is actually its 'emblem' (331) rests on a misconception of both immersion and metalepsis (see note 14 in this essay).

precisely this: under what conditions may metalepsis disrupt immersion, as is assumed to be the case by the majority of researchers, and under what conditions may it, on the contrary, appear to be more or less compatible with immersion in spite of its theoretical unnaturalness? This discussion will first require the clarification of relevant concepts (metalepsis, the unnatural, naturalization, immersion and aesthetic illusion) before I can discuss the conditions mentioned and draw some conclusions that should contribute to a poetics of (un)naturalness.

2. Terminology and Relevant Research: Metalepsis, the Unnatural and Naturalization, Immersion and Aesthetic Illusion

The term 'metalepsis' stems from Genette's structuralist narratology and was originally defined as the improbable transgression of the 'sacred' border between the world of narration and the narrated world[7] or, in more general terms, between the world of representation and the represented world. It has since been variously redefined and sometimes also expanded (see, for example, Nelles; Herman; Wagner; Genette *Métalepse*; Ryan, "Metaleptic Machines" and *Avatars of Story* 204–11; Pier and Schaeffer; Wolf "Metalepsis as a Transgeneric and Transmedial Phenomenon"; Klimek, "Metalepsis and Its (Anti-) Illusionist Effects" and *Paradoxes Erzählen*). The most important expansions concern a redefinition of metalepsis not only as a narrative but also as a transmedial device open to all (representational) media, and the inclusion of lateral metalepsis ('impossible' leaps between parallel worlds)[8] as well as the suggestion of paradoxical border crossings occurring between a representation and the world of its author. As I have said elsewhere, "the prototypical case of metalepsis can be defined as a salient phenomenon occurring exclusively in representations, namely as a usually nonaccidental and paradoxical transgression of the border between levels or (sub)worlds that are ontologically (in particular concerning the opposition reality vs. fiction) or logically differentiated (logically in a wide, not only formal sense, including, e.g., temporal or spatial

---

7. Genette describes this border as follows: "[...] la limite [...] franchi[e] au mépris de la vraisemblance [...]: [la] frontière [...] sacrée entre deux mondes: celui où l'on raconte, celui que l'on raconte" (Genette, *Figures III* 245). ("[...] the boundary [...] in defiance of verisimilitude [...]: [the] sacred frontier between two worlds, the world in which one tells, the world of which one tells" (Genette, *Narrative Discourse* 236).

8. This is a convincing proposal made by Wagner (247), which is, however, rejected by Klimek (see *Paradoxes Erzählen*, ch. 2.3.2).

differences)" (Wolf, "Metareference across Media" 50).⁹ In short, metalepsis is the paradoxical violation of the outer border of a represented world or of the border(s) between represented worlds (cf. Thoss, *Metalepsis in Contemporary Popular Fiction, Film, and Comics* 179). Metalepsis thus "violates" the represented "world's (conventionally assumed) autonomy" (Thoss, "Unnatural Narrative and Metalepsis" 190).

According to Nelles (93–95) one can distinguish between 'rhetorical metalepsis,' the 'impossible' suggestion (restricted to verbal narratives) that a narrator is affected by the story he tells (e.g., profiting from a pause in the action to insert a lengthy narratorial comment), 'epistemological metalepsis,' the existence of a paradoxical border-crossing only in the minds of characters or other fictitious agencies (this form is limited to media being able to represent thought and speech), and 'ontological metalepsis,' the apparent paradoxical transgression of a border by (represented) persons or objects.[10] As this is the most radical variant of metalepsis and hence seemingly the most unnatural, it will be the focus of the following discussion.

The defining paradoxicality of metalepsis obviously affiliates it with 'unnatural narration' (although metalepsis transcends the realm of narratives, for the sake of the present volume's focus I will henceforth restrict my discussion to narrative metalepsis). Metaleptic 'para-doxical' unnaturalness can refer to logical impossibilities (the contamination of the ontologically different realms of 'nature' and 'art'/'artifacts')[11] or to what goes beyond, and is therefore impossible according to, reigning 'doxa' (e.g., the 'orthodox' idea that the present cannot influence the past). Metalepsis thus affects precisely the two fields that Alber mentions in his definition of the unnatural: "physically impossible scenarios and events, that is, impossible by the known laws

9. Klimek, in her purist conception of metalepsis, restricts this device to paradoxical leaps, in the Genettian sense, between the narration and the narrated world (see *Paradoxes Erzählen* 43–44). A generally accepted case of this classical form of metalepses occurs in verbal frame-structures as a paradoxical crossover between framing and framed parts. In other media, however, even this simple case can cause classificatory problems owing to representation as a postulated precondition of metalepsis. Since in another publication on defamiliarized framings and frame-breaks I also attributed the quality of metalepsis to a crossover between an abstract painting and its frame (Giacomo Bella, "Velocità astratta + rumore" [1913]; Wolf, "Defamiliarized Initial Framings" 322), I would like to clarify here that this and similar examples constitute borderline cases, which—if one insists on the absence of representation (which in the painting mentioned is, by the way, debatable)—would perhaps best be termed 'quasi-metaleptic' structures.

10. In other typologies only the distinction 'rhetorical vs. ontological' metalepsis occurs (see Ryan "Metaleptic Machines," and Pier, "Metalepsis" 191–92).

11. A given phenomenon such as a character or person can be either fictional/a construct or real/natural but cannot possess both qualities at the same time (following the logical principle of *tertium non datur*).

governing the physical world, as well as logically impossible ones, that is, impossible by accepted principles of logic" ("Impossible Storyworlds" 80). What this definition does not explicitly mention, though, is the fact that the knowledge of the physical laws in question and the acceptance of logic as well as what is generally considered 'natural' are not stable givens but can vary according to cultural and historical parameters. For the Renaissance mind, for instance, the intrusion of witches into the world of everyday experience as represented in the opening scene of Shakespeare's *Macbeth* was not necessarily an 'unnatural' impossibility, while the idea of such intrusions increasingly became so in later periods. As a consequence, impossible narration must in itself be regarded as a category dependent on historical and other cultural frames.

The same is true for the means of 'defusing' the unnatural: naturalization. The term was popularized by Jonathan Culler, who, drawing on Barthes' *Le Degré zéro de l'écriture,* employed it in *Structuralist Poetics* to designate the means by which written literature "reduce[s] its strangeness" (134, cf. also 137). Alber ("Impossible Storyworlds" 80–83) uses the term in the very general sense of "mak[ing] sense of the unnatural" (80) and proposes five ways of "cop[ing] with the unnatural" (83). These are as follows: (1) "reading [unnatural] events as internal states" (e.g., dreams); (2) understanding them as an aesthetic device to "foreground [. . .] the thematic" or (3) as a form of allegory; (4) recuperation of the unnatural by blending it with "pre-existing frames" or (5) by "stretch[ing existing] frames" (83).[12] Fludernik (*Towards a "Natural" Narratology*) also uses the concept in a broad sense, albeit not as a general means of recuperating strange elements in the reading and interpreting of *all* literature since she focuses on narratives only. Drawing on Ricoeur's three forms of mimesis (vol. 3, ch. I.3), she indicates three possibilities for doing this: (a) attempting to reintroduce what is seemingly outside experientiality into real-life experience (Alber's strategy no. 1 points in the same direction); (b) activating general "explanatory schemas" (43) which would help provide access to the unnatural (this coincides with Alber's strategies no. 4 and 5); and (c) integrating the strange into certain communicative situations, in particular literary "genres" as "large-scale cognitive frames" (44) (this is echoed in Alber's strategies no. 2 and 3).

In both Alber's and Fludernik's conceptualizations of naturalization, reference is made to man-made, artificial phenomena as a means of meaningful recuperation (e.g., reference to allegory and to generic conventions). At first

---

12. In his contribution to this volume, Jan Alber reorders and extends these navigational tools.

sight this appears to depart from what one intuits to be the actual meaning warranted by the term 'naturalization' itself, namely to reintroduce something strange into the realm of the natural so that the strangeness is reduced or lost, in other words, to align it with what is regarded as ordinary, generally the case, and in accordance with the 'nature' of things, which is considered to follow principles rooted in the essence of reality and therefore to be resistant to the ever-changing moldings and constructs of human culture. Culler appears to have this meaning in mind when he says that "[n]aturalization emphasizes the fact that the strange or deviant is [...] made to seem natural" (137). However, Culler does not promote an essentialist view of the natural and appears to indicate by the formulation "seem natural" that in this 'seeming of nature' there may be a lot of culture and conventions. Indeed, although Culler does not mention this any more than Alber, one can generalize and say that in cultural representations the seemingly natural also, and arguably to a large extent, includes cultural-historical factors and conventions (although these tend to be taken for granted and need not be foregrounded in the process of reception).

Yet the question remains: is 'naturalization' an unspecified general recuperation or defusing of the 'strange' in literature (and other media), in other words, is it *any kind* of making sense of the 'unnatural' as Alber and Fludernik (most recently in 2010) appear to suggest in their broad conception of the term, or is 'naturalization' a *specific* way of recuperation in which the strange after all becomes seemingly natural in a narrower sense, so that one may at least momentarily forget about 'artificial,' cultural explanations and reduce the unnatural to apparently natural or ordinary causes, be it only within the logic of given storyworlds? The two interpretations of 'naturalization' are not identical. The situation of the protagonist Winnie in Beckett's *Happy Days* (1961), who is "[i]mbedded up to above her waist in [the] exact centre of [a] mound" (II. 148) is, for instance, most unnatural indeed, yet it is a situation for which 'naturalization' in the broad sense, including 'allegorical reading' in particular, is better suited than the narrow meaning, for Beckett's text never offers any explanation for how Winnie came to be immersed in this mound in the first place nor how a human being can exist for a prolonged time under such unnatural circumstances.

In accordance with my focus on the possibilities of rendering compatible with immersion or aesthetic illusion what may be formally classified as a metalepsis and hence as a form of the unnatural, I shall opt for the narrower meaning of 'naturalization,' since it is clear enough that what can be made to appear natural should not present difficulties with immersion. In other words: 'naturalization,' as used in the following, is more than merely making sense of seemingly strange phenomena of the story level; rather it means rendering such phenomena plausible by means apparently originating in the represented storyworld so that they become compatible with immersion: this, for instance, precludes an open 'determination' of strange story-level phenomena by discursive strategies such as foregrounding and allegory (Alber's devices no. 2 and 3). As far as the broader alternatives of making sense of the unnatural discussed by Alber and Fludernik are concerned, I would rather term them means of 'defusing' or simply of 'understanding' the unnatural.[13]

This leads me to the last of the relevant concepts to be clarified here: immersion and aesthetic illusion. I have defined aesthetic illusion elsewhere ("Illusion (Aesthetic)" 144) as

> "a basically pleasurable mental state that emerges during the reception of many representational texts, artefacts[,] or performances. These representations may be fictional or factual and include in particular narratives. Like all reception effects, aesthetic illusion is elicited by the conjunction of factors that are located (a) in the representations themselves, (b) in the reception process and the recipients, [and] (c) in cultural and historical contexts. Aesthetic illusion consists predominantly of a feeling, of variable intensity, of being imaginatively and emotionally immersed in a represented world and of experiencing this world in a way similar (but not identical) to real

---

13. One may even question whether 'naturalization' in this broad sense is not always possible in the reception of works of art and hence whether a specific term is necessary in the first place for what, after all, is simply the 'natural' attempt to 'make sense' of apparent 'nonsense' when it comes to communication involving works of art. Indeed, making sense even of what seem to be the most nonsensical and impossible things is what we are trained to generally attempt when confronted with the frame 'artwork'—and such sense-making is also what authors throughout history have always assumed as their recipients' attitude toward seemingly nonsensical or impossible fictions or statements (a case in point being the rhetorical figure of the adynaton, a "form of hyperbole [...] which involves the magnification of an event by reference to the impossible" [Cuddon 9]). The motivation for such persistent sense-making is a specific constituent of the frame 'artwork,' namely what I term *Sinnprämisse* ('premiss of meaningfulness'): we automatically assume that artworks are meaningful constructs and that even obscure or seemingly nonsensical wholes or parts of them are not actually meaningless nor merely errors or slips of the tongue (an interpretation we would much more readily attribute to everyday communication) but that they are intentional and must mean something. In a recent essay Fludernik ("Naturalizing the Unnatural") applies blending theory to various forms of 'unnatural' storytelling elements and scenarios including metalepsis (cf. 21–22), contending that it is by blending familiar domains of scenarios that even metalepsis is 'naturalized.' Yet here, too, what she actually has in mind is the question of how we are able to *understand* metalepsis in the first place, not how we are made to forget its unnatural quality. To show what difference the broad and narrow conception of 'naturalization' implies, one could even argue that the blending of (individually understandable) domains in an incompatible, paradoxical way *produces* the effect of unnaturalness rather than naturalizing it—at least in the narrow sense used by myself.

life. This constitutive impression of immersion is, however, counterbalanced by a latent rational distance, which is a consequence of the culturally acquired awareness of the difference between representations and reality."[14]

Immersion is often used as a synonym of 'aesthetic illusion,' yet, strictly speaking, it only denotes the 'immersive pole' of aesthetic illusion and is not burdened with the historical connotations of presupposing a latent awareness of art and artifactuality as aesthetic illusion is. For a discussion of metalepsis that also extends to mythical narratives and archaic contexts, in which the concept of aesthetic illusion cannot (as yet) be applied, it is clear that a broader concept of immersion is more appropriate. What reception effects (immersion in both its narrow and broad meaning) share, and this is most important in the following, is the feeling of experientially participating in a representation, a feeling that is gradable in intensity in both cases.

3. Conditions Eliciting Anti-Immersive Effects of Metalepsis

We can now come back to the first scenario as an example of a standard metalepsis and clarify the conditions which contribute to the fact that the stepping down of a filmic character from a cinema screen as occurs in *The Purple Rose of Cairo* is truly unnatural, so that it cannot be naturalized in the narrow sense and consequently impairs immersion.

Effects of artifacts on recipients always depend on an interaction between several constituents of medial communication. There is, of course, always the

14. For details see also Wolf, "Aesthetic Illusion." Schaeffer (332) radicalizes this ambivalence of aesthetic illusion (which he calls 'immersion') as an oscillation between letting oneself be drawn into the represented world and the awareness of the reality of the reception situation, for example, the cinema ("[...] il y a coexistence, chez le spectateur, entre l'immersion perceptive, qui se laisse guider par les amorces mimétiques [...] et l'attention perceptive périphérique, qui continue à traiter les informations provenant de la salle") ("there is a co-existence, in the spectator, of perceptive immersion, which lets itself be guided by mimetic triggers [...] and peripheral perceptive attention, which continues to deal with the information coming from the surrounding cinema room"). However, the problem with this conceptualization is that Schaeffer omits to mention a decisive feature of aesthetic illusion: in this state the feeling of being recentered within a represented world is dominant, and therefore devices that run counter to this impression, such as many if not most metalepses, activate a subdominant reality awareness that is normally latent. As a consequence, Schaeffer's claim that metalepsis, by its transgression of the border between different levels of 'reality' on the part of the recipient, is 'emblematic' of, rather than antagonistic to, immersion (331, 333) must be rejected. It is based on a reductive conception of aesthetic illusion and is unable to account for the disruptive effects most metalepses in fact have.

individual recipient (about whom it is difficult to say anything specific), and moreover the artifact or 'message': this not only implies the structure and content of the work in question but also the medial conditions of 'code' and 'channel.' In addition, the framing cultural conditions (i.e., in Foucault's terms, the factors of the ruling 'episteme') that shape the audience's preconceptions, as well as those of the author (the 'sender'), play a particularly important role as well.

In our case, an American film released in 1985, we may assume as such framing epistemic conditions essentials of the dominant secular worldview of the Western world of our times, a worldview that includes a belief in the validity of the physical laws of nature as explained by contemporary science and above all a conviction that representations cannot come alive or have a will of their own; in short, that medial artifacts such as films, be they factual or fictional, and the reality of the recipients are separate spheres divided by an insurmountable boundary. As far as *The Purple Rose of Cairo* is concerned, this film does nothing to disturb these basic assumptions for a considerable stretch of time. On the contrary: the realism both of the story or subject (a social critical variant of realism referring to economic circumstances as well as to the low-paid job and marital conditions of the lower-class heroine) and its filmic 'discourse' or transmission actively suggest, as is typical of realism in general, that there is a continuum between our universe and the represented world, in this case the world of the 1930s. This world may be divided from ours historically as well as by the ontological boundary between a represented world and the world in which the representation takes place, but the same natural laws and the same logic as in our experience essentially apply to it. Realism thus radicalizes what Marie-Laure Ryan called the epistemological "principle of minimal departure" (*Possible Worlds* 51). According to this principle the default option, which governs our access to storyworlds in all reception processes, is the assumption that the same basic laws are valid in both realms unless we are made aware of special conditions applying to the respective storyworld. Realism as prevailing in the initial phase of *The Purple Rose of Cairo* avoids signaling such special conditions, and this is what actually radicalizes the principle of minimal departure to a 'principle of apparently no departure at all.'

The metaleptic screen passage of the actor *mise en abyme* Tom Baxter therefore comes as a considerable shock. Interestingly, it comes as a shock both to the real recipients and to the fictional patrons of the represented cinema—at precisely the moment when Baxter, who has as yet only been engaged in an epistemological metalepsis by directly addressing the diegetic heroine Cecilia ("My God, you must really love this picture"), "*begins to leave the black-and-white screen*" and is thus shown in the process of an ontological metalepsis.

> TOM: I gotta speak to you
> *He begins to leave the black-and-white screen. The audience, reacting, begins to gasp. The film cuts to a shocked Cecilia, immobilized in her seat. As the other patrons cry out in the background, the film quickly cuts back to Tom. He actually walks off the black-and-white movie screen, turning into living color as he enters the theater.*
> *The film cuts to a woman in a hat, sitting in the last row of the theater. She screams and falls over in a faint [. . .] The audience, in color, is in an uproar.* (*The Purple Rose of Cairo* 351–52)

The gasps of the audience, the shock of Cecilia, the fainting of a lady in the audience—all of these are *mises en abyme* of the intended shock reaction of the real recipients by what I call 'reception figures.' The reaction of these figures testifies to the unnaturalness of the represented metalepsis, an unnaturalness that is never physically or logically explained (Tom Baxter's psychological interest in his admirer Cecilia being insufficient by way of naturalization in the narrow sense of the term[15]). This unnaturalness is obviously not only a theoretical one but is meant to be felt by the real audience as well. As a consequence, it is safe to assume that Baxter's 'impossible' address to Cecilia and eventual leaving of the screen endangers the real recipients' immersion, at least if they mentally compare what is possible in reality according to their convictions and what is 'impossibly' represented on screen. Through the ensuing irreconcilability of the two worlds, they will feel strongly reminded of the fact that they are 'merely' watching a film. If so, the repeated *mises en abyme* of the real cinematic reception situation which we have watched so far are at the same time belatedly foregrounded as additional reminders of artificiality, mediality, and fictionality. *The Purple Rose of Cairo* thus assumes a strong metareferential quality, a quality that is subsequently unfolded in an ambivalent criticism of what (Hollywood) film and its sought-after effect, namely strong immersion, can do to its audience for better or worse, that is, provide an acceptable escape from drab reality but also offer a potentially dangerous narcotic.

To sum up: the unnatural, immersion-hostile effect of metalepsis is based in the case of *The Purple Rose of Cairo*—a case representative of one frequent type of metalepsis—on several conditions:

---

15. Wishes or interests normally do not alter levels of reality.

1. the existence of an extracompositional epistemological framework ruling the (contemporary) audience and according to which the represented metalepsis is physically or logically impossible;
2. an intracompositional representation which in form and content at first seems to fulfill the epistemic assumptions as adduced under condition 1;
3. the lack of intracompositional explanations by which the metalepsis under discussion can be naturalized in the narrow sense of the term;
4. the indication of the actual unnaturalness of a given metalepsis through intracompositional 'reception figures,' who react in a corresponding way, betraying shock, disbelief, and so forth.

It should be noted that conditions 1 to 3 are necessary for the illusion-breaking or anti-immersive effect of nonnaturalizable unnaturalness, while condition 4 is optional, albeit frequently fulfilled. When this is the case, we may safely assume that the real recipient, too, experiences unnaturalness.

4. Conditions Permitting Various Degrees of Compatibility between Metalepsis and Immersion

However, one question merits some further attention: is it really the case that a feeling of unnaturalness as in Woody Allen's film always leads to a reduction of immersion or a breaking of illusion? Formerly (cf. Wolf, *Ästhetische Illusion* ch. 3.5.4, in particular 358; Wolf, "Metalepsis as a Transgeneric and Transmedial Phenomenon" 101) I was convinced that this is so on the grounds that the contrast between the metaleptic event in the represented world and the assumptions we apply in our experience of reality inevitably foregrounds the fictionality of the storyworld and thus distances the recipient from the representation by metareferentially drawing attention to its artificial, made-up status. Thus one may in fact argue that in *The Purple Rose of Cairo* the metalepsis is clearly a case of implicit yet nevertheless powerfully distancing metareferentiality: on the one hand, it comments on the problem of recipients who permit themselves to become too deeply immersed in storyworlds (represented by Cecilia dreaming of being on speaking terms with cinema celebrities and participating in their world of glamour) while, on the other hand, it also contributes to a celebration of film's immersive power (again, illustrated by Cecilia's attitude towards film). I am, however, now inclined to qualify the claim that metalepsis is generally a strong means of distancing the recipient by conceding that, under special conditions, metalepsis may be compatible with immersion. These special conditions, which include devices of naturalization in the narrow sense but may also go beyond them, function as 'filter factors' that influence the recipient's reaction to the unnatural. Of course, what can be said in this respect without extensive empirical research is mostly speculation based on introspection and, perhaps, a few reception testimonies. Yet, some reflections, even if not based on statistical proof (which, by the way, would be unavailable anyway as soon as we recede in history), may be allowed nevertheless and could show the direction in which future research could go.

One of the conditions that may neutralize the anti-immersive effect even of strongly felt unnaturalness is certainly a high degree of emotional involvement in the storyworld. Apart from the specific predispositions of the individual recipients, which are too elusive for theoretical evaluation (and shall therefore here be bracketed off), it is, of course, the intracompositional makeup of the work in question that regulates this involvement. In this context the general tone of the work is of particular importance: seriousness favors both emotional involvement and immersion, while comedy or humor tends more toward distance, both in emotional terms (laughter having, according to Bergson, as one of its preconditions "une anesthésie momentanée du coeur"[16] [*Le Rire* 4][17]) and in aesthetic terms (i.e., tending toward the reduction of immersion and aesthetic illusion).[18] If—contrary to what has been assumed in my discussion of *The Purple Rose of Cairo*—one would like to argue that the immersion at least of some recipients may not be remarkably impaired by the metalepsis in question, one could point to an unmitigated emotional involvement, perhaps even a strong empathy with poor Cecilia, and one could also say that this involvement is in turn supported by the prevailing serious mode of the film, which is a tragicomedy rather than a light comedy.

Sustained seriousness is, however, generally uncharacteristic of most of Woody Allen's works. More typical than *The Purple Rose of Cairo* concerning Allen's predilection for humor is one of his short stories that has become something of a classic and standard example of metalepsis (cf., e.g., Ryan, *Avatars of Story* 208): "The Kugelmass Episode" (originally published in 1977). If, in *The Purple Rose of Cairo*, the 'impossible' event of a character leaping from a hypodiegetic universe to a diegetic one can leave a conceivable margin

---

16. This translates as "a momentary anaesthesia of the heart" (Bergson, *Laughter* 11).

17. Cf. also: "Le rire n'a pas de plus grand ennemi que l'émotion" (*Le Rire* 3) ("Laughter has no greater foe than emotion" [*Laughter* 10]).

18. For the comic as generally favoring distance and as thus preparing the ground for illusion-breaking, cf. Wolf, *Ästhetische Illusion* ch. 3.7.

for compatibility with immersion as a result of a high degree of emotional involvement, this relativizing condition certainly does not apply to similar (and inverted) leaps in "The Kugelmass Episode," which therefore shall be dealt with in a brief contrastive digression. In this highly metareferential story Kugelmass, "a professor of humanities [...] unhappily married" (347), is looking for an amorous adventure and becomes the client of a New York magician, who claims that he is able to transfer Kugelmass into the storyworld of any work of world literature provided the respective book is thrown into a magic machine of his. In this story, too, a reception figure signals the impossibility of such a proposed ontological metalepsis: Kugelmass himself, on listening to the magician's self-advertisement, "made a grimace of disbelief" (350). Later, when the metalepsis 'really' happens and Kugelmass meets the eponymous heroine of *Madame Bovary* within Flaubert's storyworld, "students in various classrooms across the country" wonder "Who is this character on p. 100? A bald Jew is kissing Madame Bovary?" (352)—another intracompositional indication of the startling nature of the metaleptic event. And when Kugelmass finally asks the magician Persky to revert the metaleptic direction so that the hypodiegetic Emma can cross the border into diegetic Manhattan, the magician, while promising help, at the same time also signals the strangeness of the projected border-crossing, a strangeness that is immediately underlined by the narrator: "'Let me think about it,' Persky said. 'Maybe I could work it. Stranger things have happened.' Of course, neither of them could think of one" (354). Formally, everything thus points in the same direction as *The Purple Rose of Cairo*: in both cases we are confronted with a nonnaturalizable ontological metalepsis that characteristically elicits reactions of disbelief and puzzlement in 'reception figures.'

And yet the effect of the two metalepses may arguably differ: in contrast to the emotional investment that the representation of unhappy Cecilia will certainly elicit in most viewers of *The Purple Rose of Cairo*, and which may override the distancing effect of the cinematic metalepsis as well as the concomitant metareferentiality to a certain extent, the lighter tone of "The Kugelmass Episode" does not permit such emotional involvement and creates humorous distance right from the start. As a consequence, the metalepsis brought about by the improbable and incongruous character of a magician as an inhabitant of today's Manhattan (!) may well be said to widen the distance to the point where (strong) immersion is certainly no longer possible. Rather, we are invited to follow Kugelmass's adventure from a detached, amused point of view located outside his universe, a distance that is widened by the metareferentiality and overt intertextuality that characterizes the text even apart from its metalepses.

As we have seen in analyzing two tendentially contrastive works by Woody Allen, the intracompositional milieu in which a metalepsis occurs (concerning the general mood prevailing in a text, its emotional quality but also its degree of metareferentiality) are all factors that can considerably influence the actual effects of what technically seem to be similar if not identical metalepses. What is more, and as the above examples also show, this influence also extends to clearly nonnaturalizable metalepses as in *The Purple Rose of Cairo* and "The Kugelmass Episode."

Of course, if what can be formally classified as a metalepsis occurs in the context of factors that help mitigate its strangeness, the reduction or even lack of an anti-immersive effect is all the more understandable in cases where the text provides plausible (if physically impossible) explanations for the metalepsis in combination with a strong emotionality and possibly also specific generic frames. A case in point is Mary Shelley's Gothic novel *Frankenstein* (1818), which sports all three of these pro-immersive factors. The event relevant to our context in this novel is, of course, the transformation of an artifact (even if made out of organic material) into a living being. As long as the 'monster' is in the making, it is a representation of a human being, a "lifeless thing," "an inanimate body" (318); after Frankenstein has "infuse[d] a spark of being" (ibid.) into it, the artifact leaps onto the diegetic level of his creator, characteristically changing grammatical gender from "it" to "he" (see 318–19), all of which conforms to the formal conditions of metalepsis—provided we import our contemporary knowledge of the physical impossibility and unnaturalness of this animation into the text.

However, this is precisely the point: we are not supposed to do so. Following the textual instructions directing our reading reduces the paradoxical, metaleptic quality of the event considerably. Already at the paratextual threshold of this Gothic novel a strategy of naturalization by means of quasi-scientific explanation is initiated, starting with the reference to the experimentations with "galvanism" by "Dr Darwin" in Mary Shelley's "Author's Introduction" of 1831 (263).[19] This strategy is then continued in the description of Frankenstein's preparatory studies and activities in the main text. As a result of these attempts at 'scientifically' explaining the central event, *Frankenstein* is commonly also viewed as one of the first instances of science fiction besides being classified as a Gothic novel.

19. P. B. Shelley, in the "Preface" in which he assumes his wife's voice, also takes up this strategy, albeit in an ambivalent way: "The event on which this fiction is founded has been supposed, by Dr Darwin, and some of the physiological writers of Germany, as not of impossible occurrence. I shall not be supposed as according the remotest degree of serious faith to such an imagination" (Shelley 267).

Admittedly, the generic extracompositional frame of science fiction was not yet established in 1818 and thus—contrary to the later historical development—cannot yet be adduced as an additional factor eliciting immersion-compatibility. However, what already existed in 1818 was the generic frame of Gothic fiction, a genre that had emerged with Horace Walpole's *The Castle of Otranto* in 1765. As is well known, this genre is focused on strongly eliciting specific emotions, in particular suspense, fear, and terror (or horror). It is thus predestined for unfolding strategies that overrule the anti-immersive effect of 'impossible' representations as occurring in metalepses by integrating them into the genre-specific strangeness of the represented storyworlds as well as by strongly appealing to readers' emotions so that the essentially intellectual operation of comparing represented phenomena with real-life notions of probability and possibility is suppressed. This is what also happens at the very moment of the 'metaleptic' coming to life of the monster: the scene is narrated in gruesome tones, with the setting of "a dreary night of November" (318) providing the appropriate atmosphere. Again a 'reception figure' prefigures the intended emotional reader-reaction: Frankenstein's "horror" (319), initially such a strong emotion that it can only be transmitted by the topos of unspeakability ("How can I describe my emotions at this catastrophe [. . .]?" [318]). Clearly, such emotional loading, in combination with the aforementioned naturalizing strategy and generic expectations, renders the entire scene fully compatible with aesthetic illusion. One may even claim that the accomplishment of the monster's animation intensifies immersion—a graphic illustration of the fact that the seeming unnaturalness of what formally may be classified as an instance of metalepsis depends in its pro- or counter-immersive effect very much on intracompositional conditions, in particular on strategies of naturalization employed in the text, on emotionality, as well as on extracompositional generic frames.

'Scientific' explanation is, of course, not the only possibility for naturalizing metalepsis and taming its anti-immersive potential. A 'safety-bracket' in this respect, which is well known and figures as number 1 in Alber's "reading [unnatural] events as internal states," is intracompositional framing by dreams. This is what generally naturalizes the impossible in the dreamlands of Lewis Carroll's Alice stories, in particular the notorious epistemological metalepsis in chapter IV, "Tweedledum and Tweedledee," of *Through the Looking-Glass*. Here Tweedledee claims that Alice is only "a sort of thing in [the Red King's] dream" (Carroll 238) and that therefore Alice is "not real" (239). This amounts to an epistemological metalepsis: a hypodiegetic character (Tweedledee) claims that another hypodiegetic character (Alice inhabiting her dream) depends on the dream of yet a third hypodiegetic character (the Red

King): Alice thus appears to have paradoxically acquired a hypo-hypodiegetic status while 'in reality' being a hypodiegetic imagination of diegetic Alice's dream. Yet in dreams all sorts of impossibilities may 'naturally' happen, and this naturalization neutralizes the anti-immersive effect that metalepses such as this one would otherwise produce.[20]

Linked with this kind of naturalization qua 'internal states' is the possibility of intracompositionally relegating the unnaturalness of metalepsis to embedded fictional texts (variants of artistic 'dreams'). An interesting case in point because of its ambivalence is Flann O'Brien's experimental novel *At Swim-Two-Birds* (1939). In this almost proto-postmodernist metanovel, characters of a hypo-hypodiegetic level profit from the sleep of their hypodiegetic author, which allows them to free themselves and thus perform an ascending metalepsis. Since all of this happens in an embedded novel, introduced as part of the "spare-time literary activities" (9) of a Dublin student, one could argue that it does not harm the credibility and immersive potential of the framing story per se, which by way of contrast with the manifest fictionality of the embedded stories may even appear to be particularly credible. However, while this would be true if one removes these metalepses from their context, a rather different effect is more likely if one takes the milieu and its general metareferential function into account. As the entire text is to an extraordinary degree shot through with metareferentiality that constantly and critically lays bare fictionality and the conventions of narrative, aesthetic illusion is hardly permitted to establish itself in the first place, nor is there a sufficiently powerful emotional or suspense-related pull to override the reader's distance. Thus we have the curious instance of factors pulling in different directions: while the possibility of naturalizing the narrated metalepses between various hypodiegetic levels defuses the unnaturalness and may in principle serve to block their anti-immersive potential, the unemotional, 'brainy' metareferential context of the novel as a whole favors distance. All in all, the metalepses in question not only clearly function as instances of implicit metareference but also contribute to the anti-illusionist effect of the entire novel: in conformity with the antimimetic and moreover anti-illusionist aesthetic of the Dublin student-author, these metalepses fulfill the self-critical function of exposing the entire novel as a "self-evident sham" peopled by "illusory characters" (25).

20. Carroll's metalepsis is, however, not as harmless as it may seem at first sight, for it, so to speak, 'spills over' from the hypodiegetic to the diegetic level when Alice wakes up and at the end of the concluding chapter, characteristically titled "Which dreamed it?" is no longer sure about her true ontological status to the extent that the narrator feels compelled to directly confront the reader with the problem, leading the novel to a concluding question "Which do *you* think it was!" (344); for more details on this metalepsis and the general metareferential implications of the Alice stories see Wolf, "Lewis Carrolls 'Alice'-Geschichten."

A factor that is at least as important as the intracompositional conditions surrounding a given metalepsis are the extracompositional framing conditions. These include not only generic frames, which could already be seen at work in *Frankenstein* and with which we will be concerned again presently, but also extracompositional epistemic and cultural-historical frames. This brings us back to the second of my initial examples, the assumed historical scenario of a recital of the Pygmalion myth in ancient Greece. For the sake of argument let us suppose that the audience is an archaic one whose epistemic frame and corresponding worldview admit the possibility of gods intervening in human affairs as well as the ontological instability of objects, plants, animals, and persons that may be metamorphosed into shapes and beings located on other levels of, to use a later concept, the Great Chain of Being. Clearly, for such an audience, a narrative about a beautiful statue changing into a beautiful woman as a result of the graceful intervention of a goddess would not constitute a breach of the possible. While such a metamorphosis would perhaps not actually be conceived of as 'natural' in the sense of something that 'might happen every day' even by our archaic audience, it would be neither unnatural nor paradoxical for them. As a consequence, if for us today the transformation of a representational artifact into a living being and thus the crossing of the border between hypodiegetic fiction and diegetic 'reality' would technically constitute a metalepsis, it would arguably not be conceived in such a way by the contemporaries of our scenario (had they a concept such as metalepsis at their disposal). In fact the metaleptic quality of the event would not appear since the defining feature of paradoxicality would be lacking. As a further consequence, any immersive quality that the narration, perhaps owing to the performative skills of the rhapsode, may possess would not be impaired by the recounting of the metaleptic metamorphosis. Nor does Ovid's text betray a reception figure's marked incredulity of the kind "this is impossible!" In Ovid's discourse there is no more than a mere remark amounting to the fact that Pygmalion is happily overwhelmed by what has happened: "dum stupet et timide gaudet fallique veretur" ("The lover stands amazed, rejoices still in doubt, fears he is mistaken" [Ovid 85]). If Pygmalion is 'stupefied,' he is so because he can hardly believe his luck, not because the metamorphosis he is about to experience is in principle impossible to his way of thinking; and if he is afraid that this may be deception, this fear is again not linked to a categorical impossibility of what he after all feels with his own hands—his rigid, cool statue having acquired the malleability and warmth of living flesh—but rather testifies to an awareness that senses and wishful thinking may conjure up irrealities. So even Ovid's written form of the myth pays tribute to the fact that in myth such miraculous transformations are part of the possible rather than the unnatural.[21] It therefore does not disturb immersion, all the more so since in Ovid's version of the Pygmalion myth in his *Metamorphoses* the story is set in an intracompositional literary context in which 'miraculous' metamorphoses abound as a consequence of the fact that 'mythical transformation' forms a main unifying element of the text as a whole; the metamorphosis of the statue is therefore not unnatural but rather obeys an expected pattern within a textual frame in which special 'laws' apply.

To come back to epistemic frames as part of certain worldviews that are apt to permit a compatibility of metalepsis and immersion: in this context one should also mention medieval religious drama, for in this text type a device that is classifiable as epistemic metalepsis frequently occurs: *ad spectatores* or *parabasis*. In technical terms it consists of an 'unnatural' awareness of the existence of spectators on the part of characters and thus of a contamination between the world of representation and the represented world. However, in its original context, this kind of drama is conceived of as a reenactment of truths that are relevant to, and co-present in, the represented world as well as the audience's reality. As a consequence, the formally metaleptic quality of *ad spectatores*, in particular when focusing on religious or moral instruction, presumably did not (yet) lead to an anti-immersive effect (let alone a breaking of aesthetic illusion, a concept whose existence cannot be assumed for this type of text and cultural frame [cf. Wolf, "Shakespeare" 282])—no less than the many anachronisms that can also be observed in medieval drama. Rather, it may even have contributed to consolidating a community under religious auspices (cf. Hacker 261).

What in the case of an alleged preliterary Pygmalion story as well as in medieval religious drama may phylogenetically be classified as an early, archaic mythical or religious worldview that permits immersion-compatible metalepsis has certain ontogenetic parallels in the as yet unsophisticated worldview of children. For them, too, 'absurd' or impossible events may well fall into the realm of the acceptable. It is therefore no coincidence that illusion-compatible metalepses also occur in children's literature (e.g., the animation of a wooden jumping jack in Carlo Collodi's fairy tale *Le avventure di Pinocchio* [1881–83]) or all-age 'fantasy' fiction parading as such (cf. Klimek, "Metalepsis and Its (Anti-)Illusionist Effects" 181–83).

If the compatibility of metalepsis and immersion both in archaic myths and modern fantasy and children's fiction is largely an effect of certain extra-

---

21. For those among Ovid's contemporary readers for whom such a metamorphosis on the basis of a mythical worldview would no longer be acceptable, the reminiscence of such a worldview in conjunction with the awareness of the frame 'literature' or 'fiction' would arguably have contributed to the same immersion-friendly effect.

compositional epistemic frames, such a compatibility may also stem from the other extracompositional frame that has already been mentioned: generic conventions. Michael Ende's *Die unendliche Geschichte* (1979), a fantasy novel (parading as children's literature while in reality also appealing to adults), is a good case in point. Admittedly, the text of the initial chapters of this novel structured along the lines of an extended frame tale reads like a realistic novel. However, the paratexts (the cover illustration depicting, in the German paperback edition, an ouroboros circling an idyllic scene with an alley leading to an ebony tower amidst meadows and woods in which unicorns jump around) and the 'fantastic' initials that open all chapters dedicated to the hypodiegetic novel are sufficiently strong generic markers to indicate the genre fantasy right from the beginning.

The novel, which besides being fantasy fiction is also a metafictional allegory celebrating the salutary immersive and imaginative power of literature, is full of genuine metalepses. The first occurs when the diegetic hero Sebastian Bux, reader of the novel within the novel entitled "Die unendliche Geschichte," in a nice *mise en abyme* of reading effects, is himself so immersed in an adventure of the hypodiegetic Atreju being attacked by an evil spider that he utters a cry of terror. Paradoxically, this cry also resounds in the hypodiegetic world Phantásia and is immediately registered by its discourse so that Bastian is able to read about it and characteristically wonders: "'Sollte es am Ende mein Schrei gewesen sein, den sie [die Spinne] gehört hat?' dachte Bastian zutiefst beunruhigt. 'Aber das ist doch überhaupt nicht möglich'" (Ende, *Die unendliche Geschichte* 81).[22] Bastian here functions as yet another 'reception figure' documenting the unnaturalness of metalepsis by his reaction of disbelief. Yet to argue that at this point the real reader's 'suspension of disbelief' is terminated would be to entirely misjudge the effect of this metalepsis. For, when it occurs, the generic frame 'fantasy' has sufficiently been established not only by means of paratextual illustrations but also by the embedded novel, a highly fantastic narrative about an empire threatened by an increasing lack of readers' interest in *Fantasie* (imagination) that occupies 90 percent of the entire book. As a consequence, the reader learns to accept so many 'impossible things' (the unicorn on the framing cover functioning as a nice foreshadowing or '*mise en cadre*')[23] that this metalepsis would at best produce a mildly startling effect. Therefore, the wonder (echoing Bastian's) that readers will feel is arguably less prone to be metareferentially resolved by jumping out of the fictional world

22. "'Could it [the spider] have heard my cry?' Bastian wondered in alarm. 'But that's not possible'" (Ende, *The Neverending Story* 77).

23. For framings functioning as the reverse of *mise en abyme*, a device I have termed '*mise en cadre*'; see Wolf, "*Mise en cadre*."

and considering the entire event from this extratextual vantage point as a mere fiction, thus destroying aesthetic illusion. Rather, this emotional reaction will immerse readers more deeply in the storyworld—by kindling their interest in the outcome not only of the adventure with the spider but also of the contact that has apparently been established between the diegetic and the hypodiegetic worlds by means of an epistemological metalepsis.

The mildly startling effect produced by Bastian's metaleptic cry is repeated in the second instance of an as yet epistemological metalepsis, namely when a hypodiegetic character gazes at a magic mirror representing diegetic Bastian, a fact that is again commented on by the boy: "Es war doch überhaupt nicht möglich, daß in einem gedruckten Buch etwas stehen konnte, was nur in diesem Augenblick und nur für ihn zutraf" (*Die unendliche Geschichte* 115).[24] Shortly after this, another metalepsis occurs which consists in the curious fact that Bastian's will begins to clearly influence events in Phantásia. Arguably because both Bastian and the readers are beginning to become used to the repeated metalepses, this 'impossibility' is no longer accompanied by markers of 'unnaturalness' from the reception figure Bastian. However, such markers turn up again ("Bastian erschrak"[25] [184]) when some pages later the metaleptic direction is reverted from a descending one (leap from diegetic to hypodiegetic level) to an ascending one (leap in the opposite direction): Bastian suddenly sees the face of the Kindliche Kaiserin, the Childlike Empress, the ruler of Phantásia, appear in the garret where he is reading about this hypodiegetic character. However, this astonishment is once again not exploited for the purpose of undermining immersion; rather, it induces Bastian (and with him the actual reader) to continue reading, if possible more avidly (cf. 185). After this it hardly comes as a surprise that characters in Phantásia start to reckon with Bastian as part of their own storyworld ("Ob er es weiß oder nicht—er gehört jetzt schon zur Unendlichen Geschichte" [197]).[26] What still elicits some wonder in both Bastian ("Bastians Gedanken verwirrten sich" [208])[27] and the real reader is the fact that leading hypodiegetic characters including the Kindliche Kaiserin consult an old man ("[den] Alten vom Wandernden Berge" [206]),[28] who turns out to be engaged in another epistemological metalepsis: he is supposedly the author not only of "Die unendliche

---

24. "How could there be something in a book that applied only to this particular moment and only to him?" (Ende, *The Neverending Story* 106).

25. "Bastian gave a start" (Ende, *The Neverending Story* 169).

26. "'Whether he knows it or not, he is already part of the Neverending Story'" (Ende, *The Neverending Story* 180).

27. "Bastian's thoughts were in a whirl" (Ende, *The Neverending Story* 192).

28. "[the] Old Man of Wandering Mountain" (Ende, *The Neverending Story* 189).

Geschichte" *mise en abyme* but of the framing novel as well (cf. 208–16). Interestingly, the recounting of the old man's writing threatens to become an endless *mise en abyme,* since it contains the act of reading the story up to the point where the Kindliche Kaiserin meets the old man. At this point Bastian decides to interfere and jumps into the hypodiegetic novel (see 216). This is actually the most impossible metalepsis, a classic case of 'descending' ontological metalepsis, but at this point the markers of impossibility and even of wonder cease—arguably a sign that even the last traces of an anti-immersive potential of metalepsis have miraculously vanished.

However, this vanishing is not so miraculous after all. It is an effect primarily of the generic frame 'fantasy' which shapes the readers' expectations so that they accept 'impossibilities' more readily. In addition, the text is written in a serious mood and is full of suspense, all of which increases the readers' emotional engagement while at the same time decreasing their readiness to metareferentially distance themselves from the fascinating storyworld(s).

The combined workings of generic frames and emotional tone can also be observed in drama with reference to the occurrence and effect of the aforementioned device of *parabasis* or *ad spectatores.* It is no coincidence that, as a rule, tragedy shuns *ad spectatores* and thus avoids endangering the audience's emotional involvement, while comedy sports *ad spectatores* much more frequently. In comedy, the effect of *parabasis* is often enough the reduction of dramatic illusion and immersion. However, if this reduction is not total, this may again be due to the workings of a generic frame: *ad spectatores* is after all a frequent and thus expected device in comedy. When it occurs in laughing comedy in particular it may in addition create or reinforce a 'carnivalesque' (*sensu* Bakhtin) community between audience and the stage world. This community is different from 'immersion' as the imaginary participation in a represented world as explained in section 2, but still it remains a noteworthy kind of contact between two worlds.

Yet another condition must be mentioned which also contributes to defusing the anti-immersive potential of metalepsis: habituation. Remarkably, the metalepses of *Die unendliche Geschichte* are introduced according to a pattern of intensification (from various forms of epistemological to ontological metalepsis), but this also means that the potentially startling effect of Bastian's culminatory ontological leap into Phantásia is counteracted by the multiplicity of half a dozen preparatory ('merely' epistemological) metalepses, so that the scandal of this unnaturalness is considerably weakened (in this, one need not even take recourse to an allegorical 'naturalization' *sensu* Alber). Habituation is indeed an important factor, fueled by both intracompositional and extracompositional repetition, when it comes to assessing metalepses in fantasy, postmodernist literature, and other media:[29] in fact, metalepses have become such frequent devices that, inevitably, the occurrence of yet another instance of this increasingly well-known phenomenon can certainly no longer muster the effect of 'scandalous' unnaturalness it may have had in former times. As a consequence, one would be inclined to say that such habituation reduces if not destroys the anti-immersive effect of metalepsis, were it not for the fact that the immersive quality of aesthetic illusion is often not sought after in postmodernist literature and art in the first place, especially not in its radically experimental variants. Yet there is also a 'muted' variant of postmodernism in which relatively traditional storytelling is combined with metareferentiality and forms double-layered works that can cater to different readers and expectations. There, habituation is certainly a relevant factor that discernibly tunes down the unnatural as well as its anti-immersive effects in an at least partially illusionist context. The compatibility of metalepsis and immersion resulting from habitation in muted postmodernism may already be observed, within the narrow confines of a short story, in "The Kugelmass Episode," in which the crossing of an ontological border is effected not once but repeatedly; it is even more discernible in contemporary novels such as Jasper Fforde's *The Eyre Affair* (2001), in which a machine similar to that of the magician's in Woody Allen's story repeatedly allows characters to enter hypodiegetic fictional worlds of literary texts.

5. Toward a Poetics of (Un)naturalness

What does all of this amount to? Metalepsis as a particularly clear case of unnaturalness and the varying immersion-relevant effects it may have in different circumstances provide a revealing case study for a poetics of (un)naturalness. When mentioning a 'poetics of (un)naturalness' as a part of—in the context of the present essay—narratology and a theory of aesthetic illusion, one should, however, make clear right from the start that what is at issue is not a new, 'unnatural narratology' as has recently been suggested (cf. Richardson; Alber, Iversen, Nielsen, and Richardson) but an extension or modification of existing theory. One should also be aware that in this the traditional categories, including those that are modeled on 'mimetic' narratives and what in Western culture has been regarded as 'natural' for a considerable time, cannot be suspended or rejected altogether but must be used as a necessary back-

---

29. Habituation is all the more important in this historical context since, as Richardson has emphasized, postmodernist (as well as modernist) literature is generally prone to produce 'extreme' and unnatural forms of narration.

ground against which the 'unnatural' can be perceived and described in the first place. The abolishing of 'natural' categories would entail abolishing the description of the 'unnatural' as well. In this concluding section some elements of such a complementary poetics of unnaturalness shall tentatively be extrapolated from the preceding case study, building blocks that derive from what has been said so far. This concerns in particular the following results:

1. The natural and the unnatural (such as metalepsis) and their reception-theoretical effects must always be conceived of as a co-production of several factors of communication; apart from the 'message' (the text or artifact where the phenomenon under discussion occurs) these include in particular the extracompositional factors of the given epistemological cultural context as well as those of specific generic conventions framing the work under discussion.
2. As a consequence, the natural and the unnatural are not stable, transhistorical, and transcultural essences but historically and culturally variable; this gives these categories a slippery nature and makes them difficult to handle, in particular when it comes to discussing texts and artifacts from outside present Western culture.
3. Similarly, there is no clear one-to-one relationship between what formally may be classified as unnatural and specific effects such as defamiliarization, the prevention of immersion or the breaking of aesthetic illusion; at best one may assume a certain tendency as a starting point or reception-theoretical hypothesis, in particular a marked anti-immersive or illusion-breaking potential of 'unnatural' devices such as metalepsis.
4. However, the extent to which this theoretical potential is actualized in given cases (and in particular the actual impossibility of naturalization in the narrow sense) depends on a variety of 'filter factors' that may apply individually or jointly and sometimes even pull in different directions. As far as extracompositional factors are concerned, see above, number 1; as far as intracompositional factors are concerned, the following may contribute to an assessment of the effects of unnaturalness as embodied in metalepsis:

    • the degree of affiliation a given work or artifact assumes with reference to dominant cultural frames and to well-known generic conventions (see also above, nos. 1 and 2): generic frames such as fantasy, science fiction, or children's literature can defuse the unnatural;

- the existence of intracompositional elements that can render the seemingly unnatural plausible, that is, explicable as a result of the workings of science and technology or as dreams, magic, or as parts of hypodiegetic texts or fantasies (sometimes in combination with specific generic frames);
- the degree of emotional involvement (including suspense) elicited in the context of the unnatural occurrence: a high degree can also neutralize the anti-immersive potential of the unnatural;
- in conjunction with the presence or absence of a strong emotional appeal: the general mood (serious or comic) of a given work; seriousness favors immersive 'adhesion' since it is frequently combined with a strong emotional involvement and therefore can counteract the defamiliarizing effect of devices such as metalepsis, while the comic tends to loosen the immersive relationship, thus generally facilitating or favoring anti-immersive effects (at the same time, the comic can produce a carnivalesque community effect, which can also reduce the felt unnaturalness of, for example, metaleptic parabasis);
- a variant of the 'general mood' may also be the given or absent tendency towards metareferentiality in a particular work; a high degree of metareferentiality may reduce the recipients' immersion so that when unnaturalness occurs it does so in a context that facilitates a further reduction of immersion, perhaps even a reading of the unnatural as a means of implicit metaization (a foregrounding of the fictionality of the work in question)[30] which would break the aesthetic illusion;
- where the unnatural fulfills a metareferential function the specificity of this function may also play a role in the overall effect: where metareferential unnaturalness is (self)critical of the representationality of the work in question it will reduce immer-

---

30. The following should be noted, though: theoretically, a prevailing metareferential milieu promotes anti-illusionism and therefore should actually reinforce the disturbing effect of metalepsis when it occurs, since metalepsis itself is in principle a form of implicit metareference. Yet this milieu may be overruled by other factors such as emotional involvement. This can, for instance, be observed in Ende's *Die unendliche Geschichte*. Its general metafictionality, while remarkable enough, is, however, not strong enough to provide a sufficiently anti-immersive milieu for the several metalepses to function as obstacles to immersion. For the novel is engaging in terms of suspense and emotions such as empathy to such a degree that the distancing effect of both the metareferential milieu and the metalepses is neutralized. In contrast to this, the equally general metareferentiality of *At Swim-Two-Birds* does promote the anti-immersive effect of the metalepses because, as stated above, this novel does not lure the reader emotionally into its storyworld.

sion, while in the case of metareferential unnaturalness that in some way contributes to praising or supporting aspects and qualities of the work in question, the contrary effect may be produced;[31]
- the degree of habituation resulting from repeated occurrences of the unnatural within the work or text in question: as with high emotional involvement, here, too, a high degree may mitigate the effect of unnaturalness.[32]

5. Sometimes the existence of intracompositional 'reception figures' mirroring intended reader responses may be used as indicators of unnaturalness (or the absence of it); however, as we have seen, these signs are not always reliable, since other factors, in particular the aforementioned 'filter factors,' may yield different results.

Assessing the (probable) effect of individual metalepses—and something similar may be claimed for unnaturalness in general—thus turns out to be a complicated multistage affair. The starting point will always be the hypothesis that a given metalepsis (or unnaturalness in general for that matter) has a potentially defamiliarizing and/or anti-immersive effect. However, before one rushes to conclusions, the parameters mentioned in the foregoing discussion must be taken into account. One must, for instance, ask whether certain epistemic, cultural, or generic contexts may neutralize the hypothesized effect, and/or whether certain intracompositional filter factors may work in a similar immersion-compatible way. In addition, the existence and reactions of reception figures should also be considered. Only when none of this yields indications that a given metalepsis (unnaturalness) is in some way neutralized may one safely assume that it will unfold its 'native' anti-immersive potential.

As a consequence of all this, the question forming the title of this essay, "'unnatural' metalepsis and immersion—necessarily incompatible?" can now clearly be answered in the negative. There are, as we have seen, cases in which

31. Cf., for example, the contrast between *At Swim-Two-Birds*, in which metareference including metalepsis as an implicit variant undermines the representationality and credibility of the novel, and *Die unendliche Geschichte*, in which Bastian's 'impossible' entry into Phantásia is an implicitly metareferential allegory of the fascination exercised by both the embedded "unendliche Geschichte" and literature in general and in which metareference and metalepses thus ultimately serve to reinforce immersion.

32. To a certain extent these 'filter factors' correspond to the 'additional factors' regulating the effect of metafiction that I have detailed elsewhere (Wolf, *Ästhetische Illusion* 256–57; 472–74): plausibility (→ naturalization); position in the text; frequency (→ habituation); saliency, extension, and the content of the metareferential reflection (whether, for example, aggressively laying bare the fictionality of the work in question or claiming authenticity for it).

the unnaturalness of metalepsis appears to be compatible with immersion and aesthetic illusion, and hence there is not a necessary incompatibility in all cases. Having said this, one must, on the other hand, put this result into perspective: since the central question of this contribution was formulated in this particular way, the focus was automatically on 'exceptions.' What remained outside the focus was the fact that the majority of metalepses may still be regarded as following the hypothesis that unnaturalness produces defamiliarization and, as a consequence, may obstruct or even disrupt immersion. It is the task of research to constantly question its own assumptions and generalizations. The claim that metalepsis has a "strong anti-illusionist effect" as a "common function," which I myself have voiced (Wolf, "Metalepsis as a Transgeneric and Transmedial Phenomenon" 101), belongs to those generalizations. It may still be said to apply to the majority of cases (testing this, at least for contemporary recipients, would form a further research project), but, as Klimek is quite right in suggesting ("Metalepsis and Its (Anti)Illusionist Effects" 184), it is a generalization that must be relativized—at least for a noteworthy minority of cases.

Works Cited

Alber, Jan. "The Diachronic Development of Unnaturalness: A New View of Genre." In *Unnatural Narratives, Unnatural Narratology*, ed. Jan Alber and Rüdiger Heinze. Berlin and New York: de Gruyter, 2011. 41–67.

———. "Impossible Storyworlds—And What to Do with Them." *Storyworlds* 1 (2009): 79–96.

———. "Unnatural Narratives." *The Literary Encyclopedia*. 2009. http://www.letencyc/php/stopics.php?rec=true&UID=7202.

Alber, Jan, Steven Iversen, Henrik Skov Nielsen, and Brian Richardson. "Unnatural Narratives, Unnatural Narratology: Beyond Mimetic Models." *Narrative* 18.2 (2010): 113–36.

Allen, Woody. "The Kugelmass Episode." In *Woody Allen: Complete Prose*. London: Picador, 1997. 345–60.

———. *The Purple Rose of Cairo*. 1985. In *Woody Allen: Three Films: Zelig, Broadway Danny Rose, The Purple Rose of Cairo*. London: Faber and Faber, 1987. 317–473.

Beckett, Samuel. *Happy Days*. 1961. *Samuel Beckett: Dramatische Dichtungen in drei Sprachen*. Frankfurt a. M.: Suhrkamp, 1981. 146–232.

Bergson, Henri. *Laughter: An Essay on the Meaning of the Comic*. 1899. Transl. Cloudesely Brereton and Fred Rothwell. Rockville, MD: Arc Manor, 2008.

———. *Le Rire: Essai sur la signification du comique*. 1899. Paris: Presses universitaires de France, 1975.

Carroll, Lewis. *The Annotated Alice: Alice's Adventures in Wonderland* and *Through the Looking-Glass*. 1865/1872, ed. Martin Gardner. Harmondsworth: Penguin, 1970.

Cuddon, J. A. *The Penguin Dictionary of Literary Terms and Literary Theory*. 1976. Rev. C. E. Preston. Harmondsworth: Penguin, 1999.

Culler, Jonathan. *Structuralist Poetics: Structuralism, Linguistics and the Study of Literature.* London: Routledge & Kegan Paul, 1975.
Döpp, Sigmar. "Narrative Metalepsen und andere Illusionsdurchbrechungen: Das spätantike Beispiel Martianus Capella." In *Millennium 6/2009: Jahrbuch zur Kultur und Geschichte des ersten Jahrtausends n. Chr.*, ed. Wolfram Brandes et al. Berlin: de Gruyter, 2009. 203–21.
Ende, Michael. *Die unendliche Geschichte.* Munich: Heyne, 1979.
———. *The Neverending Story.* Transl. Ralph Manheim. New York: Penguin, 1983.
Fludernik, Monika. "Naturalizing the Unnatural: A View from Blending Theory." *Journal of Literary Semantics* 39.1 (2010): 1–27.
———. *Towards a "Natural" Narratology.* London and New York: Routledge, 1996.
Foucault, Michel. *Les Mots et les choses: Une archéologie des sciences humaines.* Paris: Gallimard, 1966.
Genette, Gérard. "De la figure à la fiction." In Pier and Schaeffer eds., *Métalepses: Entorses au pacte de la représentation*, 21–35.
———. *Figures III.* Paris: Seuil, 1972.
———. *Métalepse: De la figure à la fiction.* Paris: Seuil, 2004.
———. *Narrative Discourse: An Essay in Method.* Ithaca, NY: Cornell University Press, 1980.
Hacker, Hans-Jürgen. *Zur Poetologie des mittelalterlichen Dramas.* Heidelberg: Winter, 1985.
Herman, David. "Toward a Formal Description of Narrative Metalepsis." *Journal of Literary Semantics* 26 (1997): 132–52.
Klimek, Sonja. "Metalepsis and Its (Anti-)Illusionist Effects in the Arts, Media and Role-Playing Games." In *Metareference across Media: Theory and Case Studies—Dedicated to Walter Bernhart on the Occasion of His Retirement*, ed. Werner Wolf in collaboration with Katharina Bantleon and Jeff Thoss. Amsterdam and New York: Rodopi, 2009. 169–87.
———. *Paradoxes Erzählen: Die Metalepse in der phantastischen Literatur.* Paderborn: Mentis, 2010.
LaGrandeur, Kevin. "The Talking Brass Head as a Symbol of Dangerous Knowledge in *Friar Bacon* and in *Alphonsus, King of Aragon.*" *English Studies* 5 (1999): 408–22.
Martin, Diester. "Pygmalion." In *Mythenrezeption: Die antike Mythologie in Literatur, Musik und Kunst von den Anfängen bis zur Gegenwart*, ed. Maria Moog-Grünewald. Stuttgart: Wissenschaftliche Buchgesellschaft, 2008. 631–40.
Nelles, William. "Stories within Stories: Narrative Levels and Embedded Narrative." *Studies in the Literary Imagination* 25.1 (1992): 79–96.
O'Brien, Flann. *At Swim-Two-Birds.* 1939. Harmondsworth: Penguin, 1967.
Ovid. *Metamorphoses.* 10. With an English translation by Frank Justus Miller. 2 vols. London: Heinemann; Cambridge, MA: Harvard University Press, 1968.
Pier, John. "Métalepse et hierarchies narratives." In Pier and Schaeffer, eds., *Métalepses: Entorses au pacte de la représentation*, 247–61.
———. "Metalepsis." In *Handbook of Narratology*, ed. John Pier, Wolf Schmid, Jörg Schönert, and Peter Hühn. Berlin and New York: de Gruyter, 2009. 190–203.
Pier, John, and Jean-Marie Schaeffer, eds. *Métalepses: Entorses au pacte de la représentation.* Paris: Ecole des Hautes Etudes en Sciences Sociales, 2005.
Richardson, Brian. *Unnatural Voices: Extreme Narration in Modern and Contemporary Fiction.* Columbus: The Ohio State University Press, 2006.
Ricoeur, Paul. *Temps et récit.* 3 vols. Paris: Seuil, 1983.
Ryan, Marie-Laure. *Avatars of Story.* Minneapolis: University of Minnesota Press, 2006.
———. "Metaleptic Machines." *Semiotica* 150 (2004): 439–69.

———. *Possible Worlds, Artificial Intelligence and Narrative Theory*. Bloomington: Indiana University Press, 1991.
Schaeffer, Jean-Marie. "Métalepse et immersion fictionnelle." In Pier and Schaeffer, eds., *Métalepses: Entorses au pacte de la représentation*, 323–34.
Shelley, Mary. "Frankenstein." In *Three Gothic Novels*, ed. Peter Fairclough. Harmondsworth: Penguin, 1968. 257–497.
Stoichita, Victor I. *The Pygmalion Effect: From Ovid to Hitchcock*. Transl. Alison Anderson. Chicago and London: University of Chicago Press, 2008.
Thoss, Jeff. "Unnatural Narrative and Metalepsis: Grant Morrison's *Animal Man*." In *Unnatural Narratives, Unnatural Narratology*, ed. Jan Alber and Rüdiger Heinze. Berlin and New York: de Gruyter, 2011. 189–209.
———. *Metalepsis in Contemporary Popular Fiction, Film, and Comics*. Unpublished PhD Thesis, University of Graz, 2012.
Wagner, Frank. "Glissements et déphasages: Note sur la métalepse narrative." *Poétique* 130 (2002): 235–53.
Wolf, Werner. "Aesthetic illusion." In *Immersion and Distance: Aesthetic Illusion in Literature and Other Media*, ed. Werner Wolf, Walter Bernhart, and Andreas Mahler. Amsterdam: Rodopi, 2013. 1–62.
———. *Ästhetische Illusion und Illusionsdurchbrechung in der Erzählkunst: Theorie und Geschichte mit Schwerpunkt auf englischem illusionsstörenden Erzählen*. Tübingen: Niemeyer, 1993.
———. "Defamiliarized Initial Framings in Fiction." In *Framing Borders in Literature and Other Media*, ed. Werner Wolf and Walter Bernhart. Amsterdam: Rodopi, 2006. 295–328.
———. "Illusion (Aesthetic)." In *Handbook of Narratology*, ed. John Pier, Wolf Schmid, Jörg Schönert, and Peter Hühn. Berlin and New York: de Gruyter, 2009. 144–60.
———. "Lewis Carrolls 'Alice'-Geschichten als sprach- und erkenntniskritische Metafiktionen: Ein Beitrag zur Geschichte des metafiktionalen Romans im 19. Jahrhundert." *Germanisch-Romanische Monatsschrift* 37 (1987): 423–46.
———. "Metalepsis as a Transgeneric and Transmedial Phenomenon: A Case Study of the Possibilities of 'Exporting' Narratological Concepts." In *Narratology Beyond Literary Criticism: Mediality, Disciplinarity*, ed. Jan Christoph Meister in cooperation with Tom Kindt and Wilhelm Schernus. Berlin and New York: de Gruyter, 2005. 83–107.
———. "Metareference across Media: The Concept, its Transmedial Potentials and Problems, Main Forms and Functions." In *Metareference across Media: Theory and Case Studies— Dedicated to Walter Bernhart on the Occasion of his Retirement*, ed. Werner Wolf in collaboration with Katharina Bantleon and Jeff Thoss. Amsterdam and New York: Rodopi, 2009. 1–85.
———. "*Mise en cadre*—A Neglected Counterpart to *mise en abyme*: A Frame-Theoretical Supplement to Classical Narratology." In *Postclassical Narratology: Approaches and Analyses*, ed. Jan Alber and Monika Fludernik. Columbus: The Ohio State University Press, 2010. 58–82.
———. "Shakespeare und die Entstehung ästhetischer Illusion im englischen Drama." *Germanisch-Romanische Monatsschrift* 43 (1993). 279–301.

Realism and the Unnatural

MARIA MÄKELÄ

Realism, in this study, [. . .] refers to the illusionistic evocation of a verisimilar fictional reality whose convincing presentation correlates particularly with psychological or motivational verisimilitude.

—Fludernik, *Towards* 131

[. . .] reality is neither the subject nor the object of true art which creates its own special reality having nothing to do with the average "reality" perceived by the communal eye.

—Nabokov, *Pale Fire* 106

1. Introduction

How to recover the unnatural essence of the *conventional* in narrative fiction? The emergent trend of unnatural narratology has drawn its impetus mostly from the strikingly transgressive, illogical, or antimimetic elements of narrative construction (Richardson *Unnatural Voices*; Alber; Alber, Iversen, Nielsen, and Richardson). Consequently, texts that have established the firm ground of literary conventions—such as classical realist novels—have been playing the part of default narratives in their representational design as well as in their experiential parameters. I take this collection of essays to be an opportunity to demonstrate that narratives under the heading of realism may even have *more* narratologically transgressive potential than the manifestly antiexperiential or antinarrative extremes. The approach sketched in this essay may not, however, be as much against the unnatural grain as it might first appear, since the common aim remains the same: to contest—through theory-defying examples—the homogenizing side effects of much contemporary narratology.

VIKTOR SHKLOVSKY, the Russian formalist and the eminent hero of classical narratologists, left us with an ambiguous concept, estrangement (*ostranenie*). Is art supposed to defamiliarize us from our experience of life or from conventional modes of representation? Or even a trickier question: to what extent do the conventions of representation affect our perception of life? At least it seems evident that life *as such*—without art—appeared to him to be an insipid series of repetitions.

> And so life is reckoned as nothing. Habitualization devours work, clothes, furniture, one's wife, and the fear of war. [. . .] And art exists that one may recover the sensation of life; it exists to make one feel things, to make the stone stony. The purpose of art is to impart the sensation of things as they are perceived and not as they are known. The technique of art is to make objects "unfamiliar," to make forms difficult, to increase the difficulty and length of perception because the process of perception is an aesthetic end in itself and must be prolonged. *Art is a way of experiencing the artfulness of an object: the object is not important.* . . . (18; italics in original)

Shklovsky's classical formulation triggers at least two possible reactions: to consider art (1) as a series of revolutions catalyzed by the avant-garde, or (2), even in its most familiar forms, as a vehicle for prolonging the leap from representation to assimilation (see Striedter 7; Holquist and Kliger 629–31). The former take is supported by the formalist notion of literary evolution, suggesting that an artistic technique, once freshly estranging, wears off quite in the manner of the charms of one's wife (or husband). Yet it seems to me that Shklovsky's above quoted impressionistic definition makes one incline toward the latter notion, to believe that also literary *conventions* "increase the difficulty and length of perception" and are thus intervening in the otherwise sluggish dialogue between our minds and our environment. Were this not the case, we should accept that a work ceases to be art once its technique becomes automatized by successors.

When Shklovsky draws our attention to the "technique of art" and to the "process of perception" at the same time, he is inviting us to the same frontier where most of the cognitive narratologists are presently camped: the fuzzy area where the meeting point of mental and literary representations should be found. This is a realm of study where the question of narrative construction concerns both the text and its reader. But after a closer look at the premises of cognitive narratology, one cannot but notice that the cognitive agenda favors familiarization over defamiliarization: instead of sticking to the materiality of the sign (to the Jakobsonian poetic function), cognitive narratologists are anxious to merge mental representations with literary ones. For instance, Manfred Jahn suggests that reading a narrative "possibly even *requires* 'deictic shifts' to imaginary co-ordinates and places" ("Focalization" 102; my italics, M.M.); or, consider Uri Margolin's stance towards fictional agents:

> [. . .] we are operating within the confines of a make-believe world, *pretending* that narrators and storyworld participants exist independently of the text which *actually* creates them via semiotic means, and that they are *sufficiently* human-like so that concepts developed in cognitive science to model the activities of actual human minds are applicable to them, *even if* only through analogical transfer. (273; my italics, M.M.)

Eager in demonstrating the general applicability of our mental narrative schemata, cognitive narratologists tend to speak of literary narratives in terms of "sense-making" (see, e.g., Alber 79–80); the reader is a navigator, the text is a map, and the target is mental assimilation (or apperception; see Jahn "Focalization"). The much favored approach to allegedly frame-breaking ("new") literary narratives is to celebrate their potential in *enriching* the mental framework of readers, the result of which is that these once transgressive texts become *naturalized;* "fiction as a genre comes to represent precisely those impossible naturalized frames and to create readerly expectations along those lines" (Fludernik, "Natural Narratology" 255; see also Alber; Fludernik "Naturalizing the Unnatural"). It seems evident that from the point of view of cognitive narratology, reading fictional narratives is all about *diminishing* the difficulties and the required time in remodeling verbal presentation into internal representation—and not the other way around as Shklovsky would have it.

The emergent trend of unnatural narratology has been extremely efficient in digging out new, even *sui generis* cases of narrative (de)construction; yet it seems to me that this is innovativeness with regard to one's corpus but not always theoretically adventurous enough. Still a demand appears to arise for some denaturalization of basic theoretical categories that shape our understanding of the reading process. On the one hand, cognitive narratology is by definition resistant to narrative contingencies since it grounds itself in *prototype* modeling: the cognitive-narratological prototype reader always opts for the most likely, the primary, and the coherent. On the other hand, as far as another dominant narratological branch, the Chicago school of rhetorical narratology, is concerned, their insistence on the situatedness of narrative communication more often than not frustrates any attempt to focus on details that might downplay the communicative situation or even make the story incommunicable.

The recent exposition of unnatural narratology by Alber, Iversen, Nielsen, and Richardson makes headway in challenging the easy analogies that have been drawn either between real-world schemata and constructed storyworlds (116–19), or between actual human agency and verbally constructed voices (119–29). Yet if we wish to challenge the idea of the narrative prototype, we should not only look for deviations but also work *within* the alleged prototype, which includes established literary conventions and narratives that Alber et al. call "ordinary realist texts" (114). Furthermore, we may remember that Fludernik's *Towards a "Natural" Narratology*, the most influential advocate for the universality of narrative frames, is introducing us not to a class of particular texts but instead to frames of reading and interpretation. Consequently, not even for Natural Narratology does there exist such a thing as a "natural novel." In fact, Fludernik herself presents us with many of the peculiarities of novelistic *vraisemblance* or synthetic verisimilitude (*Towards* 129–77). For her, the default narrative is a naturally *occurring* one—even if it is a ghost story and, as such, representing things unnatural.

In what follows I will choose a denaturalizing angle to (1) **perception;** (2) **psychological and motivational verisimilitude,** and (3) **discursive agency** in a few examples from Flaubert, Tolstoy, and Dickens. However, my central assertion is targeted less at particular novelistic modes than the diversity of *readerly frames:* I wish to demonstrate that many realist conventions are peculiarly balanced between the cognitively familiar and the cognitively estranging—and, as such, question the reader's loyalty to naturalization, to "'converting' the non-natural into a basic cognitive category" (Fludernik, "Natural Narratology" 256). Finally, I will try to sketch a fresh approach to unnatural narratology, one that would construe "the reader" not as a mere sense-making machine but as someone who might just as well opt for the improbable and the indeterminate.

2. Novelistic Perception: Detail and Disturbance

Let me start with a digression on visual art. In 2009 Jan Alber gave a visiting lecture at the University of Tampere on impossible storyworlds and their cognitive reification that started with a reference to unnatural spaces in perspective drawing. One of the mentioned artists was M. C. Escher, whose *Concave and Convex* (1955) is shown in figure 7.1—a drawing that obviously aims at irking and needling our cognitive capacity. Everything is wrong here, and yet our basic schemata concerning space, as well as perspective drawing, are triggered. Everyone would agree that the world presented is unnatural—in the sense of being physically or architecturally impossible.

For the sake of comparison, in figure 7.2 you find another piece of art, *Young Girls at the Sea* (*Jeunes filles au bord de la mer*) by Puvis de Chavannes, from the late nineteenth century. I am first to admit that there is nothing *strikingly* troubling in this painting, no alarming perspectival tricks, no impossible shapes. Yet one might ask: which one of the works is more disconcerting—*at the end*? The majority of readers would still say Escher, obviously, but we might yet stop for another minute with the Puvis painting, with its clear-cut contours and semiflat appearance. Acclaimed for his masterful exploitation of perspectival conventions, Puvis recovers the flat techniques of the pre-Renaissance period and merges them with stylized, partial perspective to create a pastichelike reference to early-Renaissance Italian art as well as to relief sculpture: the three women presented do not form a single layer as they would in a medieval painting but rather represent three overlapping layers. In the middle, the steep shore bank cuts the picture in two and appears to form a unified layer with the woman lying on the right; this edge or joint may be the most unsettling detail counteracting the naturalization of the scene. The resultant effect is that of oscillation between flatness and perspective; between a sense of surface and a sense of depth. *Young Girls by the Sea* does not merely attempt at a formal pastiche but is a commentary on the contemporary realistic and perspectival aesthetics: Puvis rehabilitates the ornamental and the medium-specific facet of painting.

Jeunes filles may lack the alleged cognitive shock effect of Escher, yet the prudence and the scarcity with which the painting demonstrates the deviation in perception and space seems to be enough to reflect the type of not-quite-familiarity we experience with much artistic presentation. Whereas the observer is likely to recognize the architectural impossibility of *Concave and Convex* within seconds, to appreciate Puvis's pseudo-perspectivity is a slower process that, furthermore, never really ceases—it would be impossible to imagine a moment of recognition, assimilation, or reification. The process of

FIGURE 7.1
M. C. ESCHER'S *CONCAVE AND CONVEX* © THE M. C. ESCHER COMPANY—HOLLAND. ALL RIGHTS RESERVED. www.mcescher.com

FIGURE 7.2
YOUNG GIRLS BY THE SEA, BEFORE 1894 (OIL ON CANVAS), PUVIS DE CHAVANNES, PIERRE (1824–98), MUSÉE D'ORSAY, PARIS, FRANCE/GIRAUDON/THE BRIDGEMAN ART LIBRARY

perception itself is defamiliarized and left lingering between the naturalizable and the irremediably strange; Puvis is able to, in Shklovsky's words, "increase the difficulty and length of perception" and to demonstrate that "the process of perception is an aesthetic end in itself and must be prolonged" (18). Yet it is the same element of two-dimensionality that makes both Escher's impossible spaces and Puvis's semiflat representation possible and restores any attempt at 3D modeling as unnatural.

The reverse and yet complementary relation between Escher's drawing and Puvis's painting has its literary equivalent in the relationship between postmodernist techniques and—say—Gustave Flaubert. Neither Flaubert nor Puvis is a realist proper, but rather their work is a commentary on realism—they usher us into the backstage of artistic verisimilitude and serve as intermediaries between the before and the after of prototypical realism. Quite in the manner of Puvis, *Madame Bovary* also flaunts the uncanny incongruence between the alleged storyworld and its "flat" (textual) construction. The first emblem of this tendency is the much-discussed hat of young Charles Bovary, described at the very beginning of the novel:

> It was one of those hats of the Composite order, in which we find features of the military bear-skin, the Polish chapska, the bowler hat, the beaver and the cotton nightcap, one of those pathetic things, in fact, whose mute ugliness has a profundity of expression like the face of an imbecile. Ovoid and stiffened with whalebone, it began with three big circular sausages; then, separated by a red band, there alternated diamonds of velours and rabbit-fur; after that came a sort of bag terminating in a cardboard polygon, embroidered all over with complicated braid, and, hanging down at the end of a long cord that was too thin, a little cluster of gold threads, like a tassel. (4)

Are we dealing with an "unnatural" hat? Would Escher or Puvis draw this hat? (as Vladimir Nabokov has done; see Nabokov, *Lectures* 131). The hat is not physically or architecturally impossible, yet it seems inconceivable. The farcical accessories and the multilayered structure cannot be assimilated with prior knowledge—despite all the schemata made available by the narrator (chapska, military or bowler hat, and so on).[1] It seems that the ultimate motivation for

---

1. In fact, the entire description reminds one of the cognitive challenge that Lisa Zunshine deals with in her cognitive-narratological applications of Theory of Mind studies: the human mind is only capable of tracking down four to five levels of intentionality (Zunshine 28–29)—that is, when trying to figure out embedded mental actions such as "x knows y believes a to be mad at c" and so on. A careful reading of Charles's hat discerns at least five different levels of

this allegedly hyperrealist description is the same as in *Jeunes filles:* to give us a sense of paper, or of writing, as juxtaposed with the illusion of immediate perception. The flat discourse is incapable of representing the multilayered monster of a hat, that is, textuality thwarts mimetic intention.

To top this off, there is "hanging down at the end of a long cord [...] a little cluster of gold threads, *like a tassel*" ("[...] *en manière de gland*"). The description of Charles and Emma's wedding cake, no less outrageous and incomprehensible than the hat, culminates in an analogous simile: at the very top, there is "a little Cupid, perched on a chocolate swing, its two poles finished off with two real rose-buds, *just like knobs,* on the top" ("[...] de rose naturels, *en guise de boules,* au sommet"). These ridiculous minutiae not only are part of a pseudo-description but are themselves *representative of other* artifacts. Flaubert's mock-referentiality seems to suggest that a realist novel in itself is a pathetic—if also flamboyant—simile, just as the gold threads in the hat or the tacky rosebuds on the cake are there only *en manière de* something else.

Yet who perceives, or where is the focus of perception (Genette, *Narrative Discourse Revisited* 64)? A common take on perception in a realist novel emphasizes either omniscience, omnipresence, and control of the strong narrator-figure (as in Dickens), or the psychologically realistic conveyance of character focalization (as in Tolstoy or Flaubert). Yet the theoretical notion of narrator as focalizer manifests one of the much-discussed breaches between classical and postclassical narratology: whereas Chatman (144–45) and Genette (*Narrative Discourse Revisited* 74–77) insist on treating the narrator as a world-*generating* agency, both cognitive and rhetorical narratologists would rather allocate all fictional agencies—both narrators and character-focalizers—the same cognitive schemata for world *construction* (Jahn "Windows"; Phelan, "Why" and *Living to Tell* 114–19). This debate goes too deep into the epistemological problems of fiction to be reproduced here, but one might still throw on some gasoline by asking whether interpretive confusions in assigning story-internal or story-external cognitive activities to textual agents are, in fact, fundamental to literary fiction. Who is ultimately constructing, perceiving, or reading the storyworld? Consequently, the ambivalent role of the narrator as both the generator and the (re)constructor of the storyworld might

---

ornament or material. Zunshine refers to authors such as Woolf and Nabokov to demonstrate how "fiction engages, teases, and pushes to its tentative limits our mind-reading capacity" (4) but at the same time suggests that the process of mind construction is eventually the same, whether we read fiction or our social reality. Yet one would suspect—just as is the case with Charles's hat, as juxtaposed with a real encounter with an extraordinarily ugly headpiece—the act of mind construction to be crucially dependent on the difference between textual and perceptual evidence. In the last section of this article, I will briefly discuss the *leveling down* of intention in realist consciousness representation.

even affect the interpretation of conventionally realist novels. Moreover, as I will demonstrate toward the end of my essay, the roles of the narrator and character are constantly on the verge of collapsing into one another in canonical realist consciousness representation (see also Mäkelä "Possible Minds").

Again, this underlying unnaturalness is *thematized* in Flaubert, notably in the famous discrepancy between the beginning and the overall design of the novel: the story opens with the word "nous," referring to the schoolmates of young Charles Bovary, forming their first unfavorable impression of him and his hat; soon after the opening, first-person references gradually give way to omniscient narration, the narration thus generating what Jonathan Culler calls Flaubert's elusive narrator (*Flaubert*).

Another crucial observation on narrative disturbances in *Madame Bovary* is also made by Culler, albeit over thirty years after his seminal Flaubert study ("The Realism"). Let us look at the passage Culler refers to, which happens to be one of my personal favorites as well. Here Charles pays a visit to père Rouault, yet supposedly to meet Emma, whom he finds alone in the kitchen:

> He arrived there one day about three o'clock; everybody was out in the fields; he went into the kitchen, but at first didn't notice Emma; the shutters were closed. Through the cracks in the wood, the sun cast along narrow stripes of brightness that broke across the angles of furniture and trembled on the ceiling. Flies, on the table, were crawling up the glasses left there, and buzzing about in the bottom, drowning in the cider dregs. The daylight that came down the chimney, turning the soot on the fire-back to velvet, touched the cold cinders with blue. Between the window and the hearth, Emma was sewing; she wore no fichu, on her bare shoulders you could see little drops of sweat. (21)

Several details invite the reader to naturalize the entire description of the stagnant, grotesquely aesthetic setting as perceived by Charles: we are told that first he does not see Emma, so presumably we should get a report on what he did see. Yet, as Culler notes, at the same time we are hard-pressed to imagine such exquisite sense of detail (the prismatic effects of light, the drowning flies, and the drops of sweat) emanating from Charles's dull and indelicate disposition. For Culler, the passage marks one of the cornerstones of Flaubertian aesthetics, his desire to frustrate any readerly attempt to personalize narrative stances ("The Realism" 690–91). Consequently, *Madame Bovary* displays a world that is *realistic:* "Realism, one might say, is based on a sense that there is a world there, independent of any human meaning or desire, as well as on the theme of the world's resistance to human purposes" (692).

How do Culler's observations and the Flaubertian realism pertain to contemporary narratological concerns? First of all, the definition of realism that Culler derives from Flaubert's oeuvre seems somewhat contradictory to the notion of "natural" parameters and cognitive verisimilitude. For cognitive narratology, the storyworld always appears as perceived by *someone* (even if this agent is hypothetical; see Herman "Hypothetical"). As Fludernik's definition of realism has it, from the readerly perspective it is psychological anchoring and "motivation" that guarantee the plausibility of the storyworld (*Towards* 131, 167). Second of all, the predominant definition of narrative as an experiential mode that grounds itself in the human qualia, in the "what is it like" essence of events and worlds (Herman, "Cognition" 256–57), would insinuate that the unanchored and unmotivated worlds of realism are, in fact, essentially nonnarratable. From the vantage point of cognitive narratology, a *narrated* world which merely "is there" is—unnatural. At this point, a cognitive narratologist would be eager to place an anthropomorphized narrator-figure in the scene to anchor the experience. Yet, as in the above-cited example from *Madame Bovary*, it is precisely the frustration of the figural experience as the allegedly firm interpretive footing that creates the experiential void and the sense of displacement.

In fact, one may find an analogous controversy in the archives of classical narratology. Roy Pascal, fixing his critical eye on psychological verisimilitude, *accuses* Flaubert of improbable eloquence, sophistication, and exactitude in the representation of figural perception and labels this alleged shortcoming "narrative usurpation" (107–10); whereas Brian McHale, in his review of Pascal's study, considers this "usurpation" and the resultant indeterminate impressionism as one of the fundaments of Flaubertian poetics (400).

It seems to me that in spite of the fact that Flaubert is an extraordinary writer, the indeterminacy of perceptual agency is not something that only he cultivates; rather, as is the case with Puvis's semiperspectivism, Flaubert only highlights a feature that is always already present in textualized, literary constructions of human perception.[2] At this point we may be reminded of Henry James's "house of fiction," a metaphor that Manfred Jahn revives in his discussion on focalization: narrators are seated outside the house of fiction looking in through their respective windows; focalizing characters inhabit the house of fiction, holding mirrors that reflect the insides of the house, thus providing new coordinates for the narrators' perceptions (Jahn, "Windows"

---

2. For some apt remarks in the same vein, see Tammi.

251–52). Jahn insists that the Jamesian notion of perceiving narrators admits the *reader* to an imaginary perceptual position in (relation to) the storyworld (258). What Jahn's conceptual metaphor does not account for is the inevitable fact that a representation that entails layered perceptual agency (character/narrator/reader) is not a static setting or scene but involves constant traffic in and out the house of fiction; perception and construction overlap inextricably. The entering Charles Bovary and the drowning flies issue exactly such a challenge to our reading by questioning a naturalized relationship between perception and verbal construction on any level of cognitive mental functioning—diegetic, extradiegetic, or extratextual. A cognitive approach resting uncompromisingly on natural perceptual agency in narrative texts is not able to account for this traffic and disturbance.

The example of Charles and the flies betrays one further characteristic typical of realist textual architecture. A frequent argument in favor of the immersive and illusionist quality of realist fiction arises from the level of detail. Yet one might argue, as does literary critic James Wood from his privileged position outside narratological debates, that the obsession with verisimilar detail in realist fiction is, in fact, rather countercognitive. Wood is affected by Flaubert's devotion to detail, which, according to Wood, manifests as *selection* (not as randomness imitating on-line perception); Flaubert's details are "frozen in their gel of chosenness" (33). The effect is that of both recognition and estrangement. It is as if the flies in the kitchen of Rouault are dipped not only into the cider dregs but into the "gel of chosenness": the traces of selection imply intentional construction, and yet the effect is that of a "world just being there"—all sorts of beautiful banality taking place beyond the mediocre interests of Charles Bovary.

Moreover, the metonymic essence of realist descriptions creates an effect of—not precision but—disproportion. As the famous definition of Barthes goes, the code of *effet de réel* should be invisible to a reader accustomed to novelistic conventions ("The Reality Effect"); in other words, the extrapolation of the storyworld from metonymic evidence should be a naturalized procedure. Yet if we were to follow Wood in recognizing the "gel of chosenness," we might want to conclude that the constructed perception of the Rouault kitchen is more grotesque than natural; the flies obtain an unmerited position, they swell with nonmeaning (see also Mäkelä, "Heavy Flies"). From this perspective, realism would seem to be an art more of distortion than of reproduction. The uncanny construction of storyworlds in realism might even suggest that there are some fundamental narrative elements that disconfirm the Gestalt-psychological assumption of the human mind as coherence-driven.

3. Distortions of Psychological and Motivational Verisimilitude

As already mentioned, the notion of narrativity as mediated experientiality lays heavy emphasis on "psychological and motivational verisimilitude" (Fludernik, *Towards* 131), on story-internal elements as being convincingly situated within the parameters of embodied human experience. My earlier discussion centered on distortions of on-line perception on a narrative micro level that manifested as ambivalent perceptual agency and as nonholistic world construction. The tricky subject of motivation should, however, be addressed on a larger narrative scale. In the following, I wish to make a short note on problems having to do with the incongruence between compositional and psychological motivation in literary realism. Typically, the hackneyed conception of realism as faithfully depicting the harsh human condition goes hand in hand with a heavy reliance on psychological motivation. In such a reading, every detail and every narrative choice is interpreted as shedding light on a particular experience in particular circumstances. Yet the most beloved realists are like Tolstoy or Dickens: the ones capable of creating vividness and richness of life which is almost unimaginable and always dislocated.

The following passage from Tolstoy's *Anna Karenina* describes the moment when Anna is just about to arrive to comfort her sister-in-law. Dolly has learned that her happy-go-lucky husband, Stepan Arkadyevich, is having an affair with their children's governess:

> When Anna came in, Dolly was sitting in the small drawing room with a plump, tow-headed boy who already resembled his father, listening as he recited a French lesson. The boy was reading, his hand twisting and trying to tear off the barely attached button of his jacket. His mother took his hand away several times, but the plump little hand would take hold of the button again. His mother tore the button off and put it in her pocket. (66)

Read in its immediate context, psychological motivation starts to emanate from this description. First, one would assume that it is Anna who witnesses this comforting domestic scene on her arrival to a home where "all was confusion"; perhaps the "plump little hand" is investigated with an endearing eye that might very well belong to Anna, the sweet aunt of the Oblonsky children. Furthermore, it is noted that Grisha, the little boy, "already resembled his father," an observation that Dolly herself would not be prone or eager to make in her circumstances; whereas the sister of Stepan Arkadyevich, not having seen the family in a long time, obviously would. This evident interpretation is launched at the outset by pinning down the scene to a moment "when Anna came in." Strangely enough, the perception becomes dislocated in the light of the following events: after the episode with the loose button, Dolly returns to her own knitting and the narrator takes off to describe Dolly's anguish and anxiety that she must bear in the middle of domestic bustle. Then, after one page, another description of Anna's entrance follows:

> Hearing the rustle of a dress and light footsteps already at the door, she turned, and her careworn face involuntarily expressed not joy but surprise. [. . .]
> "This is Grisha? My God, how he's grown!" said Anna [. . .]
> She took off her scarf and hat and, catching a strand of her dark, curly hair in it, shook her head, trying to disentangle it.
> "And you are radiant with happiness and health," said Dolly, almost with envy. (67)

Would the confusion be a mere blunder on the part of the reader, who would now conclude that Anna was entering the house in the beginning of the chapter and only later reaching the small drawing room where Dolly and Grisha are seated? That is unlikely, since the juxtaposition of contradictory "first impressions" proves thematically productive. To whom belongs the eye for small domestic charms—or is the tableau and the little button more a reflection of anxiety than of comforting ordinariness? When Anna and Dolly meet, we also witness an encounter between two "unhappy families" (cf. Dolly's musings on Anna's marriage: "there was something false in the whole shape of their family life," 66). The ambivalent descriptions of Anna's entrance resonate with the transformation that Anna is to experience during her stay in Moscow: after the fateful night at the ball when Anna lets Vronsky enrapture her, the Oblonsky children who were formerly charmed by Anna start to neglect her. This reversal of destinies and positions is foreshadowed in Dolly's thoughts on Anna's arrival: "After all, she's not guilty of anything" (66). The narration evokes a possibility that Anna would be the one to appreciate the "plump little hands"[3] but later thwarts this interpretation to give more emphasis to Anna's own glamorous appearance.

Yet the web of possible motivations does not limit itself here; another psychological motivation, just as plausible, has been there all along. What if the

---

3. Peculiarly enough, the impersonal perception of Grisha's hands points toward authorial usurpation: it is Tolstoy the author who seems to be obsessed with children's—and Napoleon's!—plump little hands; they occur at least in *War and Peace*, *The Cossacks*, and *Childhood, Boyhood, and Youth*.

entire scene with the button and the plump little hands is focalized through Dolly? That said, the composition appears to be completely different: if Grisha's resemblance to his father is Dolly's observation, then the "plump and tow-headed" boy is not that sweet anymore, and the plump little hands that pull the button are more annoying than charming. Why else would Dolly have *torn* the button off? A change of motivational perspective makes little Grisha a potential future adulterer, already as restless and self-indulgent as his father.

A common claim adopted from modernists such as James and Lubbock is that Tolstoy's prose lacks artistic form but, as a compensation, is able to provide us with a sense of uncontrollable flow of life (see Greenwood); yet there are critics who are claiming just the opposite and demonstrating how Tolstoy's narrative choices—and their frequent indiscernibility (why mention the button?)—reflect his grand theme of determinism and freedom of choice, the undecided balancing between predestined form and existential randomness (Alexandrov 290–98). This seeming indecision between significant and insignificant detail is highlighted in the contradictory angles to Anna's arrival: the loose button would, at a first blush, seem to be in the service of *l'effet de réel*, furnishing our impression of Dolly's domestic reality; whereas the charming details of Anna's presence ("light footsteps"), attire ("rustle of a dress"), and coiffure ("dark, curly hair") evidently provide a striking contrast to Dolly's "careworn face." For a moment at least, the loose button seems to imply that realism defies relevance just as domesticity defies romance and tellability. (See also Mäkelä "Heavy Flies.")

Again, as in the Flaubert example with Charles and the flies, the convention of figural perception is *abused*: in lieu of allowing a smooth deictic shift into the fictional reality, the narration searches for an angle to the storyworld in a process of constant, unstable deictic shifting. The narrative does not display itself as relevant but as in search of relevance; the role of detail is under negotiation. What is striking is that this ambivalence grounds itself precisely in the possibility of a fictional world "just being there," independent of any narrative interest. With a realist text full of psychologically or structurally seemingly unanchored elements, we might want to return to Lotman's always fresh observation on the reading experience as a networking of multiple relations: "[w]hat is extra-systemic [or: asystemic, see Alexandrov 291] in life is represented as polysystemic in art" (72). As Lotman explains it, the multiplicity of possible connections and motivations creates an illusion of freedom (and, thus, perhaps, of "life"), whereas a detail that is clearly linked to some holistic framework has a very constricted thematic potential.

All this brings me back to the question of "natural" and "unnatural" narratives. Alber outlines five strategies with which readers make sense of "extreme" narratives that defy the parameters of human experientiality. According to Alber, the readers either (1) graft the disturbing nonmimetic element onto some other than mimetically motivated structure ("reading events as internal states"; "foregrounding the thematic"; "reading allegorically"), or (2) accept the nonmimetic element as an extension of their own parameters ("blending scripts"; "frame enrichment").[4] These strategies appear to me as most general readerly procedures taken in search of coherence—and as such, they are an apt and welcome addition to the cognitive-narratological toolkit. Yet one is left wondering whether this approach would issue any challenge to prevalent approaches.

One of Alber's examples, Caryl Churchill's postmodernist play *Heart's Desire*, displays mutually exclusive plotlines or "retakes" of a character entering a scene, which Alber naturalizes as manifestations of the characters' fantasies, traumas, and narrative perfectionism. What is the fundamental difference between the contradictory entrances in Churchill's play and the perceptually and motivationally ambivalent entrance scene in *Anna Karenina*—if both of their effects can be enveloped with the same holistic schemata? Just as perspective drawing enables both Escher's and Puvis's distorted visions of space, textual story construction makes it possible for both Tolstoy and the postmodernists to transcend real-life parameters. Conversely, both are also unable to provide a full immersion and a complete congruence with real-life experience—a state of affairs which, I think, is much more foregrounded by novelistic conventions than many a narratologist would ever acknowledge. Alber's analyses seem to suggest that a cognitive apperception through psychological or thematic motivation is *necessary*: that there would be no two ways about it, no balancing between chance randomness and motivated structure.[5] Such a reading seems, paradoxically, to transform physically or logically impossible storyworlds into narratives that are more vulnerable to easy naturalization than any text from mainstream classical realism. In Flaubert or Tolstoy, compositional motivation repeatedly overrides embodied and situated perception and reflection, which creates an imbalance that never really gets restored.

Much of the unnaturalness associated with postmodernism has to do with temporality (see Richardson, "Narrative Poetics" 24–32). However, from the readerly point of view, reading Tolstoy and reading postmodernist fiction is just as unnatural: the relationship between the succession of words and the succession of fictional events is just as incongruent, and the entire temporal

---

4. In his contribution to this volume, Alber reorders and extends these navigational tools.

5. To be fair, one must mention that Alber indeed recognizes the "other" interpretive stance, the one that enjoys ambiguity and does not encourage naturalization. Alber calls this stance the "Zen way of reading" but is obviously doubtful of its validity and prevalence (83–84).

dimension is a mere metaphor in both cases. The unnaturalness of temporal conventions in fiction is brilliantly revealed by James Wood's analysis of novelistic descriptions that lump together dynamic and habitual detail—a mode perfected by none other than good Flaubert. Wood discusses an example from *Sentimental Education,* where Frédéric strolls idly through the Latin Quarter in Paris and the omniscient narrator both is and is not tracking the perception of the hero: "At the back of the deserted cafés, women behind the bars yawned between their untouched bottles; the newspapers lay unopened on the reading-room tables; in the laundresses' workshops the washing quivered in the warm draughts" (cited in Wood 33). As Wood writes, "the women cannot be yawning for the same length of time as the washing is quivering or the newspapers are lying on the tables" (34). Such illusions of simultaneity acquired through nonnaturalizable, multitemporal perception are veritable commonplaces in post-Flaubertian fiction, and yet, from a cognitive vantage point, they must be unnatural. But, then again, there is nothing really new in contradictory plotlines, either. What unnatural narratology should do is to reach for what is beyond the conventional/unconventional or the legitimate/disruptive divide and pay closer attention to the subtleties in the use of nonnaturalizable frames.

One of the most notorious concepts to undervalue the unnatural elements in realist fiction is immersion, as referring to an illusionist transition both into the storyworld and into the experiential plane of characters. Even in Marie-Laure Ryan's otherwise elegant study on immersion and interactivity in literature and electronic media, the novels of "high realism" have been allotted the role of immersive texts that, by rendering their worlds as seemingly independent of language (Ryan 158–59), do not activate the element of "play" in the reading process (175–76, 199). For Ryan, one of the authors creating highly worldlike and immersive narratives is Dickens, a writer who, it seems to me, has a tendency to try out different angles on his storyworld in a fluid manner that, in fact, counteracts easy immersion. Consider the following passage from *Bleak House:*

> What connexion can there be, between the place in Lincolnshire, the house in town, the Mercury in powder, and the whereabouts of Jo the outlaw with the broom, who had that distant ray of light upon him when he swept the churchyard step? What connexion can there have been between many people in the innumerable histories of this world, who, from opposite sides of great gulfs, have, nevertheless, been very curiously brought together!
>
> Jo sweeps his crossing all day long, unconscious of the link, if any link there be. He sums up his mental condition, when asked a question, by

replying that he 'don't know nothink.' He knows that it's hard to keep the mud off the crossing in dirty weather, and harder still to live by doing it. (256)

Instead of transporting the reader into the muddy and smoggy fictional London, the Dickensian narrator simulates the process of ostensible immersion itself. First, it seems that the narrating presence hovers above the strangely connected fictional universe, contemplating the dynamics of detail and motivation. After that the narration makes a dive into the experiential plane of the proletarian Jo and the realm of diegetic ignorance of the holistic composition, and yet this is a dive that is pronouncedly *simulated:* the spatial sensation of the transition is not that of outside-in but of top-down, a vertical movement down the staircase of narrative hierarchy. The shift proves a mere parody of immersion when Jo is being asked (by the metaleptic narrator who has stepped down to the diegetic level, presumably) about his experience of being-in-the-fictional-world: he "don't know nothink."

What is more, the passage goes on to reveal the mechanisms of discursive simulation behind the representation of fictional consciousness; this is how the narrator of *Bleak House* continues his fake expedition in the figural experiential plane, wondering how illiteracy must affect Jo's perspective on life:

It must be a strange state to be like Jo! [. . .] To see people read, and to see people write, and to see the postmen deliver letters, and not to have the least idea of all that language—to be, to every scrap of it, stone blind and dumb! It must be very puzzling to see the good company going to the churches on Sundays, with their books in their hands, and to think (for perhaps Jo *does* think, at odd times) what does it all mean, and if it means anything to anybody, how comes it that it means nothing to me? To be hustled, and jostled, and moved on; and really to feel that it would appear to be perfectly true that I have no business, here, or there, or anywhere; and yet to be perplexed by the consideration that I *am* here somehow, too, and everybody overlooked me until I became the creature that I am! [. . .] His whole material and immaterial life is wonderfully strange; his death, the strangest thing of all. (257–58)

As Dickens demonstrates, the illusion of immersion concerns figural language as well: his authoritarian narrator's voice smooths out his plunge into Jo's constructed consciousness by setting out in a hypothetical mode ("It must be very puzzling . . ."), which only gradually accumulates into an illusion of figural inner discourse with first-person reference (". . . how comes it that it means nothing to me"). In here and elsewhere in *Bleak House,* Dickens clearly undermines the authority of the conventional omniscient narrator, the alleged landmark of the literature of his own era, by creating impenetrable minds whose workings can only be guessed at. As Terry Eagleton notes in his preface to the 2003 Penguin edition of *Bleak House,* it is as if the characters were surrounded by the same fog of mystery as the London setting and the notorious Chancery Court (viii). The literary narrator is only capable of constructing a verbal version of the illiterate Jo's confused mind—a construction which, conversely, Jo himself would be unable to read. Although at this point Dickens seems to be rather unconventional, the process of constructing the fictional mind of Jo reveals the essential mechanisms of "realist" consciousness representation at large.[6] Moreover, unlike Flaubert and Tolstoy, Dickens is no master of free indirect discourse, and perhaps that is precisely why he can give such an elaborate demonstration of the mode's boundary conditions, of its strange locus between authorial hypothesis and constructed figural idiom. In the next section we will develop these lines of thoughts further.

4. Schematic Consciousnesses and Nonderivable Discursive Agency

As Ryan points out in her discussion of immersive realism, "[t]he 'reality effect' of nineteenth-century fiction is achieved by the least natural, most ostentatiously fictional of narrative techniques—omniscient narration, free indirect discourse, and variable focalization" (159). By reading Ryan or almost any other contemporary narratologist one might conclude that the conventions of omniscience and third-person experientiality have been most painlessly naturalized and have long since ceased to interfere with the reading process (see, e.g., Fludernik, *Towards* 48): "telling can be dispensed with, readers simply orient themselves to a position within the fictional world [. . .] frames naturally available only for one's own experience become accessible for application to a third person." The example from *Bleak House* speaks against this ease and accessibility and reveals the significant thematic import of the ultimate unreadability of minds.

Paradoxically, however, the naturalized unnaturalness of omniscience is replaced by a truly natural method of mind construction: the narrator of *Bleak*

---

6. In fact, Wilhelm Füger's classical, yet only recently translated, study on the limits of narratorial knowledge ("Limits") suggests that epistemic restrictions in the allegedly omniscient narratorial mode might be more the rule than the exception. Füger's test case is Fielding's *Joseph Andrews,* a novel frequently used as a textbook example of "omniscience."

House constructs Jo's mind via schematization and typification; mechanisms that, according to Fludernik, are a common means to reproduce someone else's spoken or inner discourse (*Fictions* 398–433). The narrator seems to reach Jo's inner discourse by applying plausible frames of verbalization: "the good company going to the churches on Sundays, with their books in their hands, [...] what does it all mean, and if it means anything to anybody, how comes it that it means nothing to me?" As Fludernik has shown, discourse representation relies on prototypical discourse schemata and results in approximations, not reproductions. All of this has to do with the cognitive scientific notion of sense-making as frame application: our approach to new situations is always based on our constructive knowledge of previous contexts. It is through this evoking of discursive schemata, writes Fludernik, that the ghost ("linguistic hallucination," 453) of the figural voice arises from our interpretation of free indirect discourse. Consequently, one might say that the aura of unnaturalness or pronounced literariness of representing consciousness or omniscient narration has started to fade in the wake of cognitive approaches: just as we are all weaving narratives out of our own experience, we are also constructors of other people's experiences.

Both the narrative and the readerly mechanisms of constructing the characters' interiority have severe consequences for the interpretation of the so-called psychological realism. What is more, realists such as Dickens, Tolstoy, and most notably Flaubert precisely juxtapose narrative and readerly construction: the characters, the narrators, and the readers are ultimately tackling the shared problem posed by the alien mind. Consider, for example, Anna's stiff and dispassionate husband, Karenin, slowly and laboriously adjusting his one-track mind to the fact that his wife is having an affair with Vronsky. For Karenin, the point of irreversible revelation is also a disturbing moment of intermental recognition and involuntary mindreading:

> For the first time [Karenin] vividly pictured to himself [his wife's] personal life, her thoughts, her wishes, and the thought that she could and should have her own particular life seemed so frightening to him that he hastened to drive it away. It was that bottomless deep into which it was frightening to look. To put himself in thought and feeling into another being was a mental act alien to Alexei Alexandrovich. He regarded this mental act as harmful and dangerous fantasizing. (143–44)

One of the most illuminating findings in cognitive narratology has to do with the analogousness of figural, narratorial, and readerly construction processes: as Lisa Zunshine's (*Why We Read*) and Alan Palmer's (*Fictional Minds*) studies suggest, much of novelistic interpretation relies on our *natural* ability to infer mental states and actions from outward behavior. The approaches underscoring Theory of Mind and intersubjectivity shed a critical light on classical narratology's linguistic interest in speech categories (indirect/direct/free indirect discourse) and thus on the problematic construction called figural *voice* (see, e.g., Palmer 9–12, 57–69). This is all well-deserved, and in the study of fictional minds, cognitive narratology has proved a genuine blessing.

Yet there is one shortcoming that both classical and cognitive narratology share in their approaches to fictional minds, something that could be termed the *easy-access fallacy*. According to the classical theorist Franz K. Stanzel, "[r]ealistic presentation of consciousness seems to require the illusion of immediacy. [. . .] Interior monologue, free indirect style and figural narrative situation [. . .] suggest immediacy, that is, the illusion of direct insight into the character's thoughts" (127). For Zunshine, the main task in reading fiction is "keep[ing] track of who thought, wanted, and felt what and when" (5). Both approaches rather outspokenly suggest that there is an inside to be found if we just dig deep enough. However, if we look at even the most canonized pieces of free indirect discourse in *Madame Bovary*, we may notice how the entire division into inside and outside appears strikingly illusory:

> Charles's conversation was as flat as any pavement. [. . .] He couldn't swim, or fence or shoot, and he wasn't able to explain, one day, a riding term which she had come across in a novel. (38)

> Why could she not be leaning out on the balcony of a Swiss chalet, or hiding her sadness in a cottage in Scotland, with a husband wearing a long-tailed black velvet coat, and soft boots, appointed hat and frills on his shirt! (38)

> Now the bad days of Tostes came back again. This time she thought herself far more unhappy: for she was experienced in sorrow, with the certainty that it would never end. Any woman who had imposed such great sacrifices on herself could well be permitted a few fancies.[7] She bought a Gothic prie-dieu, and in one month she spent fourteen francs on lemons for cleaning her nails. [. . .] (115)

The prominent characteristic of free indirect discourse is its capacity to *level*

---

7. In the French original, this reads as follows: "Une femme qui s'était imposé de si grands sacrifices pouvait bien passer des fantaisies" (217).

down the hierarchy of voices—or the levels of intentionality, as Zunshine would have it—so as to downplay the discursive agency supposedly lurking behind the expression. Sentences such as "Charles's conversation was as flat as any pavement" or "Any woman who had imposed such great sacrifices on herself could well be permitted a few fancies" can and will, obviously, be naturalized as displaying Emma's postures, but the form is not that of immediate impression but of *narrative takeover,* even rhetorical intention. Already Pascal's dual-voice hypothesis suggests that "narrative usurpation" may happen either way around (107–10): (1) The flat, nonderivable essence of fictional utterances permits the character to authorize her own view by appropriating the discursive locus of the narrator (see Mäkelä "Masters"). (2) Conversely, narrators such as the heterodiegetic one in *Bleak House* flaunt this freedom by constructing the apparent inner discourse of characters through discursive schemata that best serve their narrative purposes. Thus an apparently realist rendering of inner figural discourse is also bound to demonstrate its own inherent impossibility: a narrative can only represent the narrative construction of an experience, not the "raw feels" of immediate impression. Thus also the notion of psychological immersion turns out to be highly debatable.

Consequently, the last facets of novelistic conventions that I suggest for further denaturalization are voice or discursive agency and the fictional mind in general. Whether we foreground the narratorial or the figural intentions in consciousness representation, the result is far from displaying clear-cut, derivable cognitive agencies. All we have is narrative usurpers. Flaubert's free indirect discourse is a case in point. Consider the above-cited passage describing the pseudoverbalized tableau of romantic mountain scenes and a husband "wearing a long-tailed black velvet coat, and soft boots, appointed hat and frills on his shirt" evolving in Emma's mind. The sentence is capable of conveying both distance from and association with Emma's emotional state. The exclamatory syntax that accumulates into a disturbingly minute description of the imaginary husband's gallant costume would obviously reflect Emma's ennui and fancies. Yet the entire tableau, in its lovingly rendered detail, reminds the reader more of the same elusive novelistic agency that might be responsible for recording the above-presented drowning flies in cider dregs. In fact, Genette has paid attention to this very same phenomenon, noting that the accuracy in the descriptions of Emma's fantasies counteracts internalization: one would rather expect hazy and nonspecific impressions instead of poetically detailed descriptions of the fantasy milieus (*Figures I* 227–28). Again, it seems that the natural frames of story-internal experientiality are evoked merely with an eye on exploiting them and recovering the flat, nonderivable essence of novelistic discursive agency.

5. Conclusion: Unnatural Reading

From the point of view suggested in this essay, the literary tokens of unnaturalness would obviously seem countless. I have only been able to touch upon some specimens: dislocations in perception; ambivalence between motivation and arbitrariness; and finally, the ultimate impossibility of deriving cognitive—and particularly discursive—agencies from novelistic representation. Yet my chief aim has been to shift the focus of unnatural narratology from taxonomy of narratives more toward offering a counterforce to those current narratological trends that are eager to assimilate all types of narrative construction under the same umbrella framework.

I have also been trying to demonstrate that, as is the case with artists such as Escher and Puvis, the distinction between conventional and deviant narratives is far from clear-cut. Should we embrace Alber's classification of possible strategies with which we approach impossibilities in narratives—something, as I think, we can very well do—we should conclude that the unnaturalness of the storyworlds or plotlines (causing readerly "discomfort, fear, or worry," Alber 83) is only a textual surface under which the reader is tempted to find the psychologically, motivationally, or thematically verisimilar. To me, it seems just as unimaginable to assume a storyworld independent of representation as it would be to base my interpretation of *Concave and Convex* or *Jeunes filles au bord de la mer* on the assumptions about the "real" sceneries preceding the act of representation.

Consequently, I should think an emphasis on *unnatural reading* to be a more tenable footing for unnatural narratology. The approaches probed in this essay are counterimmersive, and yet I do not believe them to be counterintuitive. The novelistic techniques of Flaubert, Tolstoy, and Dickens seem to be in a constant motion between surface and depth, appealing to both cognitive familiarity and cognitive estrangement. On my reading, it is precisely this unresolvable motion that introduces a Shklovskian delay between text and cognition. A denaturalized approach to allegedly naturalized conventions might even attest that the uncanniness of textual world and mind construction plays a significant role in the "normal"—or "prototypical"—reading experience, since many narrators/authors "trust the reader appreciates the strangeness of this, because if he does not, there is no sense in writing poems, or notes to poems, or anything at all" (*Pale Fire* 164–65). In fact, this hypothesis is my primary reason for *not* replacing the notion of the unnatural with the more established concept of estrangement: the impetus for unnatural narratology springs from a desire to provide some new coordinates for narrative theory at large.

Works Cited

Alber, Jan. "Impossible Storyworlds—And What to Do with Them." *Storyworlds* 1 (2009): 79–96.
Alber, Jan, Stefan Iversen, Henrik Skov Nielsen, and Brian Richardson. "Unnatural Narratives, Unnatural Narratology: Beyond Mimetic Models." *Narrative* 18.2 (2010): 113–36.
Alexandrov, Vladimir E. *Limits to Interpretation: The Meanings of Anna Karenina*. Madison: University of Wisconsin Press, 2004.
Barthes, Roland. "The Reality Effect." In *The Rustle of Language*, trans. Richard Howard. Berkeley and Los Angeles: University of California Press, 1986. 141–48. [The French original "L'Effet de réel" in *Communications* 11, 1968.]
Chatman, Seymour. *Coming to Terms: The Rhetoric of Narrative in Fiction and Film*. Ithaca, NY: Cornell University Press, 1990.
Culler, Jonathan. *Flaubert: The Uses of Uncertainty*. London: Elek, 1974.
———. "The Realism of Madame Bovary." *Modern Language Notes* 122.4 (2007): 683–96.
Dickens, Charles. *Bleak House*. 1853. London and New York: Penguin, 2003.
Eagleton, Terry. "Preface." *Bleak House*, by Charles Dickens. London and New York: Penguin, 2003.
Flaubert, Gustave. *Madame Bovary*. 1857. Paris: Librairie Générale Française, 1999.
———. *Madame Bovary. Provincial Lives*. Trans. Geoffrey Wall. London and New York: Penguin, 2003.
Fludernik, Monika. *The Fictions of Language and the Languages of Fiction: The Linguistic Representation of Speech and Consciousness*. London and New York: Routledge, 1993.
———. "Natural Narratology and Cognitive Parameters." In *Narrative Theory and Cognitive Sciences*, ed. David Herman. Stanford, CA: Center for the Study of Language and Information, 2003. 243–67.
———. "Naturalizing the Unnatural: A View from Blending Theory." *Journal of Literary Semantics* 39 (2010): 1–27.
———. *Towards a "Natural" Narratology*. London and New York: Routledge.
Füger, Wilhelm. "Limits of the Narrator's Knowledge in Fielding's Joseph Andrews: A Contribution to a Theory of Negated Knowledge in Fiction." *Style* 38.3 (2004): 278–89. [Abbreviated version of "Das Nichtwissen des Erzählens in Fieldings Joseph Andrews: Baustein zu einer Theorie negierten Wissens in der Fiktion," 1978.]
Genette, Gérard. *Figures I*. Paris: Seuil, 1966.
———. *Narrative Discourse Revisited*. Trans. Jane E. Lewin. Ithaca, NY: Cornell University Press, 1988. [The French original *Nouveau discours du récit* 1983.]
Greenwood, E. B. "Tolstoy's Poetic Realism in War and Peace." *Critical Quarterly* 11.3 (2007): 219–33.
Herman, David. "Cognition, Emotion, and Consciousness." In *The Cambridge Companion to Narrative*, ed. David Herman. Cambridge: Cambridge University Press, 2007. 245–59.
———. "Hypothetical Focalization." *Narrative* 2.3 (1994): 230–53.
Holquist, Michael and Ilya Kliger. "Minding the Gap: Toward a Historical Poetics of Estrangement." *Poetics Today* 26.4 (2005): 613–36.
Jahn, Manfred. "Focalization." In *The Cambridge Companion to Narrative*, ed. David Herman. Cambridge: Cambridge University Press, 2007. 94–108.
———. "Windows of Focalization: Deconstructing and Reconstructing a Narratological Concept." *Style* 30.2 (1996): 241–67.
Lotman, Jurij. *The Structure of the Artistic Text*. Trans. Ronald Vroon. Ann Arbor: University

of Michigan, Department of Slavic Languages and Literatures, 1977. [The Russian original 1971.]

Mäkelä, Maria. "Heavy Flies: Disproportionate Narration in Literary Realism." In *The Grotesque and the Unnatural*, ed. Markku Salmela and Jarkko Toikkanen. New York: Cambria Press, 2012.

———. "Masters of Interiority: Figural Voices as Discursive Appropriators and as Loopholes in Narrative Communication." In *Strange Voices in Narrative Fiction*, ed. Per Krogh Hansen, Stefan Iversen, Henrik Skov Nielsen, and Rolf Reitan. Berlin and New York: de Gruyter, 2011. 191–218.

———. "Possible Minds. Constructing—and Reading—Another Consciousness as Fiction." In *FREElanguage INDIRECTtranslation DISCOURSEnarratology. Linguistic, Translatological and Literary-Theoretical Encounters*, ed. Pekka Tammi and Hannu Tommola. Tampere Studies in Language, Translation and Culture A2. Tampere: Tampere University Press.

Margolin, Uri. "Cognitive Science, the Thinking Mind, and Literary Narrative." In *Narrative Theory and the Cognitive Sciences*, ed. David Herman. Stanford, CA: Center for the Study of Language and Information. 271–94.

McHale, Brian. [Review of Pascal.] *PTL: A Journal for Descriptive Poetics and Theory of Literature* 3.2 (1978): 398–400.

Nabokov, Vladimir. *Lectures on Literature*. 1980. London: Picador, 1983.

———. *Pale Fire*. 1962. Harmondsworth: Penguin, 1973.

Palmer, Alan. *Fictional Minds*. Lincoln and London: University of Nebraska Press, 2004.

Pascal, Roy. *The Dual Voice: Free Indirect Speech and Its Functioning in the Nineteenth-Century European Novel*. Manchester: Manchester University Press, 1977.

Phelan, James. *Living to Tell About It: A Rhetoric and Ethics of Character Narration*. Ithaca, NY: Cornell University Press, 2005.

———. "Why Narrators Can Be Focalizers—And Why It Matters." In *New Perspectives on Narrative Perspective*, ed. Willie Van Peer and Seymour Chatman. Albany: State University of New York Press, 2001. 51–64.

Richardson, Brian. "Narrative Poetics and Postmodern Transgression: Theorizing the Collapse of Time, Voice, and Frame." *Narrative* 8.1 (2000): 23–42.

———. *Unnatural Voices: Extreme Narration in Modern and Contemporary Fiction*. Columbus: The Ohio State University Press, 2006.

Ryan, Marie-Laure. *Narrative as Virtual Reality: Immersion and Interactivity in Literature and Electronic Media*. Baltimore: Johns Hopkins University Press, 2001.

Shklovsky, Viktor. "Art as Technique." In *Literary Theory: An Anthology*, ed. Julie Rivkin and Michael Ryan. Oxford: Blackwell, 1998. 17–23. [The Russian original 1917.]

Stanzel, Franz K. *A Theory of Narrative*. Trans. Charlotte Goedsche. Cambridge: Cambridge University Press, 1984.

Striedter, Jurij. "The Russian Formalist Theory of Literary Evolution." *PTL: A Journal for Descriptive Poetics and Theory of Literature* 3.1 (1978): 1–24.

Tammi, Pekka. "Against 'against' Narrative (On Nabokov's 'Recruiting')." In *Narrativity, Fictionality, and Literariness: The Narrative Turn and the Study of Literary Fiction*, ed. Lars-Åke Skalin. Örebro Studies in Literary History and Criticism 7. Örebro: Örebro University Press, 2008. 37–55.

Tolstoy, Leo. *Anna Karenina*. Trans. Richard Pevear and Larissa Volokhonsky. London and New York: Penguin, 2000. [The Russian original 1877.]

Wood, James. *How Fiction Works*. London: Jonathan Cape, 2008.

Zunshine, Lisa. *Why We Read Fiction: Theory of Mind and the Novel*. Columbus: The Ohio State University Press, 2006.

Implausibilities, Crossovers, and Impossibilities

8

A Rhetorical Approach to Breaks in the Code of Mimetic Character Narration

JAMES PHELAN

CHARACTER NARRATION is a fertile spawning ground for unnatural or antimimetic narration, especially for sporadic outbreaks of the antimimetic within narration whose dominant code is mimetic—that is, one that respects the normal human limitations of knowledge, temporal and spatial mobility, and so on.[1] Character narration generates these breaks from the mimetic code because, as an art of indirection, it places significant constraints on the (implied) author's[2] freedom to communicate with her audience—and sometimes the author feels the need to operate outside those constraints. In employing either mimetic or antimimetic character narration, an author must use one text to communicate the different purposes of (at least) two different

---

1. The dominant mimetic code is similar but not identical to what Monika Fludernik, borrowing from work in linguistics, terms "natural" narration, that is, telling that is "regulated or motivated by cognitive parameters based on man's [sic] experience of embodiedness in a real-world context" (17). The reason that the concepts are not identical is that the dominant mimetic code includes some conventions that authorize the teller to exceed the cognitive parameters Fludernik refers to.

2. Although I am among those who find the concept of the implied author to be efficacious, for the purposes of this essay the distinction between the implied and the flesh-and-blood author is less important than the idea that narratives are shaped by an authorial agent. For simplicity's sake, then, I will, for the most part, use the term "author" and will refer to authors just by their last names rather than by "the implied X."

tellers (author and narrator) to at least three different audiences (the narratee, the authorial audience, and the actual audience; for more on these audiences, see Rabinowitz, *Before Reading* and "Truth in Fiction"). The author who employs mimetic character narration accepts the more specific constraints of the character's human limitations. Given these constraints, an author contemplating character narration as a possible technique can go one of three ways: (1) she can accept all the constraints and work scrupulously within them; (2) she can reject the mimetic code from the outset and endow the character narrator with whatever powers the author thinks will serve her larger purposes; or (3) she can accept the constraints for the most part but exercise the right to depart from them under the appropriate conditions.

In this essay I will use a rhetorical approach to narrative to analyze cases in which authors take this third route, because I believe the resulting juxtaposition of mimetic and antimimetic narration can shed light on each and especially on the nature of readerly engagements with each, light that will help us recognize "appropriate conditions." In previous work, I have discussed various kinds of departures from the mimetic code, including paralepsis, Gérard Genette's term for a narrator telling more than the character could know (*Narrative as Rhetoric*, chapter 5); paralipsis, Genette's term for a narrator unaccountably withholding what he knows (*Narrative as Rhetoric*, chapters 3 and 4); redundant telling, my term for a narrator telling a narratee something they both know the narratee already knows (*Living to Tell About It*); and simultaneous present-tense narration, in which the narrator lives and tells at the same time ("Present Tense Narration"). In all those discussions I have emphasized the ways in which these departures from the dominant code are often not noticed and have therefore argued for a broader conception of the mimetic. In addition, in *Living to Tell About It*, I have distinguished between disclosure functions (the way the narration serves the implied author's needs to communicate to the authorial audience) and narrator functions (the way that same narration, with its particular set of restrictions, serves the narrator's needs to communicate to the narratee), and I have argued that when the two kinds of functions conflict, the disclosure functions ultimately trump the narrator functions.

In this essay, I return to paralepsis, which I will call implausibly knowledgeable narration, and simultaneous present-tense character narration in order to extend—and to some extent revise—my previous work, and I will analyze a kind of narration that to my knowledge has not been noticed before, what I will call crossover narration. In this departure from the mimetic code, an author links the narration of two independent sets of events by *transferring the effects* of the narration of one to the narration of the other so that, for example, the affective responses evoked by the narration of one set of events will influence not just the audience's perception of the other set of events but the motivation of characters involved in those events. The three breaks form a useful cluster, because implausibly knowledgeable and crossover narration are typically temporary breaks, whereas simultaneous present-tense character narration is often a global, and thus more radical, break. Although the dynamics of each kind of break are different, I shall seek to identify some underlying conventions of reading that help to explain why readers often do not notice the breaks. More specifically, I shall propose two Meta-Rules of Readerly Engagement with Breaks in the Mimetic Code: the Value-Added Meta-Rule, which underlies the principle that disclosure functions trump narrator functions and stipulates that readers overlook breaks in the code when those breaks enhance their reading experience; and the Story-over-Discourse Meta-Rule, which stipulates that once a narrative foregrounds its mimetic component, readers will privilege story elements over discourse elements, and, thus, be inclined to overlook breaks in the code. Both Meta-Rules point to a broader principle of rhetorical theory that is connected to the theory's interest in accounting for the experience of reading: the logic of readerly response should trump the logic of narratological distinctions developed without reference to that response.

1. Rhetorical Theory, Conventions, and Readerly Interests

Before I turn to cases, I want to say more about the rhetorical approach, and especially the role it assigns to readerly response. The model views the dynamics of narrative communication as a feedback loop among authorial agency, textual phenomena, and readerly response. In other words, the model assumes that texts are designed by authors in order to affect audiences in certain ways, that those designs are communicated through the author's deployment of the resources of textuality—everything from style and technique to structure and genre—and that readers' responses are a function, guide, and test of those authorial designs and their realization in the textual phenomena. One methodological consequence of this view is that the rhetorical critic can begin an inquiry at any of the three points in the loop confident in the knowledge that the inquiry will lead to the other two points. In this essay it may look as if I'm starting with the textual phenomena—the breaks in the mimetic code—but I am actually starting with readerly response: I select breaks that either do not at all undercut most readers' mimetic engagement or do not undercut that engagement as much as attention to their unnaturalness would lead us to expect. From this starting point, I seek to uncover the causes of the readerly response in both the surface details of the text and in narrative conventions—including previously unacknowledged ones—governing author-audience communications. I base my claims about "most readers" on my own responses, on those of my students, and on the Sherlock Holmes "Silver Blaze" principle, that is, the absence of any barks about these breaks from other watchdog critics. Consequently, when I speak of readerly response I am referring to that of both the authorial audience and a substantial contingent of the actual audience.

At first glance, the task of distinguishing between natural and unnatural ways of disclosing information seems straightforward: in natural—or mimetic—narrative, the disclosure operates within the constraints of the known world, its laws of physics, and the powers and limitations of its human inhabitants, whereas in unnatural or antimimetic narrative, disclosure operates either without regard for such constraints or in deliberate violation of them. Thus, for example, we would regard Edgar Allan Poe as employing natural narration in "The Cask of Amontillado" with its consistent restriction to Montresor's perspective but then—if we follow Henrik Skov Nielsen's reading—as employing unnatural narration in "The Tell-Tale Heart" in that section of the narrative in which the heart speaks.

But a little further reflection shows that once again we must make room in our theory for that often annoying intruder, Fit-with-Known-Facts. Some conventions of mimetic narrative authorize what looks suspiciously like what our initial formulation would label unnatural or antimimetic narration. The somebodies who are not themselves characters and who disclose the something that happened in Western novels in the realistic tradition (*Emma, Madame Bovary, Middlemarch, Mrs. Dalloway*—the list goes on and on) have the power to access the consciousnesses of different characters in their storyworlds and to move—without the need for real-world modes of transportation and without the passage of storytime—from one location to another. In addition, character narrators often have implausible capacities that we take for granted. In "The Cask of Amontillado," Montresor gives verbatim accounts of dialogue uttered fifty years before his act of narration. Rather than questioning the plausibility of Montresor's prodigious memory, we accept the convention that the retrospective character narrator can reliably report these conversations—and thus do not regard the dialogue as breaking the mimetic code.[3] At the very least, then, we need to recognize that any account of breaks

---

3. In conversational, nonfictional storytelling, the default convention operates in a slightly

in the mimetic code needs to account for the power of conventions. More specifically, such an account needs to attend to the way that this power breaks the equivalence between the natural and the mimetic and the unnatural and the antimimetic, because mimesis depends on relationships that go in two directions: toward the world outside the text and its physical laws and toward accepted practices that are much more part of literary history than scientific and cultural history. Furthermore, conventions arise and endure, among other reasons, because authors and audiences both find benefits in what they enable.

This point about mimesis and conventions brings me to another important component of the rhetorical model, its identification of three kinds of readerly interest in narrative: the mimetic, the thematic, and the synthetic. Mimetic interests arise when the narrative represents characters, places, and events as like those we encounter in the extratextual world. Thematic interests arise from the way that the narrative highlights the ideational/political/ethical components of those characters, places, and events—or its ways of representing them. Synthetic interests arise when the narrative calls attention to its various elements as building blocks in its larger construction. Although all elements of narrative fiction are inescapably synthetic, particular narratives may foreground or background their synthetic component. Attending to the relationships among these components helps capture the difference in readerly engagement between mimetic and antimimetic fiction. Fiction that foregrounds the mimetic, as Ralph W. Rader puts it, "offers the reader a focal illusion of characters acting autonomously as if in the world of real experience within a subsidiary awareness of an underlying constructive authorial purpose" (206) designed to give the story a thematic, ethical, and affective significance and force which real-world experience does not have. Fiction that foregrounds the synthetic offers the reader either a focal illusion of characters acting autonomously in a world clearly marked as different from that of real experience or an exposure of the illusion of the autonomy for the characters and events. In either case, the purpose is to give the reader a thematic, ethical, and affective significance different from but no less powerful than that of mimetic fiction. Sometimes the foregrounding of the synthetic results in the backgrounding of the mimetic, but sometimes narratives can put both interests in the foreground.

---

different way. Listeners accept the storyteller's account of the dialogue as a plausible reconstruction rather than as a literal quotation of what was said.

2. Implausibly Knowledgeable Narration (a.k.a. Paralepsis)

In the beginning of chapter 2 of *Adventures of Huckleberry Finn,* Huck reports two events that occur on a nighttime excursion he has with Tom Sawyer. Tom helps himself to some candles from the Widow Douglas's kitchen, leaving a five-cent piece for them on the kitchen table, and then plays a practical joke on Jim, who has fallen asleep in the yard. Tom slips Jim's hat off and hangs it on a nearby tree. Before continuing with his account of the night's adventures, Huck's narration flashes forward to recount Jim's response to these events:

> Afterwards Jim said the witches bewitched him and put him in a trance, and rode him all over the State, and then set him under the trees again and hung his hat on a limb to show him who done it. And next time Jim told it he said that they rode him down to New Orleans: and after that, every time he told it he spread it more and more, till by-and-by he said they rode him all over the world, and tired him most to death and his back was all over saddle-boils. . . . Niggers is always talking about witches in the dark by the kitchen fire; but whenever one was talking and letting on to know all about such things, Jim would happen in and say, "Hm, what you know bout witches?" and that nigger was corked up and had to take a back seat. Jim always kept that five-center piece around his neck with a string and said it was a charm the devil give to him with his own hands and told him he could cure anybody with it and fetch witches whenever he wanted to, just by saying something to it; but he never told what it was he said to it. Niggers would come from all around there and give Jim anything they had, just for a sight of that five-center piece; but they wouldn't touch it, because the devil had had his hands on it. Jim was most ruined, for a servant, because he got stuck up on account of having seen the devil and been rode by witches.[4] (36)

Huck's digressive prolepsis is highly amusing, so much so that it is easy to overlook the implausibilities of his knowing all that he reports here, implausibilities related to access and to temporality. If, as Huck's narration implies, he heard directly or heard from a third party about Jim's successive embellishments of the story, then his life at the Widow's has a significant dimension that does not otherwise appear in his narrative. Either he hangs out with the slaves even when they gather to tell stories in their own space ("in the dark by the

---

[4]. I am grateful to Henrik Skov Nielsen for directing my attention to this passage.

kitchen fire") or he has a very close friend among the slaves who reports all this information to him. But each of these hypotheses preserves the mimetic in one way only to disrupt it in another. Each generates a different kind of implausibility, a withholding of information from the narratee—about how Huck spends days or about his friend among the slaves—that does not fit with his generally naïve openness.

As for temporality, the issue involves the relation of the time span of Jim's exploits as storyteller to the time span of Huck's stay at the Widow Douglas's. We soon learn that Huck is on the scene only another five or six months—it was "about a month" (41) that Tom's band of robbers goes about its business, "another three or four months" that took them well into winter (43) before Pap turns up, and then another six weeks or so until Pap takes him away from the Widow "one day in the spring" (49). Could Jim have perfected his stories and become a regional legend in such a short time? Or is Huck reporting a sequence of events that could not have occurred within the time frame of the dominant action? The vagueness of the reach of the flash forward makes it impossible to answer for certain, but that very vagueness in combination with Huck's unlikely knowledge indicates that in this passage Twain has departed from the mimetic code of Huck's narration. Furthermore, Twain's vagueness about the time span of Jim's suggests both that he does not want to call attention to this departure and that he is more concerned with disclosing certain information to his audience than with conforming to the restrictions of the mimetic code.

Twain wants, first, to entertain his audience, and he effectively draws on the combination of Jim's flight of fancy, the credulity of the other slaves, and Huck's own naïveté (notice that Huck never questions Jim's silence about the devil's magic words) to accomplish that goal. But Twain also uses the passage for his initial characterization of Jim, and, indeed, that goal guides the rest of his choices in the narration. The digression stands out not only because of the flash forward but also because it represents the first time in the novel that Huck is not himself an actor in the events. Twain designs Huck's narration so that Jim is front and center, and the passage highlights many of his traits: he has an active imagination; he stands out among the other slaves; and he is an extremely proud man. In addition, Jim is remarkably and intuitively resourceful: he takes the events of falling asleep and waking up to find his hat hung on a tree limb and a five-cent piece on the kitchen table and parlays them into the means to elevate his status among his fellow slaves. Finally, Twain shows that Jim believes in a supernatural realm that is different from, although somewhat related to, the supernatural realm of the Christianity that the Widow Douglas and Miss Watson have been trying to teach Huck. By breaking the mimetic code of Huck's narration, Twain establishes Jim as a remarkable and arresting man, one whom Huck is then very fortunate to meet up with on Jackson's Island.

This analysis leads me to propose six reasons why readers are not likely to notice Twain's departure from the mimetic code until some close-reading narratologist points it out. The first four involve details about Twain's specific execution of the break from which we can extrapolate some Rules of Thumb (that is, conventions rather than laws) about Readerly Engagement with Departures from the Mimetic Code, and the last two articulate Meta-Rules that underlie those first four.

1. The passage is relatively brief, and thus suggests the Rule of Duration: the briefer the break, the less likely it is to be noticed; the more extended the break, the more likely it is to be noticed.[5]
2. The voice in the passage remains recognizably Huck's and thus creates continuity with the dominant code. Here we have the Rule of Partial Continuity: when the break is restricted to one aspect of the narration, it is less likely to be noticed.
3. The transitions into and out of the break are smooth and matter-of-fact: it begins in mid-paragraph with the adverb "Afterwards" and ends where the quotation above ends. The next paragraph accomplishes the transition back to the present time of the action with a simple "Well," followed by "when Tom and me got to the edge of the hilltop" (36). Similarly, the passage does not call attention to the signs of its break in perceptual field (or vision). Huck's knowledge of what Jim said to the other slaves is simply presumed by his act of narration—nothing is done to explain or justify it. In these ways Twain follows the Rule of Self-Assurance: if the character narrator does not call attention to the break, it is less likely to be noticed. To put it another way, when breaking the code, it is better to ask for forgiveness than permission—and, if your break is relatively unobtrusive, chances are you won't need to ask for forgiveness.
4. When we first come upon this passage, the issue of temporality is not a concern because we do not know the length of the temporal interval between this night and Pap's taking Huck from the Widow's. Even in retrospect, the vagueness of the temporality will hide the unnaturalness from most readers. Here we have the Rule of Temporal Decoding:

5. One important qualification here: sometimes a break can extend for such a long duration and be so compelling that readers (a) accept it as the new normal and (b) focus their attention on what is being disclosed rather than on the break that makes the disclosure possible.

if the break in the code is detectable right away, it is more likely to be noticed than if it is not detectable until later in the narrative progression.[6]

5. The Value-Added Meta-Rule: Readers overlook breaks in the mimetic code when those breaks enhance the reading experience by allowing access to relevant information that would not be available without those breaks. This is the Meta-Rule that underwrites the principle that disclosure functions trump narrator functions.
6. The Story-over-Discourse Meta-Rule: Once fictional narratives establish their commitment to providing readers that "focal illusion of characters acting autonomously as if in the world of real experience," readers privilege—and seek to preserve—their mimetic interests in those characters and that storyworld. Furthermore, since the traditions of realistic fiction include conventions about narrative discourse that, on the surface of it, look antimimetic, readers will overlook breaks in the mimetic code of the discourse as long as they enhance their mimetic engagements with the story. This Meta-Rule combines with the Rule of Partial Continuity to explain why breaks in the perceptual field (or vision) of the narration are less likely to be noticed when they are not accompanied by a shift in voice. In character narration, voice is often a means to reinforce the reader's sense that the narrating-I and the experiencing-I are parts of the same person.

Let's now consider a more egregious example of implausibly knowledgeable narration in which most readers either don't notice or don't mind the break in the mimetic code. In chapter 8 of *The Great Gatsby*, F. Scott Fitzgerald has Nick Carraway report in considerable detail how George Wilson spent the night after his wife Myrtle's death.[7] The Rules of Duration and Temporal Decoding guide the judgment of this break as more egregious: Nick's report goes for more than four pages and every aspect of the break is immediately apparent—if one is looking for such a break. Furthermore, Fitzgerald's break is

6. This generalization also applies to my discussion of what I call "paradoxical paralipsis" in chapters 3 and 4 of *Narrative as Rhetoric*.

7. I discuss this same stretch of narration in chapter 5 of *Narrative as Rhetoric*, but I return to it because I believe I now have a more adequate explanation of why readers are not likely to notice the break in the mimetic code. Earlier I emphasized that our judgments of mimesis depended in part on conventions and that "those conventions are somewhat elastic and the criterion 'what is possible or probable in life' can sometimes give way . . . to the criterion 'what is needed by the narrative at this point'" (110). The Rules and especially the Meta-Rules about departures from the mimetic code add considerable precision and nuance to the previous account, even as they replace the idea of a broader standard of mimesis with the more accurate description of breaks in the dominant code of the mimetic.

more radical than Twain's because Fitzgerald gives Nick the privilege not only of reporting events he did not witness but also of focalizing the scene through other characters—primarily Michaelis, Wilson's neighbor who kept an eye on him that night, and, secondarily, Wilson himself. Consider, for example, this excerpt, which begins with Michaelis asking Wilson a question, continues with Michaelis's vision, and then shifts to Wilson's.

> "Maybe you got some friend that I could telephone for, George?"
> This was a forlorn hope—he was almost sure that Wilson had no friend: there was not enough of him for his wife. He was glad a little later when he noticed a change in the room, a blue quickening by the window, and realized that dawn wasn't far off. About five o'clock it was blue enough outside to snap off the light.
> Wilson's glazed eyes turned out to the ashheaps, where small grey clouds took on fantastic shape and scurried here and there in the faint dawn wind. (167)

Given that the implausible knowing in Nick's narration is so much more pronounced, why do most readers either not notice the break from the mimetic code or not find it troubling if they do? The Rules of Partial Continuity and Self-Assurance provide part of the answer: although we have a shift in perceptual field, we still have Nick's voice. And although Nick does explicitly call attention to a shift in his narration, he focuses on a shift in temporality rather than perception: "Now I want to go back a little and tell what happened at the garage after we left there the night before" (163–64). In line with the Rule of Self-Assurance, Nick just plunges right into his reporting.[8]

But with two rules pointing toward notice of the break and two pointing against such notice, the more compelling explanation can be found in the Meta-Rules of Added Value and Story over Discourse. Nick's implausibly knowledgeable narration adds considerable value to the narrative. It fulfills a significant gap in the audience's knowledge of events, even as it heightens our mimetic engagement with Wilson. The focalization through Michaelis means that we still see Wilson from the outside, while the dialogue and the occasional focalization through Wilson give us some sharper sense of his psychological state (notice that he sees the clouds as having "fantastic" shapes), even as it stops short of revealing all that he is thinking. This mimetic engage-

---

8. In chapter 7 Nick notes that Michaelis was the principal witness at the inquest, and the narration that immediately follows is clearly built on Michaelis's testimony. But it is implausible to conclude that Michaelis's testimony would be as detailed and as focused on the blow-by-blow of cognition as the account Nick gives in chapter 8.

ment becomes all the more important as chapter 8 continues to its climactic revelation of Gatsby glimpsing an "ashen, fantastic figure gliding toward him" (169)—Wilson. Nick's implausibly knowledgeable narration foregrounds issues of character and motive as they apply to Wilson. Since the novel as a whole also foregrounds those issues (who is Gatsby, and why does he throw his parties?), this enhancement of the reader's mimetic engagement in the elements of story either occludes or renders insignificant the reader's perception of the break in the mimetic code of the discourse.

3. Crossover Narration

Shortly after this stretch of implausibly knowledgeable narration, Fitzgerald employs a different kind of break from the mimetic code, one that I call crossover narration. This break occurs right after Nick narrates his interpretation of Gatsby's last minutes of life (narration that I will return to below). Nick's next paragraph begins this way:

> The chauffer—he was one of Wolfsheim's protégés—heard the shots—afterward he could only say that he hadn't thought anything much about them. I drove from the station directly to Gatsby's house and my rushing anxiously up the front steps was the first thing that alarmed anyone. (169)

It's Nick's report about "rushing anxiously up the front steps" that constitutes the break, as a review of the context will make clear.[9] Seven pages previously—just before Nick says that he wants to "go back a little and tell what happened at the garage" (163–64)—he has reported the following information about his actions earlier that day. In the morning he went to work in Manhattan. He fell asleep over some paperwork, only to wake up in a sweat when his phone rang. The caller was Jordan Baker, with whom he had a frustrating conversation that ended with one of them hanging up on the other. He tried to call Gatsby's house but kept getting a busy signal until he was told by an operator that the line was being kept open for a call from Detroit. At noon he decided to take the three-fifty train back to West Egg, and he then "leaned back in [his] chair and tried to think" (163).

Nick clearly is preoccupied with Gatsby, and Nick's waking up in a sweat, his repeated phone calls to the house, and his decision to leave work early

---

9. The chauffeur's claim opens the door to various interpretive consequences (see Lockridge) beyond the scope of this essay, but Nick's narration of it fits with the mimetic code.

suggest that his preoccupation includes some level of anxiety about Gatsby. Thus, Nick's going directly to Gatsby's house is well motivated. But Nick's anxiety level is not so high that it keeps him from going to work or keeps him awake once there. The level is also not so high that it leads him to decide to take the very next train. Thus, when Fitzgerald has Nick report that he rushed anxiously to Gatsby's door—with no explanation of why at the time of the action Nick's anxiety level should have changed so much—Fitzgerald takes a significant shortcut. Indeed, that lack of explanation—nothing about what Nick had been thinking, nothing about why, if he were so anxious, he still waited until the 3:50 train—makes it look to the narratologically trained eye that Fitzgerald suddenly stops respecting the need to sustain the "focal illusion" that Nick is acting autonomously. Rather than motivating Nick's high anxiety, Fitzgerald seems to assign it to him because Fitzgerald needs an efficient way to move the action along.

Now it would be possible to interpret the sentence as adhering to the mimetic code by inferring that Fitzgerald is signaling that Nick is an unreliable narrator here, retrospectively claiming greater concern for Gatsby than he actually felt. But this hypothesis runs into the recalcitrance that Nick's anxiety prods Gatsby's employees into action—and their investigation leads them to the corpses of both Gatsby and Wilson. Thus, the more elegant and more persuasive explanation is that Nick's reporting of his anxiety is reliable but that Fitzgerald has chosen not to have Nick explain why he is so much more anxious at 4:30 than he was at noon. In order to assess Fitzgerald's choice, we need to take a closer look at Nick's intervening narration.

After reporting the events at Wilson's garage the previous night, Nick moves on to report Wilson's activities earlier that day and then Gatsby's movements and likely thoughts that afternoon. This narration remains within the mimetic code: in Wilson's case Nick either indicates that he has a source for what he knows (Wilson's movements "were afterward traced") or admits what he doesn't know ("for three hours he disappeared from view" [168]); in Gatsby's case Nick implies that his sources are Gatsby's butler and chauffeur, and Nick clearly marks his report about Gatsby's thoughts as speculation. Nick's tracing of the movements of Wilson and Gatsby culminates in Nick's hypothetical account of Gatsby's last thoughts and perceptions. Gatsby must have been thinking, Nick writes, about "A new world, material without being real, where poor ghosts, breathing dreams like air, drifted fortuitously about . . . like that ashen, fantastic figure, gliding toward him through the amorphous trees" (169). Then Fitzgerald inserts a paragraph break and has Nick deliver the two sentences I quoted at the beginning of this section.

Now if Fitzgerald had Nick report that he had a high level of anxiety at the office, the effect of this intervening narration would be different: at the very least our readerly anxiety about what will happen next in the developing narrative present would increase significantly, as we wondered whether Nick's anxiety would prove to be well-founded. As it is now, however, the major effect of Nick's flashback is to shift our attention from Nick the character first to Wilson and then to Gatsby, and the major effect of the narrating-I's retracings of Wilson's and Gatsby's activities is to heighten the sense of shock and loss we feel once their paths converge. And these effects prepare the way for the crossover. Having just experienced them in Nick's narration, most readers will not stop to question the experiencing-Nick's anxious rush to the door—even though the experiencing-Nick does not know anything about Wilson's movements. To put the claim more strongly, Fitzgerald's crossover works because *it is virtually impossible to read Nick's report of his anxiety as character without connecting it to his just-concluded narration about Wilson and Gatsby.*

In terms of the Rules of Readerly Engagement, Fitzgerald's crossover works because it ingeniously combines the Rules of Duration and Self-Assurance with the Value-Added and Story-over-Discourse Meta-Rules. The break is brief and done with confidence. It adds the value of emphasizing Nick's psychic investment in Gatsby and his fate without displacing what happens to Gatsby from the center of the audience's interest at this climactic point in the narrative. But most impressively, the crossover takes advantage of our greater readerly engagement with elements of story than with elements of discourse. Within the logic of a formal narratology, we can describe Fitzgerald's crossover as the metaleptic interpenetration of the normally distinct roles of character and narrator: the narrating-Nick's reporting of what he came to know—and to imagine—later on substitutes for the time-of-the-action motivation of the experiencing-Nick's behavior. But within the logic of rhetorical theory, we can describe the crossover narration as a brilliant application of the Story-over-Discourse Meta-Rule: Fitzgerald has found a way to use our affective responses to the convergence of Wilson and Gatsby as grounds for our finding the experiencing-Nick's high anxiety plausible. The difference in these two accounts points to a corollary of the Story-over-Discourse Meta-Rule: most readers of character narration are less fastidious about the distinct roles of character and narrator than formal narratologists are.

4. Simultaneous Present-Tense Narration

This technique is such a radical break from the mimetic code that I want to acknowledge up front that the main question it raises is not "why don't most readers notice the break?" but rather "in what ways, if any, does the technique still conform to aspects of the mimetic code?" Applying the Rules of Duration and of Temporal Disclosure, we see that the antimimetic features of the technique are in the foreground, especially when the technique extends across a whole narrative. Furthermore, as I and others (see especially Cohn; DelConte; Nielsen) argue, the impossibility of living and telling at the same time means that there is no plausible occasion for the narration. But how much does that impossibility affect the other standard features of character narration, including its basic condition of being a telling from someone to someone else?

Henrik Skov Nielsen makes a rigorous argument, using the following passage from Bret Easton Ellis's *Glamorama*, that the impossibility goes all the way down.

> "See you, baby." I hand her a French tulip I just happen to be holding and start pulling away from the curb.
>
> "Oh Victor," she calls out, handing Scooter the French tulip. "I got the job! I got the contract."
>
> "Great, baby. I gotta run. What job you crazy chick?"
>
> "Guess?"
>
> "Matsuda? Gap?" I grin, limousines honking behind me. "Baby, listen, see you tomorrow night."
>
> "No. *Guess?*"
>
> "Baby, I already did. You're mind-tripping me." (19)

Nielsen comments as follows:

> [T]here is in fact a clear difference between two levels of words and the ways in which they can and cannot be ascribed to a character narrator. There is clearly a character who starts out by saying "See you, baby." These words are situated in a communicative situation and uttered by the character (Victor) to a female acquaintance. But at no point is there a narrator situated anywhere before, during or after the events, who says: "I hand her a French tulip." No communicative situation seems imaginable in which a narrator will narrate these words to a narratee. And never will Victor say, think, or mumble to himself or anyone else "I hand her a French tulip." There is no context and no occasion for telling them. The techniques used in the quote dissociate the words from the narrator's account. (59)

In short, Nielsen argues that there is no narration taking place to or from anyone at the level of the storyworld. Instead, Nielsen suggests, we're left with an author communicating to his or her audience through a technique that is a variation of reflector narration.

I admire the rigor of Nielsen's argument, but I am struck by how it depends on an appeal to the logic of the natural world: no occasion entails no narrator and no narratee. From my rhetorical perspective, Nielsen's tight chain of entailment can—and should—be broken at the link between occasion and narrator. To put it another way, once we remember that even some narration that stays within the mimetic code is governed by conventions that break the logic of the natural world, once we recognize how conventions operate to minimize the unnaturalness of breaks such as the ones I've examined above, and once we remember that most readers do regard passages of simultaneous present-tense character narration as having a narrator, we have good grounds to seek another explanation of the technique. Here's mine, which proposes the technique's enabling convention: character narrators in fiction are able to perform both of their roles (experiencing and telling) at the same time.

This proposal seeks to capture the paradoxical relation between the mimetic and the antimimetic in the technique: it is a genuine telling for some purpose(s) from a character to someone else on the impossible occasion of the time of the action. Just as we have a convention that permits a noncharacter narrator to violate real-world rules about knowing other people's minds and constraints on moving through time and space, we have a convention, developed in response to authors' practice, that authorizes a narrator's telling to a narratee while simultaneously acting in ways that would in the real world preclude such narration.

This view, I suggest, also offers a more persuasive account of the passage from *Glamorama*. The conclusion that there is no narrator or narratee encounters considerable recalcitrance from the textual phenomena, a recalcitrance that disappears when we posit the enabling convention. The narration, after all, has so many features of standard character narration. In the sentence "I hand her a French tulip I happen to be holding," a character narrator, Victor, assumes that his narratee knows what a French tulip is but does not know that Victor is holding one and does not know what Victor is doing with it. In this regard, the discourse is far more similar to than different from its natural narration past-tense counterpart, "I handed her a French tulip I happened to be holding." Furthermore, there is no reason why this character narrator could not directly address the narratee—although the impossible occasion means that the narratee would be present only in the teller's mind: "I hand her a French tulip, Jack."

The view based on the logic of readerly engagement also offers a more elegant explanation of the relation between the reporting of the dialogue and the narration itself. Without a narrator, we must assign both the reporting of the dialogue and the variant of reflector narration to someone other than

Victor: either Ellis or his impersonal stand-in in the storyworld. And we would want a good explanation for why Ellis did not just use figural narration, an explanation that would need to emphasize its difference from both standard figural narration and character narration. I do not mean that such an explanation would itself be impossible, but I do mean that it would necessarily be far more elaborate and therefore less persuasive than the straightforward account offered by the rhetorical view: Victor as character narrator, like Huck Finn and Nick Carraway, reports both the dialogue and the narration to his absent narratee.

Since the issue of the narratee looms large for Nielsen (and DelConte), let me turn to a different example, this one from Scott Turow's *Innocent*.

> **Rusty, September 2, 2008**
> The inside line in my chambers rings, and when I hear her voice, just the first word, it is nearly enough to bring me to my knees. It has been a good six months since the last time I saw her, when she came by to have lunch with my assistant, and well more than a year since we brought things to a close. (111)

How should we explain the narration in the second sentence? Without the context provided by the simultaneous narration of the first sentence, the question would not even arise, since it has all the marks of standard character narration: Rusty reports relevant backstory to his narratee, and through that reporting the implied Turow communicates to his audience not only those details but some additional information about Rusty as both character and narrator (e.g., he is vividly aware of how long it has been since he has seen "her"). But on Nielsen's account, the presence of the first sentence means that analysis of the second's rhetorical dynamics is at best misguided because both sentences are a variant of figural narration. Although it is relatively easy to regard the first sentence that way—all one has to do is substitute third-person references for first-person ones ("my" becomes "his," "I" becomes "Rusty"), it is much harder to regard the second sentence as such a variant. Once we posit the chain of communication as going from Turow to his reader, then the narration seems to escape from the orbit of Rusty's perceptions. It is at least as plausible to read the narration as Turow telling us directly that it has been a good six months as it is to read the narration as Rusty's thinking it has been that long. Again, my point is not that the case for a variant of figural narration becomes impossible to make but rather that the case is less persuasive than the more elegant explanation that the passage gives us what its rhetorical dynamics makes it seem like it gives us: a character narrator addressing a narratee.

Finally, the Value-Added and Story over Discourse Rules also support the rhetorical view. The added value comes in the technique's capacity to immerse the audience in the character narrator's continually moving present, an immersion that takes away any sense of the character narrator's own teleological progression—though this absence of storyworld teleology can be contained within a sense of the author's teleology. In addition, in narratives with a significant interest in the mimetic component of story, this effect of the technique can enhance that interest, as it does in *Innocent,* which tells the story of a man on trial.

In conclusion, I acknowledge the limits of my investigation here: rather than taking on unnatural narration in general, I have focused on just three kinds of departures from the mimetic code of character narration. Developing a full account of unnatural narration remains a task that is at once daunting and exciting. What this essay contributes to that task is both its small survey of some types of character narration and its proposal that the larger project attend not just to the relation between the natural and the unnatural but also to conventions and the influence of readerly response on our understanding of textual phenomena and authorial agency.

Works Cited

Cohn, Dorrit. *The Distinction of Fiction.* Baltimore: Johns Hopkins University Press, 1999.

DelConte, Matt. "A Further Study of Present Tense Narration: The Absentee Narratee and Four-Wall Present Tense in Coetzee's *Waiting for the Barbarians* and *Disgrace.*" *Journal of Narrative Theory* 37.3 (2007): 427–46.

Ellis, Bret Easton. *Glamorama.* New York: Knopf, 1999.

Fitzgerald, F. Scott. *The Great Gatsby.* New York: Scribner, 1925.

Fludernik, Monika. *Towards a "Natural" Narratology.* London and New York: Routledge, 1996.

Genette, Gérard. *Narrative Discourse: An Essay in Method.* Trans. Jane E. Lewin. Ithaca, NY: Cornell University Press, 1983.

Lockridge, Ernest. "F. Scott Fitzgerald's *Trompe L'Oeil* and *The Great Gatsby*'s Buried Plot." *Journal of Narrative Technique* 17 (1987): 163–83.

Nielsen, Henrik Skov. "Fictional Voices? Strange Voices? Unnatural Voices?" In *Strange Voices in Narrative Fiction,* ed. Per Krogh Hansen, Stefan Iversen, Henrik Skov Nielsen, and Rolf Reitan. Berlin: De Gruyter, 2011. 55–82.

———. "The Impersonal Voice in First-Person Narrative Fiction." *Narrative* 12.2 (2004): 133–50.

Phelan, James. *Living to Tell About It: A Rhetoric and Ethics of Character Narration.* Ithaca, NY: Cornell University Press, 2005.

———. *Narrative as Rhetoric: Technique, Audiences, Ethics, Ideology.* Columbus: The Ohio State University Press, 1996.

———. "Present Tense Narration, Mimesis, the Narrative Norm, and the Positioning of the

Reader in *Waiting for the Barbarians*." In *Understanding Narrative*, ed. James Phelan and Peter J. Rabinowitz. Columbus: The Ohio State University Press, 1994. 222–45.

Rabinowitz, Peter J. *Before Reading: Narrative Conventions and the Politics of Interpretation*. Ithaca, NY: Cornell University Press, 1987.

———. "Truth in Fiction: A Reexamination of Audiences." *Critical Inquiry* 4 (1977): 121–41.

Rader, Ralph W. "The Emergence of the Novel in England: Genre in History vs. History of Genre." In *Fact, Fiction, and Form: Selected Essays of Ralph W. Rader*, ed. James Phelan and David H. Richter. Columbus: The Ohio State University Press. 203–17. Turow, Scott. *Innocent*. New York: Grand Central, 2010.

Twain, Mark. *Adventures of Huckleberry Finn: A Case Study in Critical Controversy*. 2nd ed. Ed. Gerald Graff and James Phelan. Boston: St. Martin's, 2004.

Unnatural Narrative in Hypertext Fiction

9

ALICE BELL

1. Introduction

This essay argues that hypertext provides a distinctive context for unnaturalness in narrative fiction. It explores the structural attributes of hypertext fiction in general before analyzing two examples of unnatural narrative in Stuart Moulthrop's Storyspace hypertext fiction *Victory Garden*. The first analysis shows how the multilinear structure of hypertext facilitates narrative contradiction. The second analysis demonstrates that the fragmented structure of the text allows the unnatural status of a scene to change depending on the reading route through which it is accessed. The study thus analyzes two different types of unnaturalness in hypertext by first focusing on a logical impossibility before moving on to an example of physical impossibility. The article concludes that hypertext adds a digitally specific component to unnatural narrative that must be analyzed according to the affordances of the medium (cf. Hayles).

2. Unnatural Narratology

In the relatively new field of unnatural narratology, unnatural narratives have been defined as "strategies or aspects of discourse that do not have a natural grounding in familiar cognitive parameters or in familiar real-life situations" (Fludernik, *Towards* 11); "texts that employ unnatural narrational stances that are impossible in nonfictional discourse" (Richardson 37); and narratives that contain "physically impossible scenarios and events, that is, impossible by the known laws governing the physical world, as well as logically impossible ones" (Alber 80). While each study provides a slightly different definition of the unnatural—with Fludernik preferring the term "non-natural"—each theorist emphasizes that some types of narrative cannot occur in real-world situations. Unnatural narratives are therefore narratives that are inherently fictional because they contain events and scenarios that are impossible according to real-world physical and logical laws.

Most studies within unnatural narratology use examples from print fiction in their analyses, and few have considered how unnatural narratives operate in a digital context. Yet as studies within the field of hypertext theory have shown (e.g., Bolter; Ciccoricco; Bell, *Possible* and "Ontological"), the structural attributes that characterize Storyspace hypertext fiction in particular have significant ramifications for narrative fiction because the physical configuration of the text facilitates a unique narrative structure. Storyspace hypertext fictions are read from a computer and composed of fragments of text, known as lexias, that are connected by hyperlinks. The reader can press the "Enter" key on his or her keyboard to follow a default path through the text. Alternatively, the reader can follow hyperlinks which lead him or her to other parts of the text. While a finite number of hyperlinks exist within a text, thus setting limits as to its structural organization, readers are ultimately responsible for their journey through the text. They can choose to pursue a scene for as long as the default reading path will allow, or they can use the hyperlinks to explore other diversions that interest them. A reader may read a default path until he or she can continue no further, or he or she may abandon a particular reading path and return to the beginning of the text to choose another. Some readers might flick backward and forward through the text, retracing their earlier steps. Others might use a "search" facility, which allows them to locate lexias that contain particular words, or use a list of lexias from a dropdown menu. Readers can therefore navigate the text according to a particular agenda or read in a less considered fashion by randomly following links. Each reader's experience of the text will vary and, to the extent that he or she can select lexia titles randomly, is somewhat unpredictable. In addition, because each reading usually results in a different configuration of lexias, the same fragments of text can be read in a number of different orders.

A number of print works, retrospectively collected under the term "proto-hypertext," are often seen as the print precursors of hypertext fiction. B. S.

Johnson's *The Unfortunates* comprises a box containing twenty-seven pamphlets—each acting as an individual chapter. The reader must begin with the prescribed first and last pamphlet but can then choose to read the other chapters in any order. Also packaged in a box, Marc Saporta's novel *Composition No. 1* is composed of unbound pages that the reader can read in any order she or he chooses. In both cases, different reading orders deliver or imply different narrative outcomes so that the reader is assigned some responsibility, as in a hypertext fiction, for selecting which path to follow (also see Richardson's essay in this volume for other examples of printed texts that contain fragmented and/or multilinear narratives).

While proto-hypertexts share some of the structural attributes of hypertext fiction insofar as the reader is allotted a degree of responsibility for his or her journey through the text, digital hypertext is not, like the texts cited above, a collection of textual fragments that can be joined in any order, allowing for an indefinite number of configurations. Rather, a hypertext fiction contains fragments that are linked in predetermined paths of which the reader is not always aware, so while the reader of both types of text is allotted a degree of responsibility, the reader's level of knowledge is quite different in each case. The reader of a proto-hypertext, such as *Composition No. 1,* can access each fragment of text at will. The hypertext fiction reader, on the other hand, can unveil only one lexia at a time and is often ignorant of the forthcoming sections and reading paths. In each case, the reader is granted some responsibility, but the reader of a hypertext fiction is always constricted by the integral capacities of the digital medium to hide the forthcoming text. Moreover, while both types of text facilitate structural fragmentation, the hypertext medium allows authors to implement media-specific narrative structures. The fragments of text in a hypertext are connected by hyperlinks so that there is a prelimited but ultimately unpredictable pathway through the text. Authors are also able to implement "guard fields," which prevent readers from accessing specific lexias until they have visited others, and readers are often ignorant of the structural limitations that are placed on their experience of the text.

3. Unnatural Narrative and Hypertext Fiction

As the preceding overview shows, the reader of a hypertext fiction will inevitably experience different events, different versions of events, or a different ordering of events, depending on the path he or she chooses to take. Thus hypertext inherently facilitates fragmentation and multilinearity. Richardson suggests that the narrative multiplicity found in hypertext fiction causes an unavoidable form of unnaturalness. In particular he suggests that narrators of hypertext fiction "problematize the idea of omniscience and even third-person narration by presenting a series of narrative possibilities that a reader must then convert into a single story" (9). As Richardson notes, the structure of a hypertext usually means that readers experience a number of different versions of the narrative, some of which may contradict others. This might be because the fictional world is presented from a number of different viewpoints, or it may be because the ontological status of an event is obscured by the fragmented and/or nonchronological order in which it is read by a reader.

Hypertext theorists also identify a link between the hypertext structure and narrative multiplicity. Bolter, for example, defines hypertext as "a structure that can embrace contradictory . . . outcomes" (125–26). Douglas is more committed to the distinctiveness of hypertext, claiming that while "the physical confines of printed space . . . have prevented narratives from representing multiple, mutually exclusive representations of a single set of events" ("What" 15), hypertext is able to "embod[y] all its possibilities without giving priority to any one of them" (16). Douglas maintains that hypertext offers a narrative structure that cannot be replicated in print and is therefore concerned with the affordances that are granted by different media. Like Bolter, however, she recognizes that hypertext offers a peculiar kind of multilinear structure for narrative fiction.

The hypertext structure means that narrative contradiction and/or inconsistencies are somewhat inevitable in hypertext fiction, but, while hypertext does provide a multilinear structure, the emergent narratives are not necessarily unnatural. In some hypertexts, narrative inconsistencies can be resolved through further exploration of the text. In others, the multilinear structure is used to house different voices or to present different scenes but the narratives do not contradict one another. Thus while the hypertext structure can result in unnatural narratives, unnatural narrative is not an inevitable component of hypertext fiction.

Yet while some hypertext fiction narratives can be reconciled according to real-world parameters, Stuart Moulthrop's *Victory Garden* exploits the hypertext medium as a means of presenting a number of unnatural contradictions and ambiguities. In the story, set during the first Gulf War, protagonist Emily Runbird has been drafted to work on a Saudi Arabian military base, leaving her friends back home in the fictional town of Tara in the United States. The narrative revolves around the two settings, with the text documenting Emily's experience of the war in the Gulf as well as the effect of the conflict on her friends, family, and colleagues at home and on the campus of the University of Tara. The motives behind and consequences of the Gulf War resonate throughout the text and are debated either explicitly between characters or implicitly through the various viewpoints that are presented. Offering a mediated view of the conflict, scenes from news broadcasts depict the off- and on-air discussions between two television war correspondents. Theoretical debates between academics at the University of Tara take place over the ideological and ethical motives of the war. Quotations from real-world figures such as George Bush, Saddam Hussein, and the CBS anchorman Dan Rather are also scattered throughout the text, which, while usually a product of Moulthrop's artistic license, remind the reader that the Gulf War was an actual world event rather than a purely fictional construction.

The various scenes and voices in *Victory Garden* are linked thematically, but the hypertext structure means that they are often encountered separately and/or sporadically. Readers are therefore required to draw associations between parts of the text that might not be physically connected. Similarly, the different reading paths that result from the lexia-link configurations mean that the text can be navigated according to a number of different routes. In some cases this results in mutually exclusive versions of events being documented in each reading path. They are unnatural because the narrative contradictions they generate cannot be resolved according to real-world logic irrespective of how much more of the text is explored. Other forms of unnaturalness are caused by different types of narration. In these parts of the text, the nature of the unnaturalness depends on the route through which the lexia has been reached. The ambiguity that the hypertext structure permits is thus used to problematize and ultimately undermine the ontological status of particular parts of the text.

4. Narrative Contradiction in *Victory Garden*

The most significant unnatural elements in *Victory Garden* are those that are caused by narrative contradictions. Perhaps most strikingly, in some reading paths the protagonist Emily Runbird dies during a bomb blast in the Gulf, but other parts of the text imply that she has survived the conflict to return home to her family and friends. In a less ruthless but equally prominent narrative incongruity, the heterodiegetic narrator describes a scene three different times with minor details changed in each iteration. In each version of the encounter, university professor Boris Urquhart runs away from a pursuer and seeks solace in the office of his colleague Provost Tate. In the "In Need of Help" lexia the book on Tate's desk is entitled *Jane's All the World's Ordnance, 1989–90*, and in the "Helpful" lexia it is changed to *Jane's All the World's Kill-*

ing Machines, 1989–90. In the "In Need of Help" lexia, the book is described as "voluminous," and in the "Helpful" lexia as "massive" (see Bell *Possible*; Ciccoricco; Koskimaa for detailed analyses of these scenes).

Both Emily Runbird's simultaneous death and survival and Boris Urquhart's reiterated visits to Tate are unnatural because they present logically irreconcilable scenarios which, according to real-world logic, cannot exist concurrently. More specifically, they break the law of noncontradiction, which states that A and not A cannot be true at the same time. When this law is applied to the text, a character cannot both live and die, and the same scene cannot contain inconsistent details. In both cases it is possible to theoretically eliminate the narrative contradictions and thereby reconcile them with real-world logic by seeing the whole hypertext as a mass of possibilities with new and discrete fictional worlds emerging during each reading. Accordingly, in Ryan's application of Possible Worlds Theory to hypertext, "every lexia is regarded as a representation of a different possible world, and every jump to a new lexia as a recentering to another world" (222), so that each version of the story is considered to be a different story altogether. Ryan's strategy achieves its logical aim of "rationaliz[ing] . . . [hyper]texts that present a high degree of internal contradiction" (223). Yet while it is possible to see the text as a series of disconnected narratives, this approach ignores the fundamental structure and form of the hypertext by attempting to eradicate its multilinearity. More importantly, it wrongly assumes that we dismiss our previous experience of a text as we encounter new material. A strategy that seeks to reconcile unnatural elements with real-world experience—defined by Culler as "naturalization" and by Fludernik as "narrativisation" (*Towards*)—will inevitably fail to accommodate contradictions in *Victory Garden* because they are meant to be noticed. As Koskimaa notes in his analysis of *Victory Garden*, "for the most part the reader clearly recognizes she is reading several narratives simultaneously." As if to confirm the futility of naturalization, the narrator sometimes self-consciously alludes to the unnatural elements. In the reiterated scene between Boris and Tate, the narrator notes in one version that "the weather panels were *still* rolled back" ("temple"; my italics, A.B.) and that "U[rquhart] is *once again still* always running through that dark field" ("Ring Around"; my italics, A.B.). In this hypertext, then, the reader cannot ignore the unnaturalness of the recurring scene but is instead alerted to its presence.

In both examples of narrative contradiction in *Victory Garden*, a heterodiegetic narrator provides an apparently authentic account of an event before subsequently undermining its validity by superseding it with an alternative. Each thus fulfills the requirements of what Richardson defines as a "contradictory narrator . . . [in which] multiple contradictory versions of . . . the same events are set forth, with no mechanism offered (such as different narrators with different memories and agendas) to explain away the often outrageous contradictions" (104). Richardson's contradictory narrators are taken from print fictions, but the successful application of his categories to *Victory Garden* shows how they can be used to analyze other media. Yet while some types of unnaturalness can occur in different types of text, hypertext does change the way in which narrative contradictions operate. The narrative of Emily's death and the narrative of Emily's survival occur in different parts of the same text. Yet because the text exists as a collection of fragments and links, each possibility exists in parallel so that Emily's death and survival coexist. The reader may encounter them in a particular order, but any sequence is determined by the reader's choice of reading route rather than by its fixed position in the hypertext.

Similarly, while the hypertext's facility for housing multilinearity allows Emily's death and survival to exist in parallel, the hypertext's capacity to snare the reader in a reading route provides a unique environment in which the three contradictory versions of Urquhart's visit to Tate can be placed. Each description is presented in a continuous loop from which the reader cannot escape without terminating his or her reading. They occur one after the other in a tightly controlled configuration that the reader is forced to read again and again and again until he or she decides to return to the beginning of the hypertext to begin a new reading path. This type of infinite recursion is clearly not achievable in print without a never-ending and infinitely repeating text. Both examples of narrative contradiction are therefore housed in a structure that is peculiar, if not unique, to hypertext, and the unnaturalness is facilitated by the structures afforded by the medium.

5. Rereading and the Unnatural

While the fragmented structure of hypertext does not necessarily lead to unnaturalness, *Victory Garden* houses many lexias in which indeterminate or ambiguous forms of reference are contained and that a reader will interpret differently depending on the path through which they have been reached. This means that the same lexia can be used in a number of different reading paths, and this sometimes leads to contradictory narrative outcomes. Similarly, because readers can encounter the same lexia during several points in their reading, their interpretation of some parts of the text will be influenced by the respective reading route through which it is reached. Thus not only are narratives experienced in a fragmented and often disjointed manner, but the same scene can be experienced multiple times so that scenes are often (re)interpreted at a later stage in light of new information. Compounding the structural diversity, some reading paths in *Victory Garden* are restricted by "guard fields." As noted earlier, these structural mechanisms, implemented by the author, restrict access to particular lexias until others have been visited. Thus, while on one reading a particular configuration of lexias may be displayed, on another additional text that changes the nature of the narrative may have been released. Guard fields can be circumvented by using the dropdown menu to select individual lexia titles, but in a text that contains almost a thousand lexias, the chances of locating a particularly relevant piece of information are slim. More importantly, overriding the guard fields ignores the narrative ambiguities that are integral to the reader's experience of the text.

That hypertext fiction reading is characterized by rereading has been well documented in hypertext theory. Joyce argues that "hypertext fiction in some fundamental sense depends upon rereading" ("Nonce" 585) because a reader will often happen upon the same lexia more than once, only each time with a different experience of and knowledge about the rest of the text. In her analysis of Michael Joyce's hypertext fiction, *afternoon, a story,* Douglas notes that while the contents of each lexia must remain the same, "you can trek across a single place four times . . . and discover that it possesses four radically different meanings each time" ("Understanding" 118). Ciccoricco devotes a book-length study to the process of rereading in hypertext, arguing that "the rereading of textual elements, via the recycling of nodes, is fundamental to (hyper)textual comprehension" (12). The fact that readers regularly revisit lexias during the course of their reading might imply that hypertext readers should adopt a more flexible reading strategy. In particular, readers should expect that the meaning or relevance of some lexias will change in light of new information, but also that the same lexia can operate in a number of different reading contexts.

Victory Garden houses several stylistically ambiguous forms of narration from which multiple interpretations about the status of the narrator and the scenes that she or he documents can be drawn. While most of the text is narrated by a heterodiegetic narrator using the third person, the text also contains first-person singular, first-person plural, and second-person narration. The tense of the narration also fluctuates between past, present, and future so that readers encounter a multitude of narrative agents, styles, and temporal perspectives, many of which can be allotted to a number of different contexts. One of the thirty-nine entrance links, for example, leads to the "Slacktown" lexia, which contains the following abridged text:

∧∧∧
You always knew it would look like this.

An irrational space, a strange hotel, all atrium and concrete pillars with glassine cephalopod elevators crawling up down and yes across the walls. . . .

Here is an Information Kiosk.—Which way to . . . er . . . the *lobby*?

Ha ha. Always the jokester aren't you. Hang a left then another left, go left again and you'll stumble on it right after the hexagonal galleries.

As the extract above shows, this scene is narrated in the second-person present voice. Not all uses of the second-person voice in fiction are unnatural; a second-person monologue that is addressed to a homodiegetic addressee, for example, does not contravene real-world logic because both participants are located within the same ontological domain and the speaker does not claim to have access to the thoughts of another. Yet while some uses of "you" can be reconciled with real-world logic, the form used in the "Slacktown" lexia cannot, because the narrator claims to have an impossible level of omniscience. The narrative begins *in medias res* with a declarative, "you always knew it would look like this," and in this opening sentence the narrator attributes knowledge to the addressee. Initially at least, the reader can be seen as the intended recipient of the address because it is the reader's choice of link that results in her or his arriving at this lexia. Fludernik notes in her analysis of print fiction that "*you*, even if it turns out to refer to a fictional protagonist, initially always seems to involve the actual reader" ("Pronouns" 106). In a hypertext fiction, however, a second-person address is even more likely to implicate the reader because he or she is physically involved in the construction of the text. She or he must use a mouse to select a link and thus make a decision about the experience of the text. Consequently, the reader is intimately involved in the unfolding of the narrative (cf. Bell, "Ontological," and *Possible;* Bell and Ensslin; Walker).

Yet while the second-person address in "Slacktown" initiates a dialogue between narrator and reader, the narrator cannot know what the reader "knew it would look like" because the narrator does not have access to the reader's mind. As Fludernik argues, "second-person fiction [is] 'impossible' in the sense of narrating to the reader or an addressee what that addressee *qua* story protagonist must know much better" (*Towards* 262). The opening sentence of the "Slacktown" lexia creates an unnatural narrative in which the narrator claims to have access to the reader's mind and, as the narrative in "Slacktown" progresses, the unnaturalness continues but the referent of "you" changes. The narrator presents an increasingly precise description of a fictional scene, and this connects "you" to a more specific and fictional referent. Fludernik observes that "as second-person texts proceed to fill in more specific information about *you* . . . the status of this *you* as fictional persona becomes increasingly clear" (*Towards* 227). In the "Slacktown" lexia, the narrator describes a hotel lobby with intricate details including "concrete pillars" and "glassine cephalopod elevators" and in so doing provides an account of a space to which the reader does not belong. The visual description is also accompanied by proximal markers, "this" and "here," which locate the spatial point of view firmly within the fictional world. The reporting of direct speech, "which way to . . . er . . . the lobby?" which is followed by a critical response by the narrator, also confirms that the narrator is addressing a fictional character rather than the reader. The rest of the reading path further confirms such a deictic shift as the narrative follows "you" through a number of equally specific scenes and dialogues so that as the second-person narrative provides more detailed descriptions, the status of the opening line in "Slacktown" and the initial referent of "you" as reader is undermined.

More specifically, the second-person narrative in "Slacktown" shifts from what Richardson defines as the "autotelic" form, in which the "direct address to a 'you' . . . is at times the actual reader" (30), to the "standard" form, where "a story is told, usually in the present tense, about a single protagonist who is referred to in the second person" (20). Moreover, as the details of the scene become more precise, the status of the "you" in the opening line is also undermined. While the reader is the initial recipient of the second-person address, the "you" retrospectively becomes what Herman defines as the "doubly-deictic" you, in which the "narrative *you* produces an ontological hesitation between . . . reference to entities . . . internal to the storyworld and reference to entities . . . external to the storyworld" (338). In this case "you" refers to both a fictional and a real addressee simultaneously, causing a large degree of ambiguity and reader identification without the ontological frame of the narrative being exceeded completely.

Irrespective of whether "you" refers to the reader or the protagonist or both, the second-person narrative in "Slacktown" is unnatural throughout because the narrator appears to have access to the thoughts of another being. Moreover, the present tense of the narrative implies also that the narrator knows what is happening at the same that the story is unfolding. As

Fludernik observes, "by employing the imperative and the narrative present tense... second-person fiction foregrounds the act of invention and illustrates how telling *generates* the story in the first place, rather than representing and reproducing in narrative shape a sequence of events that is prior to this act of linguistic creation" (*Towards* 262). The unnaturalness of the second-person voice in "Slacktown" is compounded therefore by the tense in which it is presented; the fictional scene cannot be simultaneously described and created.

As the references to Fludernik's, Richardson's, and Herman's studies of print fiction suggest, the unnatural second-person narrative in "Slacktown" is certainly not exclusive to hypertext, and their narrative theories, which are based on print examples, can be successfully applied to the digital context of *Victory Garden*. However, the hypertext structure is used in *Victory Garden* to complicate and ultimately undermine the ontological status of the narrative in "Slacktown" as well as the many other lexias that follow and as such can be seen as offering a form of unnatural narration that is peculiar to the digital medium. As was noted in the discussion of hypertext fragmentation above, since readers often encounter the same part of a hypertext text via a number of different reading trajectories and/or revisit lexias in light of new information, their interpretation of lexias can change. The preceding analysis of the "Slacktown" lexia showed how a reader entering the text from one of several entrance links would encounter heterodiegetic second-person narration. However, if the lexia were to be accessed by a reader with more experience of the text or reached via a different reading route, other conclusions about the narrative in "Slacktown" could be drawn. More specifically, *Victory Garden* contains several scenes in which academics from the University of Tara are involved in researching dreams. During these parts of the text, experiments are performed in which volunteers are placed in a form of hypnotic sleep. Boris Urquhart then attempts to subliminally manipulate their dreaming experiences by speaking to them in the second-person voice. Providing a visual clue for readers, the dreamers' experiences appear in lexias that are framed by a curved line at the top of the screen, as shown in the "Slacktown" extract on page 193. Readers with previous experience of the dreaming sequences will therefore likely categorize the narrative in "Slacktown" as well as the other lexias that follow as part of a narrative in which the voice of a homodiegetic narrator—Boris Urquhart—is heard by a character who is asleep. In this case, the narrative represents the thoughts of a character, listening to the direct speech of Boris Urquhart as he attempts to guide them through a particular dream world.

This alternative scenario is unnatural because it depicts a scene that cannot be replicated in the real world. We have access to our own thoughts only and therefore cannot depict those of others. Similarly, we can never have access to a reporting experience at the same time that it is happening. However, while this scene is unnatural, it is unnatural in a way that is different from the unnaturalness of a heterodiegetic narrator's address. An address from the heterodiegetic narrator to either the reader or the protagonist or both, as shown in the initial analysis of "Slacktown," is unnatural because it implies that the future is known and also that minds can be read. An address to an unconscious character is unnatural because it suggests that it is possible for the thoughts of an unconscious character to be known as well as presented as they are simultaneously experienced.

In the "Slacktown" example, hypertext provides a distinctive context for unnatural narrative because the ontological status of the scene is dramatically altered by the knowledge that the reader has when he or she encounters the lexia. While readers of print fiction may also modify their interpretation of scenes based on new information, the hypertext structure allows both alternatives to exist in the same text. Crucially, these mutually exclusive events do not represent the same type of narrative contradiction as Emily's death and survival or the three versions of the same Urquhart-Tate scene. Once readers learn that the "Slacktown" lexia forms part of a dream sequence, any previous conclusions are superseded. Thus whereas narrative contradictions exist in parallel, narrative qualifications create a trail of disqualified possibilities. Yet while the result is different, in each case the analysis of "Slacktown" shows how the hypertext structure allows the unnaturalness of the scene to be influenced by the reading route through which it is reached, and this is something that is facilitated by the hypertext's fragmented structure.

6. Conclusion

The application of narrative theory has shown that the narrative contradictions and the second-person narrative housed in *Victory Garden* are unnatural. In the former case two logically irreconcilable scenarios are presented. In the latter the narrator claims to have access to the thoughts of others as well as an omniscient ability to document events as they unfold. From a methodological perspective, this analysis has also shown that narrative theory, which has been developed using examples from print fiction, can be used successfully to analyze unnaturalness in hypertext fiction. In addition, however, while this essay has argued that hypertext fiction is not inherently unnatural, it has shown that hypertext provides a multilinear and/or fragmentary context in which unnatural narratives can be placed. In a hypertext structure, narrative contradictions can exist in parallel and lexias and links can be combined to form inescapable loops. Consequently, different readers will inevitably experience different narratives, and, indeed, the same reader may well experience a different narrative each time he or she reads the text. More importantly in the context of this analysis, when encountered in a range of different reading paths, the same section of text can have a range of different meanings, some natural and some unnatural. When coupled with ambiguous forms of reference, such as that found in second-person narration, the multilinearity of the narrative is compounded. Ultimately a hypertextual structure offers an environment for narrative fiction that cannot be replicated in print. Thus when we apply narrative theory, which has traditionally been based on the analysis of print, we must be conscious of the affordances that a digital context permits.

In addition, it is because the hypertext configuration of lexias and links allows for structural experimentation that unnatural elements proliferate in digital fiction. This analysis has focused on narrative multiplicity and narrative fragmentation in *Victory Garden,* but unnatural elements can also be found in a range of other hypertext fictions. Like *Victory Garden,* Michael Joyce's *afternoon, a story* and Shelley Jackson's *Patchwork Girl* both use the hypertext structure to house narrative contradictions. In other cases, the fragmentary hypertext structure facilitates the merging of narrative levels. For example, in *Patchwork Girl* the protagonist has a sexual relationship with a character from the novel she is writing, and in Richard Holeton's *Figurski at Findhorn on Acid* the characters email the author to complain about the way in which he is presenting them. In all three texts, as in many others, the hypertext structure is used to house playful but ultimately unnatural narratives (cf. Bell and Alber). All of these unnatural devices can be found in print, but the hypertext structure allows them to be placed in a digital environment, and it is therefore important that media-specific tools are developed to account for this. Moreover, that hypertext fictions consistently contain unnatural elements suggests that narrative theory can exploit them as plentiful sources of data. As this essay has shown, however, any narratological analysis must be sensitive to the media-specific affordances these kinds of texts inevitably bring with them.

Works Cited

Alber, Jan. "Impossible Storyworlds—And What to Do with Them." *Storyworlds* 1 (2009): 79–96.

Bell, Alice. "Ontological Boundaries and Methodological Leaps: The Significance of Possible Worlds Theory for Hypertext Fiction (and Beyond)." In *New Narratives: Stories and*

Storytelling in the Digital Age, ed. Bronwen Thomas and Ruth Page. Lincoln: University of Nebraska Press, 2012. 63–82.

———. *The Possible Worlds of Hypertext Fiction*. Basingstoke: Palgrave Macmillan, 2010.

Bell, Alice and Jan Alber. "Ontological Metalepsis and Unnatural Narratology." *Journal of Narrative Theory* 42.2 (2012): 166–92.

Bell, Alice and Astrid Ensslin. "'I know what it was. You know what it was': Second Person Narration in Hypertext Fiction." *Narrative* 19.3 (2011): 311–29.

Bolter, J. David. *Writing Space: Computers, Hypertext and the Remediation of Print*. 2001. Mahwah, NJ: Lawrence Erlbaum Associates, 2009.

Ciccoricco, David. *Reading Network Fiction*. Tuscaloosa: University of Alabama Press, 2007.

Culler, Jonathan. *Structuralist Poetics: Structuralism, Linguistics and the Study of Literature*. London: Routledge & Kegan Paul, 1975.

Douglas, Jane Y. "Understanding the Act of Reading: The WOE Beginner's Guide to Dissection." *Writing on the Edge* 2.2 (1991): 112–25.

———. "What Hypertexts Can Do that Print Narratives Cannot." *Reader* 28 (1992): 1–22.

Fludernik, Monika. "Pronouns of Address and 'Odd' Third Person Forms: The Mechanics of Involvement in Fiction." In *New Essays in Deixis: Discourse, Narrative, Literature*, ed. Keith Green. Amsterdam: Rodopi, 1995. 99–129.

———. *Towards a "Natural" Narratology*. London and New York: Routledge, 1996.

Hayles, N. Katherine. *Writing Machines*. Cambridge, MA: MIT Press, 2002.

Herman, David. *Story Logic: Problems and Possibilities of Narrative*. Lincoln: University of Nebraska Press, 2002.

Holeton, Richard. *Figurski at Findhorn on Acid* [CD-ROM]. Watertown, MA: Eastgate Systems, 2001.

Jackson, Shelley. *Patchwork Girl* [CD-ROM]. Watertown, MA: Eastgate Systems, 1995.

Johnson, B. S. *The Unfortunates*. 1969. Basingstoke: Picador, 1999.

Joyce, Michael. *afternoon, a story* [CD-ROM]. Watertown, MA: Eastgate Systems, 1987.

———. "Nonce upon Some Times: Rereading Hypertext Fiction." *Modern Fiction Studies* 43.3 (1997): 579–97.

Koskimaa, Raine. *Digital Literature: From Text to Hypertext and Beyond*. PhD diss., University of Jyvaskyla, 2000. http://users.jyu.fi/~koskimaa/thesis/thesis.shtml (accessed October 8, 2011).

Moulthrop, Stuart. *Victory Garden* [CD-ROM]. Watertown, MA: Eastgate Systems, 1991.

Richardson, Brian. *Unnatural Voices: Extreme Narration in Modern and Contemporary Fiction*. Columbus: The Ohio State University Press, 2006.

Ryan, Marie-Laure. *Narrative as Virtual Reality: Immersion and Interactivity in Literature and Electronic Media*. Baltimore: John Hopkins University Press, 2001.

Saporta, Marc. *Composition No. 1* [1963]. Trans. Richard Howard. London: Visual Editions, 2011.

Walker, Jill. "Do You Think You're Part of This? Digital Texts and the Second Person Address." In *Cybertext Yearbook*, ed. Markku Eskerlinen and Raine Koskimaa. Research Centre for Contemporary Culture, University of Jyväskylä, Finland, 2000. http://cybertext.hum.jyu.fi/articles/122.pdf (accessed October 8, 2011).

The Unnaturalness of Narrative Poetry

BRIAN McHALE

THE UNDERLYING working hypothesis of all cognitive approaches to narrative, as I understand it, is that narrative is *natural,* in the sense that it arises spontaneously among all human groups, across eras and cultures, and that wherever and whenever it occurs it displays similar features. Its ubiquity and longevity are explained by the fact that it reflects fundamental categories and processes of human cognition and experience. The baseline form of all narrative is spontaneously occurring conversational narratives of personal experience, and according to the "natural narrative" hypothesis, the cognitive parameters of natural conversational narrative remain in force even in the most sophisticated written narratives.

The boldest statement of the natural narrative hypothesis is that of Monika Fludernik, whose account of it I have been paraphrasing. Fludernik argues that we *naturalize* texts by *narrativizing* them, that is, by attempting to assimilate them to the basic template of natural conversational narrative, even (or especially) when they appear to diverge markedly from that template. For instance, conversational narratives are by definition produced by a particular person occupying a particular spatial and temporal situation, so when readers encounter written texts that appear to lack such features, they go to great lengths to supply them by projecting entities such as narrators and implied authors (Fludernik 47). Of course, there have always been texts that test the limits of readers' ingenuity, increasingly many in the modernist and postmodernist periods, but only when narrativizing manifestly fails—for instance, in some of Beckett's late prose texts—do readers finally abandon the attempt to conform texts to the model of natural narrative. Arguably, there are no ultimately "unnatural" narratives, on this account, only texts that, though they may resist narrativization, ultimately yield to it, and those that do not, and so drop out of the category of narrative altogether.[1]

However, if in one sense there are no ultimately unnatural narratives, there are certainly *artificial* ones. Artifice and the unnatural are not necessarily identical or interchangeable. Although the two terms are near-synonyms in everyday usage, I want to distinguish between them here, at least provisionally. Unnaturalness is a question of a text's divergence from the model of natural conversational narrative. To the degree that it is naturalizable at all (see note 1), unnaturalness in narrative is naturalized by being assimilated to that model. Artifice, by contrast, cannot be naturalized in terms of the natural narrative model; it can only be *motivated* in terms of functional necessity or generic requirements or expectations.[2]

1.

From the earliest periods about which we know anything at all, natural conversational narrative has coexisted with more institutionalized narrative genres, produced under special circumstances by authorized performers instead of arising spontaneously in conversation. Conspicuous among these artificial narrative genres is *oral narrative poetry*, arguably the earliest form of *artistic* narrative, and certainly the first to leave its traces in the medium of writing. (Prose narrative, as Fludernik remarks [43], is a latecomer to writing in most vernacular literary traditions.) Thus the *diachronic* importance of narrative poetry is undeniable, as Fludernik acknowledges by making room for it in her survey of narrative in the Middle English period (though it drops out of

---

1. This argument—namely that all narratives, however unnatural they may appear to be, ultimately yield to naturalization in terms of the natural narrative paradigm—could be viewed as the *weaker* version of the "unnatural narrative" hypothesis; for an exemplary statement of it, see Alber. There is also a *stronger* version of the hypothesis, one that entertains the possibility that some manifestations of narrative unnaturalness may successfully resist naturalization without thereby ceasing to be narrative; Nielsen is exemplary. See Alber, Iversen, Nielsen, and Richardson for an attempt, perhaps not wholly convincing, to reconcile these versions.

2. My account of naturalization and motivation is indebted to Culler, *Structuralist* 134–60, and ultimately to the Russian formalist distinction among compositional, realistic, and aesthetic motivations.

her historical account thereafter). However, its historical importance notwithstanding, Fludernik doesn't actually devote much sustained theoretical reflection to narrative poetry. Her observations on the *interaction* of poetry and narrative in Middle English are incidental, piecemeal, and undertheorized. The verse line in saints' legends and verse romances, she observes, generally seems to correspond to the "idea units" of natural narrative (107, 115), so that prosodic units here parallel narrative units; in *Troilus and Criseyde*, by contrast, Chaucer lets narrative units overrun the divisions between his *rime royal* stanzas to accommodate long speeches and meditations (117–18).[3] These are valuable insights, but they are orphans, lacking a theoretical framework to call home.[4]

Fludernik's account here would have benefitted from a framework that allowed her to explore the relation between the narrative form of narrative poetry and whatever it is that qualifies it *as* poetry. Elsewhere (McHale, "Beginning") I have argued that this "whatever it is," the *differentia specifica* of poetry as such, is its *segmentivity*.[5] Natural narrative, of course, is also segmented, as are all verbal utterances of any kind whatsoever, but onto these "natural" systems of segmentation poetry imposes its own order, an *artificial* order comprising (depending on the poem) stanzas or sections, lines, metrical feet, down to the level of words, syllables, and even letters.[6] Poetry *spaces* language—it literally introduces white space (or, in oral poetry, pause or silence) in places where natural narrative (or written prose) has none. The multiple kinds of segmentation in a poem interact with each other in counterpoint (or *countermeasurement,* to use John Shoptaw's term),[7] producing "chords"

---

3. On Chaucer's use of the *rime royal* stanza, see Kinney.

4. When Fludernik revisits the question of poetry much later in the book (304–10, 354–58), her generalizations are uncharacteristically tentative and incoherent. She seems to conflate poetry with lyric (in common with many other theorists; see McHale "Beginning") and to assume that prose poetry must be allied with narrative precisely *because* its form is prose (308). In fact, much prose poetry is uncompromisingly lyrical, including that of Ponge, whom Fludernik specifically mentions in this connection.

5. My account of segmentivity derives from DuPlessis ("Codicil"). Poetry, DuPlessis writes, involves "the creation of meaningful sequence by the negotiation of gap (line-break, stanza-break, page space)." Poetry "is the kind of writing that is articulated in sequenced, gapped lines and whose meanings are created by occurring in bounded units [...] operating in relation to [...] pause or silence" ("Codicil" 51). DuPlessis did not include her one-page "Codicil on the Definition of Poetry" when she reprinted "Manifests," the essay to which it had been attached, in her book *Blue Studios* (73–95), but the "Codicil" does in fact appear elsewhere in the book, folded into an essay on George Oppen (*Blue* 198–99).

6. Words and syllables are units of natural language, of course, as letters are units of the system of writing, but in the system of poetic segmentation these can all acquire special supplementary values as units of *poetry,* above and beyond their functions as linguistic units.

7. Shoptaw defines a poem's measure as "its smallest unit of resistance to meaning" (212).

(DuPlessis, "Codicil" 51), complex interplays among segments of different kinds or scales. They also interact with the units of narrative organization, sometimes reinforcing or amplifying them—such as when verse lines parallel narrative units in Middle English saints' legends and romances—sometimes counterpointing or countermeasuring them, as in the case of Chaucer's handling of *rime royal*.

But surely it is not sufficient simply to tack an account of segmentivity onto the hypothesis of natural narrative in order to accommodate the special case of narrative poetry. To do so would be to risk treating the poetry in narrative poetry as merely *supplementary* to narrative, a little *extra* organization to enhance or complicate the narrative structure of a text. In such a framework, natural narrative still remains the baseline relative to which all divergences are gauged, and narrativization proceeds with poetry just as it would in the case of any other more or less resistant text. But the decision to narrate in verse has more radical consequences than that, surely. "To take a language and organize it in rhymed stanzas," writes Veronica Forrest-Thomson, "making use of a rhetorical tone and figurative combinations of words, is a social act which emphasizes formal features normally 'irrelevant' to the business of communication and, by adding this new dimension, comes to dominate the whole problem of producing meaning, or ordering" (60). Artifice changes everything, narrative included.

Artifice and naturalness have sustained a kind of dialectical tension right across the history of poetry. Certain periods, schools, and genres attach particular value to highly artificial devices and practices: complex meter and rhyme, special diction, densely figurative language, mythological subjects, literary allusion, distinctively poetic devices such as apostrophe,[8] and so on. Conversely, other periods, schools, and genres value relative naturalness, or at least the appearance of it: muted meter and rhyme, or their absence; prosaic or colloquial diction; downplayed figures; subjects drawn from everyday

---

Measure determines where gaps open up in a poetic text, and a gap is always a provocation to gap-filling and meaning-making: where the poem resists, the reader engages. Poetry can be *word-measured*, as it is, for instance, in certain modernist one-word-per-line poems (William Carlos Williams, e.e. cummings); it can be measured at the scale of the *phrase* (Emily Dickinson); it can be measured at the scale of the *line*, as is the case in most lyric poetry; it can be measured at the level of the *sentence*, as in prose-poetry or in the Language poets' practice of the "New Sentence" (239–51); and it can be measured at the level of the *section*, as in sonnet cycles or in sequences such as *The Waste Land* (251–55). Poetry is not only measured, but is typically *countermeasured*, so that spacing at one level or scale is played off against spacing at another level or scale: line against sentence, as in enjambed blank verse; phrase against line and stanza, as in Dickinson's poems; and so on.

8. On apostrophe's function as a distinguishing mark of lyric poetry, see Culler's classic essay.

life; and so on. The history of poetry is in part the history of one generation's reaction against the perceived artificiality of its predecessor, in the name of greater naturalness (e.g., the Neoclassicists' reaction against the artificiality of baroque poetics, the Romantics' reaction against the artificiality of Neoclassicism, the Imagists' reaction against the artificiality of late-Romantic poetry) or sometimes the other way around, a reaction against the inartfulness of one's predecessors in the name of greater artifice (e.g., the Renaissance poets' reaction against their late-medieval predecessors). Particularly since the Romantic revolution at the turn of the eighteenth century, much effort has gone into naturalizing the artifices of poetry, in the sense of avoiding certain irredeemably artificial features (conventional periphrastic diction, for instance) and developing psychological, functional, and organic motivations for others.[9] It is in this naturalizing spirit, for instance, that Wordsworth could defend poetry as a natural medium of expression—"a selection of the language really used by men," as he called it in the preface to the *Lyrical Ballads*—or that Keats could assert in a letter that poetry ought to "come as naturally as the leaves to a tree" if it was to come at all.

Both tendencies, toward artifice and toward naturalness, or naturalization, persist into the twentieth century and beyond. By the end of the century, the dominant mode of poetry (at least in the English-speaking world) was colloquial, anecdotal, unmetered and unrhymed, differentiated from prose by little more than lineation—poetry of minimal artifice and maximum naturalness. The alternative tendency is reflected in the historical avant-gardes and their successors, movements that value poetry for its power to *resist* the natural—to defamiliarize, to estrange, to alienate, to dis-illusion. Insofar as the dominant naturalizing mode articulates or implies something like a theory of poetry, it is unlikely to be one that addresses poetry's artifice. So if we are seeking a theory that captures what the hypothesis of natural narrative leaves out—namely the *poetry* in narrative poetry, its artifice as opposed to its naturalness—we would do better to turn to the alternative tradition, that of the historical avant-gardes.

2.

A late and particularly uncompromising restatement of the avant-garde attitude is that of Veronica Forrest-Thomson in *Poetic Artifice* (1978).[10] Though

---

9. I am relying here on Wesling (1980), mainly as filtered through Charles Bernstein's discussion ("Artifice" 42–46).

10. I have written about Forrest-Thomson's theory of artifice on several occasions, including McHale, "Making." See also Bernstein, whose response to Forrest-Thomson I discuss below, and Mark.

the book's subtitle specifies that hers is *A Theory of Twentieth-Century Poetry*, in fact Forrest-Thomson proposes a theory of poetry in general, as distinct from all other modes of discourse. Her argument runs like this: Poetry has no other medium than language, which is also, and primarily, the medium of our day-to-day pragmatic engagement with the world, used in everyday language-games including, for instance, spontaneous conversational narrative. Poetry's nature and function, however, is to *dis*connect language from everyday contexts, dislocating it into the special context of poetry, de- and then recontextualizing it. Forrest-Thomson quotes with approval Wittgenstein's dictum: "Do not forget that a poem, even though it is composed in the language of information, is not used in the language-game of giving information" (Forrest-Thomson x, quoting Wittgenstein 160). Poetry, Forrest-Thomson writes, "assimilate[s] the already-known and subject[s] it to a reworking which suspends and questions its categories, provides alternative orderings" (53). "Ordinary language," she continues, "provides poet and reader with a controlled and interpreted experiential context, while poetic convention disrupts, modifies, and perhaps questions" (56–57). It also synthesizes and integrates, imposing a new order of meaning on elements that in ordinary contexts of language-use would pass unnoticed or would be dismissed as just so much irrelevant noise. To contextualize language as poetry is to mobilize a set of conventions bearing on these "non-semantic" patterns—rhymes and other sound patterns, rhythms and repetitions, potential puns and other ambiguities, irrelevant associations. In the special context of poetry, with its special conventions, such nonsemantic patterns are foregrounded, elevated above the threshold of relevance, and semanticized, rendered meaningful.

Poetry, then, in Forrest-Thomson's view, is an essentially *artificial* discourse, distinct from natural conversational narrative or other genres of everyday discourse, and constitutionally resistant to naturalization.[11] Any poem that invites or courts naturalization (as many do, of course) compromises the very nature of poetry and undermines its special claim to our attention; such poetry is complicit with what Forrest-Thomson calls "bad naturalization." Interpreters of poetry inevitably naturalize, but *good* naturalization involves taking into account the primacy of the context of poetry itself—its artifice (36). "The worst disservice criticism can do poetry," she writes,

---

11. Fludernik's notion of narrativization (e.g., naturalizing a text by assimilating it to the model of natural narrative) is akin to Forrest-Thomson's naturalization—literally. Forrest-Thomson developed her concept of naturalization in concert with Jonathan Culler, to whom she was married for a time, and Fludernik explicitly credits Culler as the source of her own understanding of naturalization (31–35). See note 7.

is to try to understand it too soon, for this devalues the importance of real innovation which must take place on the non-semantic levels. Criticism's function is eventually to try to understand, at a late stage, even Artifice. (161)

Charles Bernstein, poet and theorist, and like Forrest-Thomson an heir of the avant-garde tradition, concurs: poetry "by nature emphasiz[es] its artifice" ("Artifice" 31). Revisiting Forrest-Thomson's theory of poetic artifice, and picking up on her metaphors of *absorption, assimilation, suspension,* and *hesitation,* Bernstein in his essay-poem *Artifice of Absorption* (1987, 1992) distinguishes between absorption in poetry and its opposite, antiabsorption. Absorptive poetry integrates, reconciles, and homogenizes its constitutive elements, including ordinary language; it naturalizes those elements, perhaps in the immigration-control sense of granting them citizenship in the poem, even though they originate elsewhere, outside. Absorptive poetry also absorbs in the sense of engaging and fascinating its readers, absorbing their attention. By contrast, antiabsorptive poetry, like the poetic artifice that Forrest-Thomson championed, resists integration, naturalization, and readerly fascination. "Poetry," Bernstein writes in one of his poems, "The Klupzy Girl" (*Islets* 47), "is like a swoon, with this difference: / It brings you to your senses." Or it does so at one level, at least; for, in Bernstein's account, poetry that is antiabsorptive at one level can nevertheless be absorptive—hypnotic, enchanting, entrancing, swoony—when we pull back to view it from another, higher level. Conversely, poetry that is absorptive, and *absorbing,* at one level can be antiabsorptive—off-putting, repulsive, alienating—at another. Moreover, the very same devices and features can be either absorptive or antiabsorptive, depending on context. Metrical versification, for instance, has typically been used for absorptive purposes, "the regular recurrences of sounds / & beats lulling—or pulling—the attention / inward" ("Artifice" 39). "Conversely," however,

> metricality & other
> traditional prosodic devices, especially
> when foregrounded, can be potent antiabsorptive
> techniques (& were traditionally used as such
> by many English poets prior to the rise of
> Romanticism). A sestina, in almost anybody's
> hands, seems artificial. ("Artifice" 39)

Neither Forrest-Thomson nor Bernstein explicitly addresses narrative poetry in connection with their theories of artifice and absorption.[12] Bernstein, in particular, seems suspicious of narrative, apparently regarding it as inherently absorptive—a view shared by many others in the avant-garde tradition. "Today's / bestsellers routinely 'spellbind,'" he observes ("Artifice" 53)—that is, they absorb us in the sense of immersing us so that, while reading a bestseller, we may lose track of the world around us. "'Escapist' literature," Bernstein writes, "offers no escape, / narratively reinforcing our captivity" (75), and he quotes approvingly from a poem by his colleague Bob Perelman: "If only the plot would leave people alone" (84, quoting Perelman 63). Nevertheless, there is no reason why the conceptual tools of artifice and absorption should not yield valuable insights when applied to poems that tell stories. Natural narrative is presumably absorptive: that is, it seeks to efface the traces of its fabrication (its artifice) and to immerse us readers in its storyworld, to engage and spellbind us. Its language is that of everyday life, the language used to play the language-game of communication, not the artificial language of what Forrest-Thomson sometimes calls, provocatively, the "Separate Planet" of poetry (87, 100). But what happens when the absorptiveness that is native to narrative is mediated by poetic artifice—by poetry's artificial apparatus of meter, line- and stanza-breaks, end-rhyme, musical effects, conspicuous figures, and so on?

One could begin exploring the relation between artifice, absorption, and narrative in narrative poetry by examining cases from the extreme poles of artificiality and naturalness. All poems, writes Bernstein, "require artifice," but some (the absorptive ones) hide it while others (the antiabsorptive ones) flaunt it ("Artifice" 30):

> If the artifice
> is recessed, the resulting textual transparency
> yields an apparent, if misleading, content.
> .... If the artifice is
> foregrounded, there's a tendency to say that there
> is no content or meaning, as if the poem were a
> formal or decorative exercise concerned only with
> representing its own mechanisms. (10)

At the pole of extreme artifice, where poems sometimes appear to be merely "formal or decorative exercise[s]," we find, for instance, verse romances of

---

12. Interestingly, Forrest-Thomson analyzes several quasi-narrative poems, including Eliot's *The Waste Land* and his quatrain poems, as well as J. H. Prynne's "Of Sanguine Fire," but she finds virtually nothing to say about their narrativity.

the English Renaissance, highly wrought poems on mythological topics, obviously designed to showcase the poets' ingenuity, linguistic facility, and mastery of poetic convention, but not always very seriously committed to their own narrative content, which sometimes appears as little more than a pretext for poetic exhibitionism. Examples include Thomas Lodge's *Scylla's Metamorphosis* (1589), Samuel Daniel's *The Complaint of Rosamond* (1592), Michael Drayton's *Endymion and Phoebe* (1592), Christopher Marlowe's *Hero and Leander* (1598), and the most accomplished of them all, the poem that I will consider in the next section, Shakespeare's *Venus and Adonis* (1593). How do verse-form, musicality, figuration, and other artificial features interact with the units and categories of narrative organization (events and agency, storyworld, characterization, focalization, narration, etc.) and the sources of narrative interest (curiosity, suspense, surprise) in such conspicuously artificial narrative poems?

At the other extreme, we might consider a twentieth-century verse novel such as Les Murray's *Fredy Neptune* (1998), a deliberately prosaic book-length poem that tells an eventful (literally *event-filled*) story in a highly novelistic manner. An Australian, Murray clearly subscribes here and elsewhere in his poetry to the dominant late-century poetics of colloquial diction and muted artifice. However, as Bernstein reminds us, muted or recessed artifice is not the same as absence of artifice. To see what difference even minimal artifice makes, in section 4 I will try the experiment of recasting a passage from *Fredy Neptune* (which is written in unmetered, generally unrhymed eight-line stanzas) as continuous prose, *de-versifying* it and juxtaposing my fabricated prose version with Murray's original. When one restores the poem's segmentivity, what happens to the organization of its narration and its storyworld? Does artifice (even the minimal artifice of line- and stanza-breaks) really change everything, or not?

3.

Shakespeare's *Venus and Adonis*[13] is a narrative poem in 199 six-line, end-rhymed stanzas, iambic pentameter in meter, and rhyming in the pattern *ababcc*. It retells a story familiar from Ovid's *Metamorphoses,* Book X, which had already been retold multiple times by Shakespeare's Renaissance predecessors, including Spenser in *The Faerie Queene* Book III, canto 1, stanzas

---

13. I am using the text in Reese (112–58) because of its convenient proximity to five other verse romances of the era, by Daniel, Lodge, Marlowe, Drayton, and Marston.

34–38. Spenser's version takes the form of ekphrases of tapestries hanging on the walls of Castle Joyous. Here the sequence of events is parceled into several quasi-lyric moments, most of them occupying their own stanzas in a way that anticipates the distribution of narrative events across panels in comics: the goddess Venus is smitten by love for the mortal Adonis; she seduces him; she gazes upon him as he sleeps; she cautions him against hunting; Adonis lies dead, gored by a boar, and Venus mourns him, whereupon he is transformed into a flower. Shakespeare's story differs from Spenser's in that his Adonis never succumbs to Venus, and her love for him remains unconsummated. However, Shakespeare's version preserves the narrative gap corresponding to Adonis's actual goring, which in his version as in Spenser's occurs offstage, literally between stanzas (in the gutter, to pursue the comics analogy). In narratological terms, one could say that events in Shakespeare's version are focalized through Venus and that, when Adonis parts from her to go hunting and gets himself killed, the perspective remains with her, so that we see and hear only what she does.

The principal differences between the Shakespearean version and Spenser's, however, arise in the areas of scale—sheer length—and consequently of narrative pacing. Spenser retells the Venus and Adonis story in the space of five nine-line stanzas, for a total of 45 lines, while Shakespeare's poem runs to no fewer than 1,194 lines. Shakespeare dilates at length upon the events of the story, digressing often, prolonging each event and thereby delaying the later ones in the sequence. His is a poem of suspended action and prolonged anticipation, a dilatory poem, much more leisurely in pace than Spenser's version. Here is where artifice has the most forceful impact on narrative. While Spencer's poem is certainly highly artificial, in Shakespeare's, artifice serves to slow narrative almost to a standstill: artifice changes everything.

The building blocks of Shakespeare's narrative—or perhaps we should say its *stumbling* blocks, since they impede the narrative as much as they advance it—are its formal units: its stanzas. Here it might be helpful to consider the *affordances* of this particular stanzaic form, its potential for use.[14] Every verse-form, stanzaic or otherwise, offers different affordances, different potentials for use, encouraging or discouraging different interactions with (in the case of narrative poems) narrative segmentation. Narrative may follow the line of least resistance, conforming to the stanzaic structure, or conversely it may ignore the promptings or resistances of form. It is always free to *override* the stanzaic structure, as Chaucer's narrative, for instance, sometimes does the

14. The concept of affordances is borrowed from software designers and media theorists, and ultimately from perceptual psychology; for an earlier attempt to apply it to stanzaic form, see McHale "Affordances."

rime royal stanza-form in Fludernik's example from *Troilus and Criseyde*. The affordances of form are only options, not mandates, but they are options that yield certain advantages that the poet may choose to seize—or not.

In the case of the *ababcc* stanza of *Venus and Adonis*,[15] lineation and stanza form are conducive to strong segmentation into compact, integral units, an affordance that Shakespeare normally observes throughout. There is little line-to-line enjambment of syntactical or narrative units, and almost none from stanza to stanza except in a couple of conspicuously anomalous passages (about which I will have more to say below). Strong mid-line caesura is rare, which makes the one stanza in which it is foregrounded an exception that proves the rule:

> 120
> 'Where did I leave?' 'No matter where (quoth he);
> Leave me, and then the story aptly ends,
> The night is spent.' 'Why, what of that?' (quoth she).
> 'I am (quoth he) expected of my friends;
>   And now 'tis dark, and going I shall fall.'
>   'In night (quoth she) desire sees best of all. (Reese 139)

Here, exceptionally for this poem, five dialogue turns have been collapsed into a single stanza, two of them beginning at mid-line (the caesura) and running over the line-end, foregrounding the romantic-comedy aspects of the situation, and ironically deflating Venus's seductive eloquence ("Where did I leave [off]?," i.e., "Now, where was I?").

The end-rhyme pattern organizes each stanza into two units: a quatrain (*abab*) followed by a couplet (*cc*). Shakespeare exploits the affordances of this stanza's form throughout, frequently realizing the potential for a "turn" after line 4. For instance, on at least four occasions he makes the stanza a vehicle for extended similes, with the comparison occupying the quatrain and the object being compared, the couplet:

> 10
> *Even as* an empty eagle, sharp by fast,
> Tires with her beak on feather, flesh, and bone,
> Shaking her wings, devouring all in haste,
> Till either gorge be stuff'd, or prey be gone;

15. This stanza form had been used before, in Sidney's *Arcadia* and Spenser's *Astrophel* and the First Eclogue of *The Shepherds Calendar*, but most relevantly in Lodge's *Scylla's Metamorphosis*, one of the poems that launched the fashion for Ovidian verse romances.

> *Even so* she kiss'd his brow, his cheek, his chin,
> And where she ends, she doth anew begin. (Reese 114; my italics, B.M.)

Simile, one might say, is a figure of dilation, as opposed to metaphor, generally a figure of compression. No surprise, then, that *Venus and Adonis*, a poem of dilation, abounds in similes, including stanza-length ones.[16]

Despite its length, *Venus and Adonis* really comprises only two episodes, or better, two cycles of delay. The first, occupying something like two-thirds of the poem (stanzas 1–135), involves erotic delay—in effect, elaborate foreplay: Adonis resists Venus's seduction. After a narrative pause of some ten stanzas, the action, such as it is, resumes: Venus delays confronting the fact of Adonis's death (stanzas 145–76); she *stalls for time*.[17] While the poetics of delay is characteristic of English Renaissance verse romances,[18] Shakespeare outdoes his

---

16. See also stanzas 49, 155, 173. Lodge in *Scylla's Metamorphosis* exploits the affordances of this same quatrain-plus-couplet form less than does Shakespeare. There appears to be only one stanza-length simile in Lodge's poem, and if anything, Lodge counterpoints his syntactic and narrative units *against* the rhyme-scheme, with many of his stanzas dividing counterintuitively into two three-line units (rhyming aba bcc). Rime royal, a related stanza-form, but seven lines long instead of six (rhyming ababbcc), would appear to offer similar opportunities for organizing stanza-length similes. Yet Shakespeare himself, in his other narrative poem, *The Rape of Lucrece* (1594), only rarely exploits the *rime royal* stanza as the vehicle for similes.

17. The structure of Shakespeare's other narrative poem, *The Rape of Lucrece*, parallels that of *Venus and Adonis*. It, too, has two anticipated climaxes, the first erotic (the rape), the second mortal (Lucrece's suicide), each delayed by the accumulation of artificial devices. Tarquin's rape of Lucrece—which, despite the gravity of this poem's tone, nevertheless excites a certain amount of prurient anticipation—is delayed first by Tarquin's lengthy self-address (stanzas 41–60), then by a highly figurative *blason* of Lucrece's sleeping body (stanzas 56–61), then by Lucrece's attempts at dissuasion (stanzas 82–96). Lucrece's suicide is delayed by Lucrece's wait for her letter to be delivered to her husband Collatine and for the latter to arrive. This narrative pause is filled in part by an elaborately artificial ekphrasis of a tapestry illustrating the fall of Troy (stanzas 196–209), and by Lucrece's commentary on it (stanzas 210–26). Finally, the suicide is delayed by Lucrece's retelling of her rape (stanzas 233–37), which is strictly speaking redundant: we have already seen it all.

18. Already as early as Lodge's *Scylla*, both the poet himself and his character narrator Glaucus display considerable self-consciousness and anxiety about delay in their respective narratives. Marlowe, in *Hero and Leander*, interpolates narrative episodes involving misdirected, inappropriate, or perverse sexuality in order to delay heteronormative consummation between his protagonists, while in his continuation of Marlowe's unfinished poem, George Chapman frankly acknowledges that he has interpolated irrelevant digressions in order to put off the painful duty of narrating the deaths of Hero and Leander. Michael Drayton's *Endymion and Phoebe* programmatically resists the delayed-consummation structure of other Ovidian verse romances (such as *Hero and Leander* and *Venus and Adonis*) because, since Phoebe's love for Endymion is strictly chaste, there is no erotic consummation to anticipate. Thus Drayton's elaborate descriptive pauses, digressions, insets, and so forth, are literally "pointless," not serving to delay or prolong *anything*, there being no climactic event to delay or prolong. Conversely, in John Marston's

predecessors and contemporaries in his deployment of the resources of artifice to *suspend* and *impede* forward motion.[19]

"The sexual analogy / seems inescapable," writes Bernstein in connection with the poetics of antiabsorption:

> an interruptiveness
> that intensifies & prolongs desire, a postponement
> that finds in delay a more sustaining pleasure &
> presence. That is, an erotics of reading &
> writing.... ("Artifice" 72)

It is just such an "interruptiveness" that characterizes the first cycle of *Venus and Adonis*. Everything that Venus does to seduce Adonis only defers consummation: herein lies the structural irony of this part of the poem, and the source of its unrelieved erotic tension. Venus's elaborate argumentation, playing seemingly endless variations on the theme of *carpe diem*, fills up many stanzas and only prolongs our wait for an erotic climax that finally never arrives. For instance, the minor episode of Adonis's horse breaking loose and taking advantage of its erotic opportunities (stanzas 44–54) is interpreted by Venus (stanza 66) as yet another emblem of seizing the day, but in fact both the episode itself and Venus's interpretation—amounting to a redundant retelling of events we have already been shown—are digressive, serving only to sidetrack Venus's campaign of seduction. The emblem of *carpe diem* is subverted, becoming a figure of withholding and delay. Moreover, the poem is self-conscious about its own delaying tactics, reflecting ironically at one point that "swelling passion doth provoke a pause" (stanza 37; Reese 120), and later that lovers' "copious stories, oftentimes begun / End without audience and are never done" (stanza 141; Reese 144).

In the second cycle, the narrative stages and embodies Venus's reluctance to confront the fact of Adonis's death. The delaying tactics become increasingly artificial, in Forrest-Thompson's and Bernstein's sense of the term, the closer she (and the narrative) comes to the ineluctable evidence of Adonis's death: his violated body. Initially, evidence of the hunt reaches Venus only as the distant sound of hounds (stanzas 145–49), but immediately thereafter

---

parodic *Metamorphosis of Pygmalion's Image* (1598), despite some gestures toward the delaying tactics of Lodge, Shakespeare, and others, there is virtually no delay between desire and consummation: Pygmalion lusts after the statue he has created (stanzas 1–22), petitions Venus to transform her into a real woman (23–24), and goes to bed with her (25–27), whereupon she is transformed and he enjoys her sexually (28–39).

19. Forrest-Thomson's terminology (*suspension, hesitation*, etc.) is highly appropriate here, but so is the related Russian formalist concept of *impeded form* (see, e.g., Shklovsky 22–42).

she confronts the boar itself, whose bloodied tusks are an index of Adonis's death (stanzas 150–51).[20] Despite the decisiveness of this evidence, the following twenty-five stanzas serve to prolong Venus's evasion of the truth. Events begin to ramify and multiply, and redundancies pile up. Venus's own indecision and indirection mirror the indirections and sidetracks of the narrative: "this way she runs, and now she will no further, / But back retires" (stanza 151; Reese 147); "She treads the path that she untreads again; / Her more than haste is mated with delay" (stanza 152; ibid.). She confronts not one of Adonis's hounds, but one after another, redundantly ("And here she meets another . . . Another, and another," stanzas 153–54; ibid.). Self-divided, Venus herself disintegrates into multiple component parts, semiautonomous "sub-Venuses" with which she must negotiate. Thus she tells her senses to "leave quaking, bids them fear no more" (stanza 151; ibid.), while "A thousand spleens bear her a thousand ways" (stanza 152; ibid.). All of this *takes time*, and takes up space in the poem, deferring the inevitable.

Artificial devices accumulate, including at least one stanza-length simile ("Look how the world's people are amaz'd / At apparitions. . . . / So she at these sad signs. . . . ," stanza 155; Reese 148). Venus apostrophizes Death (stanzas 156–99), and is in turn herself apostrophized by the poet (stanza 165). Then she apostrophizes Death all over again (stanzas 167–69), reversing herself and taking back everything she had said the first time: "Now she unweaves the web that she hath wrought" (stanza 166; Reese 150). Tellingly self-reflective, this metaphor obviously alludes to Penelope's nightly unweaving of the fabric she had woven during the day—the *locus classicus* of calculated delay.

The final delay, which stops the action dead in its tracks, occurs at the very moment that Venus "spies" Adonis's shattered body, in a sequence of five exceptionally dense stanzas, 172–76 (lines 1027–56):

172
As falcon to the lure, away she flies;
The grass stoops not, she treads on it so light;
And in her haste unfortunately spies
The foul boar's conquest on her fair delight;
    Which seen, her eyes, as murder'd with the view,
    Like stars asham'd of day, themselves withdrew:

---

20. The overrunning of the stanza-break between stanzas 150 and 151, the first time this happens in the poem, signals the special status of the boar, named at the very end of stanza 150 (where it rhymes ironically with *fear no more*) but caught up in a sentence that rushes on into the next stanza ("Whose frothy mouth, bepainted all with red" etc.).

173
Or, as the snail, whose tender horns being hit,
Shrinks backwards in his shelly cave with pain,
And there, all smother'd up, in shade doth sit,
Long after fearing to creep forth again;
 So, at his bloody view, her eyes are fled
 Into the deep dark cabins of her head:

174
Where they resign their office and their light
To the disposing of her troubled brain;
Who bids them still consort with ugly night,
And never wound the heart with looks again;
 Who, like a king perplexed in his throne,
 By their suggestion gives a deadly groan,

175
Whereat each tributary subject quakes;
As when the wind, imprison'd in the ground,
Struggling for passage, earth's foundation shakes,
Which with cold terror doth men's minds confound.
 This mutiny each part doth so surprise
 That from their dark beds once more leap her eyes;

176
And, being open'd, threw unwilling light
Upon the wide wound that the boar had trench'd
In his soft flank; whose wonted lily white
With purple tears, that his wound wept, was drench'd:
 No flower was nigh, no grass, herb, leaf, or weed,
 But stole his blood and seem'd with him to bleed. (Reese 151–52)

Stanza-breaks are overrun—countermeasured, in Shoptaw's terms—so that the five stanzas form one continuous syntactic and narrative block, yet the effect is not (as might be expected) one of breathless, onrushing haste, but rather of conceptual complication, daunting intricacy, and deferral. Having registered the (as yet unspecified) evidence of the boar's violence, Venus's eyes "withdraw" (stanza 172). As they had earlier, her parts begin acting independently of her, and of each other—eyes, brain, heart; the stanzas *anatomize*

Venus, another highly artificial delaying tactic, parodying the conventional erotic *blason* of the beloved's body.

As in a conventional *blason*, each body part is figured as something else, or indeed as *several* somethings else. Thus Venus's eyes withdraw "Like stars asham'd of day" (stanza 172), but then this simile is further dilated by an alternative simile, expanding to fill a stanza: "Or as the snail, whose tender horns being hit, / Shrinks backward" etc. (stanza 175). Her eyes resign authority to her brain, which tries to protect her heart (stanza 174), which is itself compared to a "perplexed" king. The king's "groans," in turn, are compared to an earthquake, as the similes pile up, one on top of another: heart likened to a king, king likened to an earthquake (stanza 174–75). Finally, the discourse circles back to its starting point, Venus's eyes, and the story, having stalled out for the course of five stanzas, resumes, along with Venus's consciousness, as she finally acknowledges seeing Adonis's corpse and his shed blood (stanza 176).

This is not the last of the delays, for even after this acknowledgment, Venus remains reluctant to accept the truth, and the narrative continues to embody her reluctance in its own dilatoriness. But the roundabout, dilatory progress toward the climactic revelation of Adonis's death tells us everything we need to know about the operations of artifice in this poem. The devices of artifice—similes and apostrophes and so on, but also the fundamental segmentivity that makes the poem a poem in the first place—have a drastic impact on the pacing of the narrative; but more than that, they upend the usual hierarchical relationship between discourse and story. Discourse here is not the handmaiden of story, but *dominates* story; story—narrative content—recedes into the background, while the artifices of poetry make a spectacle of themselves, exhibiting themselves for our inspection and delectation. The *poetry* in this narrative poem upstages the *narrative*.

4.

Les Murray's *Fredy Neptune,* a verse novel from the very end of the twentieth century, is the fictional autobiography of one Fred Boettcher, a working-class Australian of German parentage who wanders the world in the years from the Great War through the Second World War, sometimes as a merchant sailor, sometimes as a circus strongman, sometimes on one side of the century's murderous conflicts, sometimes on the other. Over 250 pages long and divided into five books of unequal length, it straddles multiple genres, combining elements of picaresque, proletarian fiction, historical fiction (or its postmodernist variant, historiographic metafiction), and magical realism. The novel even flirts with allegory—Fred witnesses a Turkish atrocity against Armenian civilians and, apparently as a consequence, loses his ability to experience either pain or pleasure—turning him into something like a realized metaphor for the historical traumas of the twentieth century. Nevertheless, there is enough ambiguity about the nature of Fred's strange disability (is it psychosomatic? the result of a leprosylike nerve disease?) that the novel stops short of toppling headlong into the fantastic or allegorical modes, remaining basically realistic.

In short, *Fredy Neptune* has closer affinities with prose fictions such as John Dos Passos's *U.S.A.* (1930–36), Thomas Berger's *Little Big Man* (1964), or Günter Grass's *The Tin Drum* (1959) than it does with verse novels in the tradition of Pushkin's *Eugene Onegin* (1831), Robert Browning's *The Ring and the Book* (1868–69), Stephen Vincent Benét's *John Brown's Body* (1928), or Robert Penn Warren's *Brother to Dragons* (1953, 1979).[21] Nevertheless, it *is* a poem, albeit one in the low-key, colloquial, minimally artificial style of late-century mainstream verse. It is composed in stanzas of eight free-verse lines, each varying from ten to fifteen syllables in length, generally unrhymed, though fugitive end-rhymes appear here and there, irregularly and opportunistically, as it were. In other words, *Fredy Neptune* does display forms of segmentation that are distinctive of poetry—lineation, stanza-breaks—but little more than that, and even such segmentivity as it possesses is minimal and muted.

Indeed, so unemphatic is this poem's artifice that one might find oneself wondering—as one never would in the case of flagrantly artificial poems such as *Venus and Adonis*—exactly what difference verse makes here, if any. There's one way to find out: by reformatting a brief passage of *Fredy Neptune* as prose, and then comparing this ersatz prose version with Murray's verse original to see how (if at all) verse segmentation influences narrative. I am proposing, in other words, to restage experimentally and *ad hoc* the process of *dérimage* or de-versification (see Kittay and Godzich) that Western vernacular literatures underwent in the Middle Ages, when verse narratives, hitherto the dominant narrative form, were recast as prose, launching the vernacular tradition of prose narrative.[22]

21. Other recent verse novels include novelized epics such as John Gardner's *Jason and Medeia* (1973), Derek Walcott's *Omeros* (1990), and Anne Carson's *Autobiography of Red* (1998), as well as a surprising number of genre fictions in verse, such as John Hollander's *Reflections on Espionage* (1976), a spy novel in verse; Frederick Turner's *The New World* (1985), a science fiction in verse; James Cummins's *The Whole Truth* (1986) and Kevin Young's *Black Maria* (2005), detective novels in verse; Vikram Seth's *The Golden Gate* (1986), a soap opera in verse; and Michael Ondaatje's *Collected Works of Billy the Kid* (1970), a Western in mixed verse and prose. For details, see McHale "Telling."

22. This experiment might be seen as the mirror image of one performed by Forrest-

216 | 10: THE UNNATURALNESS OF NARRATIVE POETRY

Let's sample a brief but eventful passage from early in the novel, less than halfway through Book I, "The Middle Sea" (16–17). Fred has been stranded in Egypt during the Great War, and lands a civilian job breaking horses for the British army in Cairo. Together with some fellow Australians, he follows the army to Jerusalem, recently captured from the Turks. He rides out one morning with his mates just as the Turks mount a counterattack. Recast as prose, the passage reads like this (I have somewhat arbitrarily inserted paragraphing to enhance the prose "look" of the passage):

Next morning after a drink of tea at daybreak our Cairo party rode off south. Bill Hines, Yall Sherritt, Poley Corrigan, myself and the Indian Army man Loocher Sibley. We were talking dogs, the ones who caught us out at cricket, the dingo that let Yall pet her, the curs Poley kept to lick his rheumatics better—we heard like whips cracking, and more and more, back past the windmill, out north of the city. Chains of sparks dotted off a far hill. *Machine gun,* cried Sibley. *And bundooks, lots of them. Dekho that!* a red star went smoking up the sky from the gully Jehosophat. *Jacko's rode down from Nablus to take Jerusalem back.* Stones kicked. You sensed sizzles in the air. Somewhere went pingg! Poley's face turned white: he reached around—*Bloody thing*—and picked a spent bullet out of his tunic like a bee-sting. *You're getting as tough as Freddy, and he's a stature,* said someone. We should have cleared out, but we stared at the war.

So this was battle. Going on, I kept turning round; battle was strings of riders hell-for-leather in a smoky wall of sound. There I saw my first aeroplanes. Three came straining over from down south, rocking, hanging their pony-trap wheels. In front of those north hills they stopped and braced above ground on their guns' fumy pencillings. Bigger guns right near poking out through riveted shields would shorten, and your ear hurt, round a king gap, then you'd hear the slung case rebound.

My life, keeping out of the human race to stay in it—I'd have to think back, to separate thoughts that were all one poem, like, at the brink of what was to happen. There were no sides for me: both were mine. I'd seen them both. Better to lie than pick one: better die than pick: and I'd died indeed flesh-dead, alive in no-life. Not in civvy, not in air, maybe in fire. Would I re-light there? Feel, feel if only death?

Thomson (22–24) and Culler (*Structuralist* 188–92), where they rewrite samples of banal journalistic prose as verse to expose the reading conventions of poetry. Compare also Fish's later (322–37) but more notorious experiment of asking students to interpret a "found" list of names as a poem.

I spurred to a bolt, gravel scattering, back north on my waler—Blue steep up white rubble, blotch and blotch went bursts in the sky; harnessed guns, turbaned Indians, Light Horse all yelling Ayy! men in rage, in their guts, men dead with sheep, butcher's parcels of floury khaki, near dropped rifles, jump-down terrace walls and straight lines whippy round me everywhere. My poor horse stopped one, stopped another one. I spilled off him, left him dying, ran in behind a stacked wall that was spitting and crying. A man, a young officer, was kneeling there. Politely he put down his telephone.

Whatever artificial features this passage possessed in the original have been obscured or submerged, barring a few insistent rhymes, perhaps: *pingg/thing/sting* in the first paragraph, *dying/crying* in the last, maybe a few others. Metaphorical figures throughout are colloquial and unemphatic—gunfire is like *whips cracking* and *chains of sparks,* an extracted bullet is *like a bee-sting,* and so forth—with only a few foregrounded exceptions: the *pony-trap wheels* of the aeroplanes, their guns' *pencillings* on the hillside, fallen soldiers like *butcher's parcels of floury khaki,* and so on.

"Natural" narrative features emerge strongly, none more so than Fred's narrative voice. His style is colloquial Australian (e.g., a *waler* is an Australian breed of horse), with inset direct quotations from other speakers, especially Loocher Sibley, whose exotic diction (*bundooks, Dekho that!*) explicitly marks him as an "Indian Army man."[23] Fred is narrating his own experience retrospectively, a temporal perspective signaled by the shift to the time of narration in the third paragraph, where Fred reflects in the present about his choices at that past moment of battlefield crisis. All of these features are readily assimilated to the model of natural conversational narrative, which this passage simulates.

Other features, while still "natural" in this sense, clearly derive from the poetics of the novel, especially the realist and modernist novel. The narrative pace shifts from summary to scene in the middle of the first paragraph, as indirect speech report ("We were talking," etc.) gives way to direct discourse, and events begin crowding in thick and fast as the battlefield action heats up. Singulative events ("There I saw my first aeroplanes") alternate with iterative ones ("battle was strings of riders," "Bigger guns . . . would shorten"), creating the characteristic texture of realist narrative. More characteristic of modernism is the impressionism of the battle scene, especially in the last paragraph,

---

23. "Someone," presumably not Sibley but one of the Australians, pronounces *statue* as *stature.*

where lists of fragmentary images (synecdoches) reflect the speed and confusion of battle as experienced by Fred. The effect is cinematic, a series of shots edited together to produce a single complex impression. Similar in its effect is the delayed recognition of what is happening, mirroring the characters' subjective experience of disorientation and shock. Like Marlow in the wheelhouse of *Heart of Darkness*, when "sticks," only belated recognized as spears, begin rattling down on the deck around him (see Watt 317), here Fred and his mates only belatedly recognize "whips cracking" and "chains of sparks" as machine-gun fire, "sizzles in the air" as bullets, and so on. An interval of time elapses between perception and recognition—an interval mimed by the syntax of the passage.

Now compare the same passage as it actually appears in *Fredy Neptune*, organized into five eight-line stanzas:

> Next morning after a drink of tea at daybreak
> our Cairo party rode off south. Bill Hines, Yall Sherritt,
> Poley Corrigan, myself and the Indian Army man
> Loocher Sibley. We were talking dogs, the ones
> who caught us out at cricket, the dingo that let Yall pet her,
> the curs Poley kept to lick his rheumatics better—
> we heard like whips cracking, and more and more, back past the windmill,
> out north of the city. Chains of sparks dotted off a far hill.
>
> *Machine gun,* cried Sibley. *And bundooks, lots of them. Dekho that!*
> a red star went smoking up the sky from the gully Jehosophat.
> *Jacko's rode down from Nablus to take Jerusalem back.*
> Stones kicked. You sensed sizzles in the air. Somewhere went pingg!
> Poley's face turned white: he reached around—*Bloody thing—*
> and picked a spent bullet out of his tunic like a bee-sting.
> *You're getting as tough as Freddy, and he's a stature,*
> said someone. We should have cleared out, but we stared at the war.
>
> So this was battle. Going on, I kept turning round;
> battle was strings of riders hell-for-leather in a smoky wall of sound.
> There I saw my first aeroplanes. Three came straining over
> from down south, rocking, hanging their pony-trap wheels.
> In front of those north hills they stopped and braced above ground
> on their guns' fumy pencillings. Bigger guns right near
> poking out through riveted shields would shorten, and your ear
> hurt, round a king gap, then you'd hear the slung case rebound.

My life, keeping out of the human race to stay in it—
I'd have to think back, to separate thoughts that were all one
poem, like, at the brink of what was to happen.
There were no sides for me: both were mine. I'd seen them both.
Better to lie than pick one: better die than pick: and I'd died indeed
flesh-dead, alive in no-life. Not in civvy, not in air,
maybe in fire. Would I re-light there? Feel, feel if only death?
I spurred to a bolt, gravel scattering, back north on my waler—

Blue steep up white rubble, blotch and blotch went bursts in the sky;
harnessed guns, turbaned Indians, Light Horse all yelling Ayy!
men in rage, in their guts, men dead with sheep, butcher's parcels
of floury khaki, near dropped rifles, jump-down terrace walls
and straight lines whippy round me everywhere. My poor horse stopped
    one,
stopped another one. I spilled off him, left him dying, ran
in behind a stacked wall that was spitting and crying. A man,
a young officer, was kneeling there. Politely he put down his telephone.
(Murray 16–17)

As it happens, this is one of the passages in the novel where end-rhymes do occur, albeit irregularly. Strikingly, these were mainly rendered "inaudible" in the prose form—for instance, *pet her/better, that/Jehosophat, war/stature, parcels/walls, one/telephone*—confirming Forrest-Thomson's analysis of the irrelevance of nonsemantic elements in ordinary language, where they are eclipsed by content. Lineation thrusts these end-rhymes into plain view, making them audible and functional.[24]

In many instances, artificial segmentation converges with and corroborates or enhances narrative segmentation. For example, lines of directly quoted dialogue are each allotted separate verse lines, so that shifts in and out of quotation coincide with line-ends.[25] Similarly, the shift into Fred's narrative present coincides with a stanza-break. More tellingly, the effect of delayed recognition that I analyzed above in connection with the de-versified version is amplified by segmentation. A stanza-break intervenes between "chains of sparks"

---

24. Conversely, at least one rhyme that *was* audible even in the prose form—*dying/crying*—proves to be internal, not an end-rhyme, defeating our expectations, and creating an effect of counterpoint.

25. Moreover, the "young officer" who "politely . . . put[s] down his telephone" at the very end of this excerpt speaks at the beginning of the next stanza, so that the shift to his direct speech coincides with a stanza-break.

and "*Machine guns,*" keeping the characters (and the reader) in suspense for just a moment longer. A line-break intervenes between "*Bloody thing*" and "spent bullet," with a comparable effect. Moreover, delayed identification of the mysterious object is further foregrounded here by the end-rhymes, which all converge on the same *thing: pingg, bee-sting*. In short, artifice in this passage, minimal though it may be, serves the function of narrative delay, just as the much more flagrant artifice does in *Venus and Adonis*.[26]

However, not every instance of artificial segmentation functions in this way to reinforce and enhance narrative segmentation. In some instances, lineation and stanza organization are countermeasured *against* narrative segmentation, creating effects of counterpoint. In the first stanza, for instance, the listing of characters' eccentric proper names (which produces a strong "reality effect") and then of their topics of conversation (dogs they have known) trails across the line-breaks, enlivening and estranging these otherwise mundane catalogues through formal counterpoint. Similarly, in the fifth stanza, the catalogue of war impressions is counterpointed against line-breaks, amplifying the effect of disorientation and strangeness. Especially interesting is the handling of the shift of narrative level in stanza 4. As we have seen, the shift *into* Fred's narrative present coincides with a stanza-break, but the shift *back* to the narrated events does not. While it does coincide with a line-break, the return from the present of narration to the narrated past straddles the larger unit, indicated by the stanza-break, spilling over into the next stanza. Artificial segmentation here cuts across narrative units.

So, what difference *does* poetic artifice make in a poem such as *Fredy Neptune* where artifice is minimal, reduced to little more than lineation, stanza-breaks, and sporadic end-rhymes, by contrast with the heightened diction, extravagant figuration, and other special effects of a poem such as *Venus and Adonis*? For one thing, as we have seen, artificial segmentation functionalizes and semanticizes nonsemantic patterns, such as rhyme, that are irrelevant and even inaudible in unsegmented prose. For another, artificial segmentation sometimes coincides with narrative segmentation, enhancing and amplifying it—but not always. Sometimes, instead, it cuts across narrative segmentation, setting up counterrhythms, syncopating and counterpointing narrative shifts.

26. Delay is even an object of reflection here, as it is in *Venus and Adonis*. The *king gap* at the end of the third stanza is presumably the hiatus in one's hearing when guns fire nearby, but can't it also be construed as referring self-reflexively to the gap between stanzas that immediately follows? No doubt this is an overly ingenious reading, but it can't be dismissed out of hand in light of the next stanza, where Fred steps back from the story to reflect on his life generally, and in particular on his thoughts at the moment of battle, "that were all one / poem, like." The self-reflective figure of one's life-story as a poem recurs throughout *Fredy Neptune;* see Murray 22, 44, 122, 128, 160, 176, 190, 253.

In any case, by introducing a series of minuscule gaps and interruptions, artificial segmentation jars us out of our automatic (natural) attitude toward this absorbing narrative. By roughening the texture of the narrative, it impedes automatic absorption. It counters the template of natural narrative with a competing template—if not exactly unnatural narrative, then at least artificial narrative, that is, poetry.

Works Cited

Alber, Jan. "Impossible Storyworlds—And What to Do with Them." *Storyworlds* 1 (2009): 79–96.
Alber, Jan, Stefan Iversen, Henrik Skov Nielsen, and Brian Richardson. "Unnatural Narratives, Unnatural Narratology: Beyond Mimetic Models." *Narrative* 18.2 (2010): 113–36.
Bernstein, Charles. "Artifice of Absorption." In *A Poetics*. Cambridge, MA: Harvard University Press, 1992 [1987]. 9–89.
———. *Islets/Irritations*. New York: Roof Books, 1992 [1983].
Culler, Jonathan. "Apostrophe." In *The Pursuit of Signs: Semiotics, Literature, Deconstruction*. London: Routledge & Kegan Paul, 1981. 135–54.
———. *Structuralist Poetics: Structuralism, Linguistics and the Study of Literature*. London: Routledge, 2002 [1975].
DuPlessis, Rachel Blau. *Blue Studios: Poetry and Its Cultural Work*. Tuscaloosa: University of Alabama Press, 2006.
———. "Codicil on the Definition of Poetry." *Diacritics* 26.3–4 (1996): 51.
Fish, Stanley. *Is There a Text in This Class?* Cambridge, MA: Harvard University Press, 1980.
Fludernik, Monika. *Towards a "Natural" Narratology*. London and New York: Routledge, 1996.
Forrest-Thomson, Veronica. *Poetic Artifice: A Theory of Twentieth-Century Poetry*. Manchester: Manchester University Press, 1978.
Kinney, Claire Regan. *Strategies of Poetic Narrative: Chaucer, Spenser, Milton, Eliot*. Cambridge: Cambridge University Press, 1992.
Kittay, Jeffrey and Wlad Godzich. *The Emergence of Prose: An Essay in Prosaics*. Minneapolis: University of Minnesota Press, 1987.
Mark, Alison. *Veronica Forrest-Thompson and Language Poetry*. Tavistock: Northcote House, 2001.
McHale, Brian. "Affordances of Form in Stanzaic Narrative Poems." *Literator* 31.3 (2010): 199–222.
———. "Beginning to Think about Narrative in Poetry." *Narrative* 17.1 (2009): 11–30.
———. "Making (Non)sense of Postmodernist Poetry." In *Language, Text and Context: Essays in Stylistics*, ed. Michael Toolan. London: Routledge, 1992. 6–38.
———. "Telling Stories Again: On the Replenishment of Narrative in the Postmodernist Long Poem." In *The Yearbook of English Studies: Time and Narrative*, ed. Nicola Bradbury. Vol. 30. London: W. S. Maney, 2000. 250–62.
Murray, Les. *Fredy Neptune: A Novel in Verse*. New York: Farrar, Straus and Giroux, 1999 [1998].
Nielsen, Henrik Skov. "The Impersonal Voice in First-Person Narrative Fiction." *Narrative* 12.2 (2004): 133–50.

Perelman, Bob. *Ten to One: Selected Poems.* Hanover, NH: Wesleyan University Press/University Press of New England, 1999.

Reese, M. M., ed. *Elizabethan Verse Romances.* London: Routledge & Kegan Paul, 1968.

Shklovsky, Viktor. *Theory of Prose.* Trans. Benjamin Sher. Normal, IL: Dalkey Archive Press, 1990 [1929].

Shoptaw, John. "The Music of Construction: Measure and Polyphony in Ashbery and Bernstein." In *The Tribe of John: Ashbery and Contemporary Poetry,* ed. Susan Schultz. Tuscaloosa: University of Alabama Press, 1995. 211–57.

Watt, Ian. "Impressionism and Symbolism in *Heart of Darkness*" [1979]. In *Heart of Darkness: An Authoritative Text, Backgrounds and Sources, Criticism,* ed. Robert Kimbrough. 3rd ed. New York: Norton, 1988. 311–36.

Wesling, Donald. *The Chances of Rhyme: Device and Modernity.* Berkeley: University of California Press, 1980.

Wittgenstein, Ludwig. *Zettel.* Ed. G. E. M. Anscombe and G. H. von Wright. Trans. G. E. M. Anscombe. Berkeley: University of California Press, 1967.

Contributors

JAN ALBER is Associate Professor in the English Department at the University of Freiburg in Germany. He is the author of *Narrating the Prison* (Cambria Press, 2007) and has edited collections such as *Stones of Law, Bricks of Shame: Narrating Imprisonment in the Victorian Age* (with Frank Lauterbach, University of Toronto Press, 2009); *Postclassical Narratology: Approaches and Analyses* (with Monika Fludernik, The Ohio State University Press, 2010); *Unnatural Narratives, Unnatural Narratology* (with Rüdiger Heinze, de Gruyter, 2011); and *Why Study Literature?* (with Stefan Iversen, Henrik Skov Nielsen, and others, Aarhus University Press, 2011). Alber has authored and coauthored articles that were published in journals such as *Dickens Studies Annual*, the *Journal of Narrative Theory, The Journal of Popular Culture, Literature Compass, Narrative, Storyworlds*, and *Style*. In 2007, he received a fellowship from the German Research Foundation to spend a year at The Ohio State University doing research on the unnatural under the auspices of Project Narrative. In 2010, the Humboldt Foundation awarded him a Feodor-Lynen Research Fellowship for Experienced Researchers to continue this research at the University of North Carolina at Greensboro and the University of Maryland at College Park.

ALICE BELL is Senior Lecturer in English Language and Literature at Sheffield Hallam University (UK). She is Principal Investigator of the *Digital Fiction International Network* (founded with funding from The Leverhulme Trust) and of *Ontological Metalepsis and Unnatural Narratology*, a collaborative research project undertaken with Jan Alber (University of Freiburg), which was funded by The British Academy. She is author of *The Possible Worlds of Hypertext Fiction* (Palgrave Macmillan, 2010) and has published articles on digital fiction, stylistics, and narratology in *Contemporary Stylistics* (Continuum, 2007); *New Narratives: Stories and Storytelling in the Digital Age* (University of Nebraska Press, 2012); *Narrative* (2011); and *Storyworlds* (2012).

RÜDIGER HEINZE is Junior Professor in the English Seminar of the Technische Universität Braunschweig in Germany. He is the author of a monograph titled *Ethics of Literary Forms* (Lit, 2005) and coeditor of a number of collections, among them *The Disappearance of Utopia?* (with Jochen Petzold, *ZAA* Special Issue, 2007) and, most recently,

Unnatural Narratives, Unnatural Narratology (with Jan Alber, de Gruyter, 2011). He has published articles in various journals, among them the *European Journal of American Studies*, the *Journal of Postcolonial Writing*, and *Narrative*, as well as in many collections. His current research interests are in narratology and popular culture. He is also working on a monograph about children of immigrants in the USA.

STEFAN IVERSEN is Assistant Professor in the Department for Aesthetics and Communication at Aarhus University in Denmark. He has coedited the anthologies *Why Study Literature?* (Aarhus University Press, 2011) and *Strange Voices in Narrative Fiction* (de Gruyter, 2011) and has written "'In flaming flames': Crises of Experientiality in Non-Fictional Narratives" (2011) and "States of Exception: Decoupling, Metarepresentation and Strange Voices in Narrative Fiction" (2011). With Alber, Nielsen, and Richardson, he coauthored "Unnatural Narratives, Unnatural Narratology. Beyond Mimetic Models" (2010). Iversen is the author and coauthor of articles and books in Danish on subjects such as narrative theory, early modernism, narrative rhetoric, and literature of testimony. He wrote his thesis on decadence and narrative structures in the works of Johannes V. Jensen. Together with Henrik Skov Nielsen, he edits the series Modern Literary Theory (Moderne litteraturteori), and he also hosts and leads the Intensive Programme in Narratology (www.ipin.dk), an international summer school in narrative theory held annually in Aarhus since 2009.

MARIA MÄKELÄ is Senior Lecturer in the School of Language, Translation, and Literary Studies at the University of Tampere in Finland, where she teaches Comparative Literature. She is the author of a Finnish PhD thesis, *Uskoton mieli ja tekstuaaliset petokset: kirjallisen tajunnankuvauksen konventiot narratologisena haasteena* (*Textual Deceptions and the Unfaithful Mind: Conventions of Literary Consciousness Representation as a Narratological Challenge*, Tampere University Press, 2011). She is coeditor of the collection *Narrative, Interrupted: The Plotless, the Disturbing and the Trivial in Literature* (with Laura Karttunen and Markku Lehtimäki, de Gruyter, 2012). Mäkelä has published several articles on classical and postclassical narratology, consciousness representation, intermediality, literary romance and adultery, and realism. Her latest articles appear in collections that are published by or forthcoming with Cambria Press, de Gruyter, and the University of Nebraska Press.

BRIAN McHALE is Distinguished Arts and Humanities Professor of English at The Ohio State University. He is one of the founding members of Project Narrative at Ohio State and served as president of the Association for the Study of the Arts of the Present (*ASAP*) in 2010–11. The author of three books on postmodernist fiction and poetry—*Postmodernist Fiction* (Methuen, 1987), *Constructing Postmodernism* (Routledge, 1992), and *The Obligation toward the Difficult Whole: Postmodernist Long Poems* (University of Alabama Press, 2004)—he has also published many articles on modernism and postmodernism, narrative theory, and science fiction. He is coeditor, with Randall Stevenson, of the *Edinburgh Companion to Twentieth-Century Literatures in English* (Edinburgh University Press, 2006); with David Herman and James Phelan of *Teaching Narrative Theory* (The Ohio State University Press, 2010); with Luc Herman and Inger Dalsgaard of the *Cambridge Companion to Thomas Pynchon* (Cambridge University Press, 2012); and with Joe Bray and Alison Gibbons of the *Routledge Companion to Experimental Literature* (Routledge, 2012).

CONTRIBUTORS | 225

HENRIK SKOV NIELSEN is Professor in the Scandinavian Institute at the University of Aarhus in Denmark. He is the author of articles and books in Danish on narratology and literary theory. His dissertation, *Tertium datur—on literature or on what is not*, is on digression and first-person narrative fiction. Nielsen has authored and coauthored articles in the *Amsterdam International Electronic Journal of Cultural Narratology*, the *Oxford Literary Review*, *Narrative*, and others. He has also contributed to several edited collections and is the editor of a series of anthologies on literary theory. Nielsen is currently working on narratological research projects on the relation between authors and narrators and on unnatural narratology in the context of the research groups NRL (http://nordisk.au.dk/forskning/forskningscentre/nrl/intro/) and "Unnatural Narratology" (http://nordisk.au.dk/forskning/forskningscentre/nrl/unnatural/). Most recently he was appointed head of the Centre for Fictionality Studies at Aarhus University.

JAMES PHELAN is Distinguished University Professor of English at The Ohio State University. In numerous essays and books, he has been working on developing a comprehensive rhetorical theory of narrative. Key installments in this work can be found in the following six books: *Worlds from Words: A Theory of Language in Fiction* (University of Chicago Press, 1981), *Reading People, Reading Plots* (Chicago, 1989), *Narrative as Rhetoric* (The Ohio State University Press, 1996), *Living to Tell About It* (Cornell University Press, 2005), *Experiencing Fiction* (Ohio State, 2007), and *Narrative Theory: Core Concepts and Critical Debates* (Ohio State, 2012) (with Peter J. Rabinowitz, David Herman, Brian Richardson, and Robyn Warhol). In addition, he is the editor or coeditor of seven collections of essays on narrative and narrative theory, including most recently *Teaching Narrative Theory* (2010) (with David Herman and Brian McHale), *Fact, Fiction and Form: Selected Essays of Ralph W. Rader* (2011) (with David H. Richter), and *After Testimony: The Ethics and Aesthetics of Holocaust Narrative* (2012) (with Jakob Lothe and Susan R. Suleiman). Since 1992, Phelan has been the editor of *Narrative*, the journal of the International Society for the Study of Narrative, and, since 1993, coeditor of The Ohio State University Press series Theory and Interpretation of Narrative. The essay in this volume is part of a larger study of the rhetoric and ethics of narrative communication.

BRIAN RICHARDSON is Professor in the English Department of the University of Maryland, where he teaches modern literature and narrative theory. He is the author or coauthor of three books: *Unlikely Stories: Causality and the Nature of Modern Narrative* (University of Delaware Press, 1997); *Unnatural Voices: Extreme Narration in Modern and Contemporary Fiction* (The Ohio State University Press, 2006, Perkins Prize winner); and *Narrative Theory: Critical Concepts and Current Debates*, with David Herman, James Phelan, Peter Rabinowitz, and Robyn Warhol (Ohio State, 2012). Richardson has edited two other anthologies, *Narrative Dynamics: Essays on Time, Plot, Closure, and Frames* (Ohio State, 2002) and *Narrative Beginnings: Theories and Practices* (University of Nebraska Press, 2008), and has guest edited special issues of *Style* on Concepts of Narrative (34.2, 2000) and on The Implied Author (44.1, 2011). He has published articles on many aspects of modernism, postmodernism, and narrative theory, including plot, time, character, narration, reflexivity, and reader response theory. In 2011 Richardson was president of the International Society for the Study of Narrative. He is currently completing a book on the theory and history of unnatural narratives from antiquity to postmodernism.

WERNER WOLF is Professor and Chair of English and General Literature at the University of Graz in Austria. His main areas of research are literary theory (aesthetic illusion, narratology, and metafiction in particular), functions of literature, eighteenth- to twenty-first-century English fiction, as well as intermediality studies (relations and comparisons between literature and other media, notably music and the visual arts). His publications include, besides numerous essays, the monographs *Ästhetische Illusion und Illusionsdurchbrechung in der Erzählkunst* (Niemeyer, 1993) and *The Musicalization of Fiction: A Study in the Theory and History of Intermediality* (Rodopi, 1999). He is also coeditor of volumes 1, 3, 5, and 11 of the book series Word and Music Studies (1999–2010) as well as of volumes 1 and 2 of the series Studies in Intermediality: *Framing Borders in Literature and Other Media* (Rodopi, 2006) and *Description in Literature and Other Media* (Rodopi, 2007). He is currently conducting a project financed by the Austrian Science Fund (FWF) on "Metareference—a Transmedial Phenomenon," in the course of which he has also edited *Metareference Across Media: Theory and Case Studies* (Rodopi, 2009) and *The Metareferential Turn in Contemporary Arts and Media: Forms, Functions, Attempts at Explanation* (Rodopi, 2011) as volumes 4 and 5 of the series Studies in Intermediality. A volume, coedited by him, *Immersion and Distance: Aesthetic Illusion in Literature and Other Media,* is currently in preparation.

Index

11:14 (Marck), 38
21 Grams (Iñárritu), 35

Abbott, H. Porter, 8, 8n11, 28, 31, 63n15, 31, 33
absorption, antiabsorption (poetry), 204–6, 211
Adventures of Huckleberry Finn (Twain), 3, 11, 172
aesthetic illusion (Wolf), 5, 11, 115, 115n5, 115n6, 116, 119, 120, 121, 121n14, 125, 128, 129, 131, 133, 135, 136, 137, 139
afternoon: a story (Joyce), 25, 26, 197
agency, 11, 69, 82, 85–89, 145, 150, 152–54, 160, 163, 169, 183, 207
Alber, Jan, 1n1, 2, 5, 6, 7, 8n11, 10, 33, 35, 67, 69, 95–96, 97, 97n2, 110, 115, 117–19, 118n12, 120, 128, 134, 145, 146, 156–57, 157n5, 164, 186, 200n1
"The Aleph" (Borges), 53–55
allegory, 49, 49n7, 56, 58, 60–62, 95, 96–97, 104, 106, 118–20, 132, 134, 138n31, 157, 215
Allen, Woody, 114, 124, 125, 127, 135
Alphabetical Africa (Abish), 55n12
alternative timelines, 38
Animal Farm (Orwell), 36
Arcadia (Sidney), 209

antimimetic narrative, 5, 6n7, 11, 16, 29, 170
Apuleius, 4
Aristophanes, 2, 4, 12, 29
Aristotle, 1
artifice, 200–207, 211–14, 217
assimilation, 143–44, 146, 149, 164, 199–200, 204n11, 204–5, 217
attribution theory, 106
At Swim-Two-Birds (O'Brien), 25, 129, 137n30, 138n31
audience, actual, 168. *See also* reader
audience, authorial, 87, 168, 170
author, 2, 23, 25, 28, 68–69, 73,76–7, 77n5, 82, 85–92, 122, 133, 155n3, 158, 167–69, 183, 192, 197
automatize, 143
avant-garde, 7, 12, 143, 203, 205–6
Le avventure di Pinocchio (Collodi), 131

Back to the Future (Zemeckis), 38
"The Babysitter" (Coover), 5, 6, 21
Bakhtin, Mikhail, 4, 45, 134
Barthes, Roland, 118
Bartleby (Melville), 104
beast fable, 6
Beckett, Samuel, 2, 5, 9, 18–19, 25, 28, 29, 32n1, 40, 83–84, 119, 200
beginnings, 25

227

228 | INDEX

Bell, Alice, 11–12, 193
Bernstein, Charles, 205–7, 211
Beowulf, 52
Bergson, Henri, 125
blending, 35, 48, 48n4, 62, 96, 118, 120n13
Block de Behar, Lisa, 53–54
"The Body" (Boully), 17
Bolter, J. David, 188
Borges, Jorge Luis, 2, 12, 53n10
The Breast (Roth), 6
Brooks, Peter, 26
Butts, Richard, 52

Calvino, Italo, 2, 25
carnivalesque, the (Bakhtin), 134
Carter, Angela, 2, 58–60
The Castle of Otranto (Walpole), 128
character narration, 167–83
Chatman, Seymour, 35n7, 45–46; model, 87–88
chronotope, 45
Ciccoricco, David, 192
"The Circle" (Nabokov, 21
classical (structuralist) narratology, 73, 100, 103, 110, 143, 150, 152, 162
Cloud Nine (Churchill), 21
cognition, 5–8, 10–11, 33n2, 35, 35n9, 40, 47–48, 48n5, 49, 51, 62–63, 63n15, 64, 71, 73, 94–96, 98–104, 107, 109–10, 118, 144–46, 149n1, 150, 152–53, 157–58, 161–64, 167n1, 176n8, 186, 199, 218–19
cognitive narratology, 1, 7, 94, 96, 98, 99, 102, 103, 104, 110, 144, 145, 152, 161–62
Cohn, Dorrit, 180
coherence, 20, 153, 157
Coleridge, Samuel Taylor, 115
communication, 86–89, 92, 120n13, 121, 136, 145, 169–70, 182, 202, 206
"Composition" (Bradbury), 26–27
Composition No. 1 (Saporta), 186
Concave and Convex (Escher), 146–47, 164
consciousness, 7, 60, 70, 75, 94, 97, 100, 102–4, 104n7, 106, 110, 150n1, 151, 159–63, 170, 210n18, 214
construction, 144, 149–50, 153, 161, 163

conventionalization, 6–7, 37, 48n5, 51, 85, 97–98, 104–5, 143
conversational storytelling, 70, 72, 91. *See also* natural narrative
Coover, Robert, 5, 6, 21, 24–25
Counter-Clock World (Dick), 38
crossover narration, 11, 168–69, 174–79
The Crying of Lot 49 (Pynchon), 29
Culler, Jonathan, 35, 118–19, 202n2, 202n8, 204n11, 216n22
cummings, e.e., 202n7
Currie, Mark, 35n10

Danielewski, Mark Z., 2, 47, 60–62
deconstruction, 2, 25, 35n10, 55, 62–63, 144
defamiliarization (Shklovsky), 6, 115, 117n9, 136–39, 143–44, 149, 203. *See also* estrangement
DelConte, Matt, 22, 180
denarration, 22, 40
Dennerlein, Katrin, 47n2
Dick, Philip K., 36
Dickens, Charles, 11, 145, 150, 154, 158–61, 164
Dickinson, Emily, 202n7
disclosure function of narrator, 168
discourse (Genette), 7, 9, 19–20, 22, 32, 32n, 34–35, 35n, 36–40, 46, 71–76, 80, 87–88, 90, 100, 122, 130, 132, 150, 159–63, 169, 175–77, 179, 181, 183, 185, 204, 214, 217. See also *syuzhet*
Doležel, Lubomír, 2, 47, 48
doppelgänger, 80
Double or Nothing (Federman), 25
Douglas, Jane Yellowlees, 188, 192
Dune (Frank Herbert), 53
DuPlessis, Rachel Blau, 201n5

Endgame (Beckett), 25
Endymion and Phoebe (Drayton), 218n8
endings, 26–27
exceptionality thesis (Herman), 69–70, 84, 99n, 102
episteme (Foucault), 122
estrangement (Shklovsky), 37, 110, 143,

153, 164, 203. *See also* defamiliarization
experientiality (Fludernik), 73, 74, 76, 77, 104n7, 118, 157, 160, 163
The Eyre Affair (Fforde), 135

fabula, 5, 9, 10, 16–29. *See also* story
fact-reporting narration, 10, 68
Faerie Queene (Spenser), 207–8
familiarization, 7, 67, 71, 144
fantasy, 36, 40, 48, 51, 105, 131–32, 134, 136, 163
farce, 149
Fehrle, Johannes, 37, 37n12
Figurski at Findhorn on Acid (Holeton), 197
Finnegans Wake (Joyce), 21
Fish, Stanley, 216n22
"Fizzle 8" (Beckett), 25
Flatland (Abbott), 56–58
Flaubert, Gustave, 11, 126, 145, 149–53, 156–58, 160–61, 163–64
Fludernik, Monika, 1n1, 3, 20, 35, 118, 120, 167, 186, 190, 193–94, 195, 199–201, 204n11
focalization (Genette), 10, 36, 67, 68, 70, 72–85, 90–92, 100, 144, 150, 152, 160, 176, 207
focalizer, 76, 150
Ford, Richard, 28
Forrest-Thompson, Veronica, 202, 203–6, 211n19, 215n22
Forster, E. M., 45
The Forever War (Haldeman), 34n6
Foucault, Michel, 55n13, 122
frames, 6–7, 7n8, 8, 35, 48–49, 62, 64, 71, 86–87, 89, 95–6, 117n9, 118, 120n13, 127–28, 130–32, 134, 136–37, 144–45, 157–58, 160–61, 163, 173, 194–95
Frankenstein (Shelley), 127, 130
Freddy Neptune (Murray, Les), 207, 214–21
The French Lieutenant's Woman (Fowles), 27, 28, 29

Genette, Gérard, 10, 32, 36, 45, 115, 116n7, 168

genre, 4, 10, 36–40, 48, 49n, 51–52, 68, 71, 97n, 97–98, 104–6, 118, 128, 132, 144, 169, 200, 202, 204, 214, 215n
Gibson, Andrew, 35n10
Gilbert, Elliott L., 57
Glamorama (Ellis), 40, 78–81, 89, 180–81
Gothic fiction, 12, 20, 59, 127–28, 162
The Great Gatsby (Fitzgerald), 11, 82–83, 175–79
Greene, Brian, 31–32
Greimas, Algirdas-Julien, and Joseph Courtés, 46
"The Grid" (Moody), 38–39, 41, 42
Groundhog Day (Ramis), 38
Gulliver's Travels (Swift), 58n14

habituation, 71, 134–35, 135n29, 138, 138n32, 143
"The Haile Selassie Funeral Train" (Davenport), 55–56
Hamilton, Natalie, 62
Hansen, Per Krogh, 35n7, 37, 40
Happy Days (Beckett), 119
Happenstance (Shields), 24
Harry Potter (Rowling), 52
Hawking, Stephen, and Leonard Mlodinow, 64
Heart of Darkness (Conrad), 218
Heinze, Rüdiger, 1n1, 5, 9, 21n2
Heise, Ursula, 21, 36n10
Henderson, Andrea, 57
Herman, David, 35, 35n10, 40, 46, 51, 64, 194
Hero and Leander (Marlowe), 210n18
heterodiegetic narration with zero focalization (Genette), 75, 77n6, 85. *See also* omniscient narration
heterotopia, 55n13
Hoffman, Gerhard, 46
Hoffmann, E. T. A., 2
homodiegetic narration with zero focalization (Genette), 75, 77, 79, 79n9, 85. *See also* omniscience, first-person
House of Leaves (Danielewski), 47, 60–62
"How" (Moore), 22
How the Garcia Girls Lost Their Accent (Alvarez), 40

human experience, 31, 42, 48, 73, 154
hyperreality, 150
hypertext fiction, 11, 185–97

If on a winter's night a traveller (Calvino), 25
Iliad (Homer), 114n3
imagined community, 91
immersion, 11, 114–16, 115n6, 119–21, 121n14, 123–25, 128, 131, 131n21, 133–39, 138n31, 157–59, 163, 183
implausibly knowledgeable narration, 172–77
implied author, 87–88, 167, 167n2, 168, 199
impossibility, 1, 9, 71, 78, 92, 104, 110, 118, 126, 133, 134, 163, 173, 186, 193; architectural, 50, 60, 61, 146; geographical, 55, 55n12; human, 6, 47n3, 90; logical, 6, 10, 33, 38, 40, 47, 117–18, 157; physical, 6, 10, 33, 40, 47, 52, 59, 97, 97n2, 98, 117–18; psychological, 72, 179; spatial, 56–58, 149
impressionism, 143, 152, 217
In the Labyrinth (Robbe-Grillet), 22
"The Index" (Ballard), 17
inductive approach, 4
The Infernal Desire Machines of Doctor Hoffman (Carter), 58–60
Innocent (Turrow), 182
intentionality, 149n1, 163
interpretation, 5, 7–8, 10, 20, 49, 62–63, 63n15, 64n16, 67–69, 72, 78–85, 87, 89n16, 89–92, 95–96, 106, 119, 120n13, 145, 151, 154–55, 161–62, 164, 177, 191–92, 195–96, 211
interruption, narrative, 209–9, 211–14, 220
intersubjectivity, 107, 162
"The Invention of Photography in Toledo" (Davenport), 55n12
Irréversible (Noé), 34, 38
Iversen, Stefan, 1n1, 3, 6–7, 8, 10, 63n15

Jahn, Manfred, and Sabine Buchholz, 45
Jealousy (Robbe-Grillet), 21
Jimmy Corrigan (Ware), 40

Joyce, Michael, 25, 26, 192, 197

Keats, John, 8n11, 203
Kinney, Claire Regan, 201n3
Kittay, Jeffrey, and Wlad Godzich, 215
Klauk, Tobias, and Tilmann Köppe, 1n1
Klimek, Sonja, 115n6, 117n9, 139
Knowlson, James, and John Pillig, 19
Koskimaa, Raine, 190
"The Kugelmass Episode" (Allen), 125–27, 135

Labov, William, 3; and linguistic discourse analysis, 71
Language Poets, 202n7
The Late Bourgeois World (Gordimer), 29
Lem, Stanisław, 36
Lessing, Gotthold Ephraim, 45
"Life Story" (Shields), 9, 17–18
lineation. *See* segmentation
Lockridge, Ernest, 177n9
Lola rennt (Tykwer), 9, 27, 38
Lunar Park (Ellis), 47

Mäkelä, Maria, 1n1, 7, 11, 29, 63n15, 67, 69
Margolin, Uri, 42
Maus (Spiegelman), 35, 40
McHale, Brian, 4–5, 12, 25, 152, 201, 203n10, 208n14
meaning, variable, 191–92
Memento (Nolan), 34, 38, 40
mentalizing, 98, 101
metalepsis, 11, 104, 159, 179; definition of, 116–17; rhetorical (Nelles), 117; epistemological (Nelles), 117; ontological (Nelles), 117
Metamorphoseon libri (Ovid), 114, 207
metamorphosis, 7, 97, 104–6, 109–10, 114n3, 130–31, 131n21, 207, 209n15, 210n16
Metamorphosis of Pygmalion's Image (Marston), 210–11n18
metaphor, 20, 24, 35, 36n10, 75, 104, 152–53, 158, 205, 210, 212, 215, 217

metareferentiality, 124, 126, 127, 129, 135, 137, 137n30
Metz, Christian, 32
Midnight's Children (Rushdie), 6, 47n3
A Midsummer Night's Dream (Shakespeare), 5, 21, 32n1
Miller, J. Hillis, 63
mimesis, 69–70, 72, 87, 118, 171; antimimetic, 1, 2n2, 3–5, 6n7, 11, 16, 23, 28–29, 70, 129, 142, 167–68, 170–71, 173–81; nonmimetic, 6n7
mimetic bias, 4
mimetic code violations, 172–83; rules of, 174–75
mimetic reductionism, 1
mind reading (Palmer), 98–99, 150n1
mind representation, 6, 68–69, 72, 77–78, 90, 92, 100, 102
mise en abyme, 113, 122, 123, 132, 132n23, 134
mise en cadre, 132, 132n23
The Mixquiahuala Letters (Castillo), 9, 23, 26
Moby Dick (Melville), 81–82, 89–90
modernism, 4, 156, 217
Moll, Andrea, 38
Molloy (Beckett), 40
mood (Genette), 10, 67–68, 73, 77, 79–80, 83–85
multilinear narratives, 20–28, 187, 191

Nabokov, Vladimir, 2, 16, 21, 149, 150n1
narratee, 168
narrative, identity as, 27
narrative contradictions, 190
narrative poetry, 200–221
narrativity, 17–20
narrativization (Fludernik), 10, 33, 35–36, 72, 199–200, 202, 204n11
narrator, 189–91, 195–96
narrator functions, 168
natural (conversational) narratives, 3, 5, 12, 16, 20, 167, 170, 199–207, 217–21. See also conversational storytelling
natural narratology (Fludernik), 70, 71
naturalization, 49, 67, 71, 79, 81, 97, 115, 116, 118, 119, 120n13, 123, 125, 127, 128, 129, 134, 136, 138n32, 151, 160–61
naturalization, bad (Forrest-Thompson), 204–5
Natürlichkeitstheorie, 71
Nelles, William, 115n6, 117
Nielsen, Henrik Skov, 1n1, 6, 10, 29, 64n16, 170, 172n4, 180–82, 200n1
Nieuwland, Mante S., and Jos J. A. van Berkum, 48n4, 52
nonmeaning (Mäkelä), 153
no-narrator thesis, 10, 68, 86
non-linearity, 38
"Notes Towards a Mental Breakdown" (Ballard), 17

"Of Sanguine Fire" (Prynne), 206n12
Olsen, Stein Haugom, 8
omniscient narration, 6, 151, 158, 160, 160n6, 161, 196 (*see also* heterodiegetic narration with zero focalization); first-person omniscience, 2 (*see also* homodiegetic narration with zero focalization)
ontology, 2, 21n1, 27, 78, 84, 87, 114, 114n3, 116–7, 117n10, 122–3, 126, 129n20, 130, 134–35, 188–89, 193–97
ordinary realist texts, 145
Orlando (Woolf), 21
Ovid, 114, 114n2, 130–31, 131n21

Pale Fire (Nabokov), 16
paralepsis, 168
paralipsis, 168–69, 172–77
parody, 58, 109, 159, 214
Partie (Cixous), 24
Patchwork Girl (Jackson), 197
Pavel, Thomas, 53
perception, 10–11, 53, 69, 75–77, 85, 143–50, 152–58, 158, 169, 176–78, 182, 218; dislocated, 155, 164
Perleman, Bob, 206
Phelan, Jim, 3, 5, 11, 29, 41n16, 168, 175n6, 175n7
Pig Tales (Darrieussecq), 11, 95, 105–7, 109
"Ping" (Beckett), 18–19

plot, 2–3, 9, 23, 26, 28, 45, 73, 80n11, 114n2, 157–58, 164, 206
Poe, Edgar Allen, 170
The Poetics of Space (Bachelard), 46
poetics of the unnatural, 37, 135–39
Ponge, Francis, 201n4
possible-worlds theory, 190
postclassical narratology, 73, 150
postmodernism, 3–5, 9, 12, 29, 32n1, 36n10, 37, 129, 135, 135n29, 149, 157, 200, 214
poststructuralism, 62, 95
present-tense narration, 168, 179–83
"Primary Sources" (Moody), 17
prototype, 116, 145, 149, 161, 164
principle of minimal departure (Ryan), 122
psychology, 4, 69, 96, 98–100, 100n4, 102n5, 102–3, 208n14; *Gestalt*, 154
The Purple Rose of Cairo (Allen), 114, 121–27
Pygmalion myth, 114, 114n2, 130–31

Rabelais, 4, 12
Rabinowitz, Peter, 35n10, 36, 36n10, 64, 168
Rader, Ralph, 171
The Rape of Lucrece (Shakespeare), 210n17
reader, 20, 22–23, 24, 169, 171, 186–87, 191–97
reader expectations, 71, 134–35, 144, 219n24
realism, 3, 11–12, 28, 36, 53, 72, 115n6, 122, 142–64, 170, 215
real-world experience, 2, 6, 8, 10, 47, 47n, 49, 55, 62, 64n, 69, 71–72, 77n, 80, 82, 87, 90–92, 96–97, 145, 170–71, 181, 186, 188–90, 193
redundant telling, 168
Reflex and Bone Structure (Major), 2
relational theory, 68, 76
representation, 68–70, 72, 77–78, 87, 89–90, 92, 100, 102–3, 110, 116–17, 119–22, 124, 126–28, 130–31, 137, 138n31, 142–44,149–53, 150n1, 159–61, 163–64, 188, 190
rereading, 191–97
restriction, 10, 67, 73, 75–76, 90, 160n6, 168, 170, 173

reversals, sustained episodic, 38
rhetorical model of narrative, 4, 10, 69, 87–88, 169, 171
Ricardou, Jean, 4
Richardson, Brian, 1n1, 3, 5, 6n7, 7, 9, 21n2, 22, 32, 32n1, 35n7, 35n10, 36, 40, 135n29, 186, 187–88, 190–91, 194
Richter, David, 42
Ricoeur, Paul, 31, 118
Rimmon-Kenan, Shlomith, 23, 31
Robbe-Grillet, Alain, 4, 9, 19–22
Ronen, Ruth, 46
Russian formalism, 4, 20, 143, 200n2, 211n19
Ryan, Marie-Laure, 28, 32, 32n1, 33, 38, 41, 46, 48, 116, 117n10, 122, 125, 158, 160, 190

Sarraute, Nathalie, 4
satire, 49, 49n7, 56–57, 62
Schaeffer, Jean-Marie, 115n6, 121n14
science fiction, 6, 12, 36, 52–53
scripts, 7, 7n8, 35–37, 38n13, 42, 62, 64, 96, 157
second-person narrative, 9, 193–96
"The Secret Room" (Robbe-Grillet), 19–20
segmentation, segmentivity (poetry), 201–14, 219–21
sense-making, 7, 95, 97, 103, 120n13, 144–45, 161
Shakespeare, 2, 4, 5, 12, 21, 32n1, 207–14
Shelley, Percy B., 127n19
Shklovsky, Viktor, 4, 143–44, 149, 211n19
Shoptaw, John, 201
Similarity Thesis, 99, 102
simulation, 10, 47, 99, 159
Simulation Theory (ST), 99, 101
Sir Gawain and the Green Knight, 52
Sliding Doors (Howitt), 38
Slocombe, Will, 61
space, 2–3, 10, 18, 146, 149, 157, 172, 181, 188, 193–94, 201, 208, 212; definition of, 45; lived space (Bachelard), 46, 48; story space vs. discourse space (Chatman), 46
Spenser, Edmund, 208–9
Sternberg, Meir, 20

story, 16–29. See also *fabula*
"A Story as You Like It" (Queneau), 22
story vs. discourse (Chatman), 35, 38–40
storyworld, 2, 6–9, 19, 22, 35n9, 37, 45, 49–50, 59, 64, 68, 72, 77, 79, 81, 86–87, 90, 92, 113, 115, 118–20, 122, 124–26, 128, 133–34, 137n30, 144–46, 149–50, 152–53, 156–58, 164, 170, 175, 180, 182–83, 194, 206–7
structuralism, 4, 20, 84, 95, 116, 118, 156, 185–87, 192, 197, 211
Superman, 37
Swift, Jonathan, 2
synthetic aspects of narrative, 171
syuzhet, 23–25, 28. See also discourse

Tammi, Pekka, 1n1
Taylor, Holly, and Barbara Tversky, 46
temporality, 5, 9, 20–22, 31–32, 33n3, 34, 34n4, 35, 35n10, 38, 40, 40n14, 55, 157–58, 172–74, 176. See also time
temporal paradoxes, 31n1, 41
textual generators, 22
thematic aspects of narrative, 171
theme: definition of, 48n6
theory of relativity (Einstein), 33n4
Theory of Mind (ToM), 95, 99–105, 110, 149n1, 162
Theory Theory (TT), 99, 101
The Third Policeman (O'Brien), 49–51
Thoss, Jeff, 115
Through the Looking-Glass (Carroll), 128–29
time: and narrative, 31–34. See also temporality
time reversal, 38
time travel, 38
Time's Arrow (Amis), 34, 38, 40
Time Bandits (Gilliam), 40, 42
The Time Machine (Wells), 9, 34, 36, 36n10, 38
Timequake (Vonnegut), 38
The Time Traveler's Wife (Niffenegger), 34, 36
Tolstoy, Leo, 11, 29, 145, 150, 154, 155n3, 156–57, 160–61, 164
Tom Sawyer (Twain), 3

Towards a "Natural" Narratology (Fludernik), 3, 118
transformation, 7, 19, 97, 105, 107, 127, 130–31, 155
transcendental realm, 49, 51, 62
transgression, 4, 11, 16, 37, 54, 67, 79, 82, 84, 92, 115–17, 121n14, 142–44
Troilus and Criseyde (Chaucer), 201, 208–9
"The Turn of the Screw" (Oates), 56
Tyrkkö, Jukka, 28

uncanny, the, 46, 80, 110, 149, 153
Die unendliche Geschichte (Ende), 132–35, 137n30, 138n31
The Unfortunates (Johnson), 24, 187
The Unnamable (Beckett), 5, 28–29
unnatural, the: and cognitive approach to, 7–8, 44–64; conventionalized instances of, 6, 7, 37, 48n5, 51, 85, 97, 105; definitions of, 3–4, 5–7; 16, 117–18; discourse level, 6n6, 22; interpretation, 5, 7–9, 62–64; methodology, 7–9; vs. natural (real-world) frames, 47; vs. natural narratives, 5, 170, 199–207, 216–21; new scientific theories, 64; story level, 6n6; reading strategies to make sense of, 10, 19–20, 35, 35n9, 48–49, 62, 64n16, 118, 118n12; vs. the unconventional, 36
unnatural characters, 2
unnatural metalepsis (= ontological metalepsis), 11, 113–39
unnatural minds, 10, 68, 94–110
unnatural narratology, 1–2, 4–5, 8–10, 12, 28–29, 33, 67, 69–70, 72, 94–95, 135, 142, 144–45, 158, 164, 185–88, 191–97; diversity within, 12; tradition of, 4–5
unnatural narrators, 2, 190–96
unnaturalizing readings (Nielsen), 8–9, 10, 67, 69, 72, 78–85, 92
unnatural spaces, 45–64, 48, 49, 51, 53, 58, 62, 63
unnatural stories, 16–29
unnatural storyworlds, 2, 89
unnatural temporality (or time), 9, 19–22, 31–42, 38, 40, 40n14, 173

Unnatural Voices (Richardson), 3, 32n1
unreadable minds (Abbott), 8, 63, 96, 104
unreliable narration, 8, 20n1, 79, 81, 87, 89n16, 90, 92n, 178

Venus and Adonis (Shakespeare), 12, 207–14
verisimilitude, 3, 11, 29, 116n7, 142, 145, 149, 152–54
verse novel, 215
Victory Garden (Moulthrop), 11–12
Virginie: Her Two Lives (Hawkes), 6n6, 47n3
voice (Genette), 2, 10, 18, 57, 67–68, 72–74, 76–77, 79–81, 82–85, 90–91, 139, 145, 159, 161–63, 174–76, 182, 188–89, 193, 195, 217

The Waste Land (Eliot), 202n7, 206n12
Watt (Beckett), 83–85
Watt, Ian, 218
We Came All the Way from Cuba So You Could Dress Like This? (Obeja), 40
Westling, Donald, 203n9
Williams, William Carlos, 202n7
Wilson, Anne, 63
Wolf, Werner, 4–5, 11
Wood, James, 153, 158
Wordsworth, William, 203

Yacobi, Tamar, 41
you-narrative. *See* second-person narrative
Young Girls by the Sea (Chavannes), 146–50

THEORY AND INTERPRETATION OF NARRATIVE
James Phelan, Peter J. Rabinowitz, and Robyn Warhol, Series Editors

Because the series editors believe that the most significant work in narrative studies today contributes both to our knowledge of specific narratives and to our understanding of narrative in general, studies in the series typically offer interpretations of individual narratives and address significant theoretical issues underlying those interpretations. The series does not privilege one critical perspective but is open to work from any strong theoretical position.

A Poetics of Unnatural Narrative
EDITED BY JAN ALBER, HENRIK SKOV NIELSEN, AND BRIAN RICHARDSON

Literary Identification from Charlotte Brontë to Tsitsi Dangarembga
LAURA GREEN

An Aesthetics of Narrative Performance: Transnational Theater, Literature, and Film in Contemporary Germany
CLAUDIA BREGER

Narrative Theory: Core Concepts and Critical Debates
DAVID HERMAN, JAMES PHELAN AND PETER J. RABINOWITZ, BRIAN RICHARDSON, AND ROBYN WARHOL

After Testimony: The Ethics and Aesthetics of Holocaust Narrative for the Future
EDITED BY JAKOB LOTHE, SUSAN RUBIN SULEIMAN, AND JAMES PHELAN

The Vitality of Allegory: Figural Narrative in Modern and Contemporary Fiction
GARY JOHNSON

Narrative Middles: Navigating the Nineteenth-Century British Novel
EDITED BY CAROLINE LEVINE AND MARIO ORTIZ-ROBLES

Fact, Fiction, and Form: Selected Essays
RALPH W. RADER. EDITED BY JAMES PHELAN AND DAVID H. RICHTER

The Real, the True, and the Told: Postmodern Historical Narrative and the Ethics of Representation
ERIC L. BERLATSKY

Franz Kafka: Narration, Rhetoric, and Reading
EDITED BY JAKOB LOTHE, BEATRICE SANDBERG, AND RONALD SPEIRS

Social Minds in the Novel
ALAN PALMER

Narrative Structures and the Language of the Self
MATTHEW CLARK

Imagining Minds: The Neuro-Aesthetics of Austen, Eliot, and Hardy
KAY YOUNG

Postclassical Narratology: Approaches and Analyses
EDITED BY JAN ALBER AND MONIKA FLUDERNIK

Techniques for Living: Fiction and Theory in the Work of Christine Brooke-Rose
KAREN R. LAWRENCE

Towards the Ethics of Form in Fiction: Narratives of Cultural Remission
LEONA TOKER

Tabloid, Inc.: Crimes, Newspapers, Narratives
V. PENELOPE PELIZZON AND NANCY M. WEST

Narrative Means, Lyric Ends: Temporality in the Nineteenth-Century British Long Poem
MONIQUE R. MORGAN

Joseph Conrad: Voice, Sequence, History, Genre
EDITED BY JAKOB LOTHE, JEREMY HAWTHORN, AND JAMES PHELAN

Understanding Nationalism: On Narrative, Cognitive Science, and Identity
PATRICK COLM HOGAN

The Rhetoric of Fictionality: Narrative Theory and the Idea of Fiction
RICHARD WALSH

Experiencing Fiction: Judgments, Progressions, and the Rhetorical Theory of Narrative
JAMES PHELAN

Unnatural Voices: Extreme Narration in Modern and Contemporary Fiction
BRIAN RICHARDSON

Narrative Causalities
EMMA KAFALENOS

Why We Read Fiction: Theory of Mind and the Novel
LISA ZUNSHINE

I Know That You Know That I Know: Narrating Subjects from Moll Flanders *to* Marnie
GEORGE BUTTE

Bloodscripts: Writing the Violent Subject
ELANA GOMEL

Surprised by Shame: Dostoevsky's Liars and Narrative Exposure
DEBORAH A. MARTINSEN

Having a Good Cry: Effeminate Feelings and Pop-Culture Forms
ROBYN R. WARHOL

Politics, Persuasion, and Pragmatism: A Rhetoric of Feminist Utopian Fiction
ELLEN PEEL

Telling Tales: Gender and Narrative Form in Victorian Literature and Culture
ELIZABETH LANGLAND

Narrative Dynamics: Essays on Time, Plot, Closure, and Frames
EDITED BY BRIAN RICHARDSON

Breaking the Frame: Metalepsis and the Construction of the Subject
DEBRA MALINA

Invisible Author: Last Essays
CHRISTINE BROOKE-ROSE

Ordinary Pleasures: Couples, Conversation, and Comedy
KAY YOUNG

Narratologies: New Perspectives on Narrative Analysis
EDITED BY DAVID HERMAN

Before Reading: Narrative Conventions and the Politics of Interpretation
PETER J. RABINOWITZ

Matters of Fact: Reading Nonfiction over the Edge
DANIEL W. LEHMAN

The Progress of Romance: Literary Historiography and the Gothic Novel
DAVID H. RICHTER

A Glance Beyond Doubt: Narration, Representation, Subjectivity
SHLOMITH RIMMON-KENAN

Narrative as Rhetoric: Technique, Audiences, Ethics, Ideology
JAMES PHELAN

Misreading Jane Eyre: *A Postformalist Paradigm*
JEROME BEATY

Psychological Politics of the American Dream: The Commodification of Subjectivity in Twentieth-Century American Literature
LOIS TYSON

Understanding Narrative
EDITED BY JAMES PHELAN AND PETER J. RABINOWITZ

Framing Anna Karenina: *Tolstoy, the Woman Question, and the Victorian Novel*
AMY MANDELKER

Gendered Interventions: Narrative Discourse in the Victorian Novel
ROBYN R. WARHOL

Reading People, Reading Plots: Character, Progression, and the Interpretation of Narrative
JAMES PHELAN

www.ingramcontent.com/pod-product-compliance
Lightning Source LLC
Chambersburg PA
CBHW020123240426
43673CB00038B/574